PSYCHOANALYTIC REFLECTIONS ON CURRENT ISSUES

PSYCHOANALYTIC REFLECTIONS ON CURRENT ISSUES

Edited by Howard B. Siegel

Laura Barbanel, Irwin Hirsch, Judith Lasky

Helen Silverman, Susan Warshaw

NEW YORK UNIVERSITY PRESS

New York and London

Library of Congress Cataloging-in-Publication Data
Psychoanalytic reflections / edited by Howard B. Siegel . . . [et al.].
p.   cm.
Includes index.
ISBN 0-8147-7909-3 (alk. paper)
1. Psychoanalysis.   I. Siegel, Howard B. (Howard Barry), 1941–
[DNLM: 1. Psychoanalytic Theory.   2. Psychoanalytic Therapy.   WM
460 P97784]
RC504.P79   1991
616.89'17—dc20
DNLM/DLC
for Library of Congress   90-13577
                                          CIP

New York University Press books are printed on acid-free paper,
and their binding materials are chosen for strength and durability.

Book design by Ken Venezio

CONTENTS

FOREWORD

When we initiated the New York University Postdoctoral Program in Psychotherapy and Psychoanalysis in 1962, the need for university-sponsored training was somewhat different than today. As early as 1952, Avrum Ben-Avi, Erwin Singer, and I proposed to New York University a postdoctoral specialization program. At the time we were matriculants at the William Alanson White Institute, and while appreciative of the good training offered psychologists, we felt troubled that the psychiatrists in our classes received certificates as trained psychoanalysts while our certificates attested only to the fact that we had completed their course work in clinical psychology (years after we had been awarded our Ph.D.s). Our training, was, of course, identical. Furthermore, we were just three of a privileged few who were permitted to receive such training; too many of our psychologist colleagues could not gain admission. We felt that if New York University allowed us to develop a training program within the department of psychology, we could admit more psychologists and not have to disguise the fact that we were being trained as psychoanalysts.[1] Our request was premature; the university was not prepared to assume the financial and academic responsibility at that time.

In 1957 I revived the idea with an additional perspective. Stuart Cook, Rollo May, Albert Thompson, Herbert Zucker, and I were involved in the effort to pass the certification law for psychologists by the New York legislature at that time. But the sponsor of the law, the New York State Department of Education, quickly pointed out that none of the doctoral programs in the state (including the one at New York University) was willing to state that their Ph.D.s were trained for the independent practice of psychotherapy. What was needed was a university-sponsored training program that would certify to the state that our profession was willing to assume that responsibility. Our postdoctoral program achieved this by simply adding intensive psychotherapy to our certificate of graduation from the psychoanalytic program. This demonstrated that we were indeed providing training in a skill defined by and taught to psychologists.

Much has changed since the late 1950s and early 1960s. In New York City, there are currently many different opportunities for psychologists to obtain training as psychoanalysts. At last count there were forty or so institutes in the metropolitan area sponsoring training programs. And certainly we no longer have to establish that clinical psychologists are trained to practice psychotherapy and psychoanalysis. Yet one of the major requirements and responsibilities of our program throughout this period has remained the same: to broaden the foundation of psychoanalytic offerings and to use our academic training to enable us to evaluate our bases for operating as we do.

In the late 1950s, most institutes were medically run and their training was very narrow. Most of them trained their candidates only in the Freudian tradition. Even the exceptions offered only one approach. For example, the American Institute limited itself to the teachings of Karen Horney, and the W. A. White Institute stressed the teachings of Harry Stack Sullivan and Erich Fromm. This situation has persisted, with the vast majority of the institutes run by psychologists continuing to offer training in only one of the psychoanalytic theories.

As a university-based training institute, we adopted a pluralistic approach by offering different psychoanalytic perspectives. As a result, the New York University postdoctoral has allowed for the analysis of the contrasting metapsychological assumptions of the differing theories; for comparisons of the different constructs, such as transference, countertransference, and resistance; and for learning the different therapeutic approaches and the rationale for the differing therapeutic techniques. Not having one defined program of training allowed us to examine our requirements and curriculum. We had no need to mimic criteria established by the medical training programs that, by and large, took candidates with no psychological background. We did not have to please a central accrediting agency such as The American Psychoanalytic Association—a group that historically frowned on the training of psychologists as psychoanalysts and that periodically occasioned rifts in the developing profession by threatening to expel members, as they did with Erich Fromm, Karen Horney, and Clara Thompson, who did not accept certain metapsychological assumptions. We did not have to limit ourselves to one particular view of psychoanalytic theory; in fact, as a university we had the responsibility to present different paradigms of psychoanalysis. Under the auspices of a major university, our program fit into the long tradition of open discussion among a diversity of views and around a certain catholicity of approach. We believed that one reason for the lack of critical theoretical evaluations stemmed from the institutes' reliance only on their graduates as teachers and supervisors. In contrast, we chose ours from among many institutes, and although we were boycotted by institutes that were members of the American Psychoanalytic Association, a few intrepid psychiatrists did join our staff.

Inasmuch as we were free of requirements that we saw as legislated, we could determine our own criteria. We did agree with the primary importance of the personal analysis; supervision; and instruction in theory, research, and practice. And the faculty did establish certain minimal criteria for frequency of personal analysis, training cases, and supervision that were still deemed necessary. Certificates were to be awarded for assessed readiness to function independently as a psychologist-psychoanalyst. Another criterion we still adhere to is to accept as training analysts graduates of other training institutes who have been in practice five years after graduation; they do not have to be graduates of New York University.

It was in our curriculum that we best expressed the function of a university, for our courses represented offerings in the Freudian, interpersonal, object-relations, and self-psychology schools as well as subjects that cut across all sectarian points of view, such as research in psychoanalysis and female psychology. As a matter of principle, students were never required to declare allegiance to one or another point of view but were free to explore without prejudice the various offerings in the program as a whole. We fully anticipated that by the time candidates received their certificates they would have developed a systematic theory, a therapeutic approach derived from their theory, and, we hoped, a respect for points of view other than their own. We believed their psychoanalytic training was built on their training as graduate psychologists, which did bias them in the direction of theory building and constructive criticism.

There have been changes in curriculum over the years. What has remained constant is a commitment to freedom of choice and opportunities to study from a variety of programs.

The essays in this current volume were written by graduates, faculty, and matriculants of the New York University Program in Psychotherapy and Psychoanalysis. The authors are scholars who ask important questions and who search not only for the answers but also for increased illumination of the issues involved. As one reads through these essays, it becomes clear that the authors are not of a single orientation. Some call themselves Freudians, some interpersonalists; others would describe themselves as object relationists or self psychologists, and still others would not want an adjectival label unless it was multialigned or non-aligned. All, however, are open to new ideas and differing points of view. They may disagree but will still respect the data and thought given to the different perspectives.

Our appreciation goes to the Psychoanalytic Society and to Dr. Howard B. Siegel and the other editors for assembling these diverse points of view. We believe this is just one of many volumes that will reflect the psychological background, scholarly precision, and the need to continue the discussion of the many issues in psychoanalytic theory and practice that need sharpening.

Bernard Kalinkowitz, Ph.D

1. A decade or so later, the W. A. White Institute began to offer identical certificates to members of both professions and offered admission to a much increased number yearly.

CONTRIBUTORS

LEWIS ARON is a faculty member in the New York University Post-doctoral Program in Psychotherapy and Psychoanalysis and is supervising psychologist at St. Luke's/Roosevelt Hospital Center. He is also associate editor of *Psychoanalytic Dialogues: A Journal of Relational Perspectives.*

EMANUEL BERMAN is senior lecturer in psychology at the University of Haifa in Israel and is on the faculty of the Israel Psychoanalytic Institute. He is also a visiting associate professor in New York University's Postdoctoral Program in Psychotherapy and Psychoanalysis.

LEANNE DOMASH is in private practice in New York City as well as being consulting psychologist at Beth Israel Medical Center and adjunct assistant professor of psychiatry at Mount Sinai School of Medicine.

NORBERT FREEDMAN teaches in the New York University Postdoctoral Program in Psychotherapy and Psychoanalysis, at the Institute for Psychoanalytic Training and Research (IPTAR), and SUNY Health Center in Brooklyn, N.Y.

HELEN GEDIMAN is clinical professor of psychology in the Postdoctoral Program in Psychotherapy and Psychoanalysis at New York University and is training and supervising analyst and faculty member at the Training Institute of the New York Freudian Society. She is also a member of the International Psychoanalytic Association.

IRWIN HIRSCH is director of the Manhattan Institute for Psychoanalysis. He is also associate professor of psychology and supervisor in the Postdoctoral Program in Psychotherapy and Psychoanalysis at Adelphi

University and is on the editorial board of *Psychoanalytic Dialogues: A Journal of Relational Perspectives.*

MARVIN HURVICH is a faculty member and supervisor at the New York University Postdoctoral Program in Psychotherapy and Psychoanalysis, a professor of psychology at Long Island University, Brooklyn Center, and a fellow at the Institute for Psychoanalytic Training and Research.

MARJORIE L. CARTER LAROWE is in private practice. She is a graduate of the New York University Postdoctoral Program in Psychotherapy and Psychoanalysis.

RICHARD LASKY is a member of the faculty and board of directors of the Institute for Psychoanalytic Training and Research. He is also clinical instructor of psychiatry, Columbia University, College of Physicians and Surgeons. He is a member of the International Psychoanalytic Association.

HARRIET LUTZKY is assistant professor at the University of Paris, a visiting scholar at New York University, and a visiting lecturer and research associate at Harvard Divinity School.

MARCIA POLLAK is on the faculty of the New York University Postdoctoral Program in Psychotherapy and Psychoanalysis and of the Manhattan Institute for Psychoanalysis.

BARBARA SCHLACHET is a faculty member in New York University's Postdoctoral Program in Psychotherapy and Psychoanalysis and is in private practice in New York City.

HELEN L. WINTROB is clinical assistant professor, Department of Psychiatry, Health Science Center, Brooklyn, N.Y. She is also in private practice in Brooklyn, N.Y.

BENJAMIN WOLSTEIN is a faculty member in the New York University Postdoctoral Program in Psychotherapy and Psychoanalysis and at the William Alanson White Institute of Psychiatry, Psychoanalysis, and Psychology.

INTRODUCTION

Psychoanalytic Reflections on Current Issues is a publication of the Psychoanalytic Society of the Postdoctoral Program of New York University. The society is composed of graduates, faculty, and supervisors of the university's postdoctoral program in Psychoanalysis and Psychotherapy.

This volume emerged from a strong belief that there should be a forum for the presentation of papers expressing the broad diversity of psychoanalytic methods, explorations, and understandings that reflect the membership of the Psychoanalytic Society.

Psychoanalytic Reflections on Current Issues represents the current and self-selected interests of the society. It, therefore, provides a compendium of the scope of psychoanalysis. The papers in this volume are heterogeneous. The volume is shaped less by the design of the editors than by the interests of those who elected to participate in the submission of contributions. The selected list of contributions is not arbitrary. The included selections are viewed as an entity that constitutes a rich sampling of the work of active investigators from a wide variety of psychoanalytic perspectives.

The purpose of this book is to stimulate further research and thought. The editors hope that the different orientations presented will help readers find points of intersection among the diverse theories and lead to the further integration of psychoanalytic theory and technique.

Howard B. Siegel, Ph.D., Editor-in Chief
Laura Barbanel, Ph.D., Associate Editor
Irwin Hirsch, Ph.D., Associate Editor
Judith Lasky, Ph.D., Associate Editor
Helen Silverman, Ph.D., Associate Editor
Susan Warshaw, Ed.D., Associate Editor

1

A "FLYING DUTCHMAN": THE PSYCHOANALYTIC
TREATMENT OF A NARCISSISTIC PERSONALITY

Emanuel Berman, Ph.D.

Fly, brother, fly! more high, more high!
Or we shall be belated:
For slow and slow that ship will go,
When the Mariner's trace is abated.
       COLERIDGE,
       The Rime of the Ancient Mariner

The legend of the "Flying Dutchman"[1] supplied a fitting metaphor for a cluster of phenomena described by many authors (for example, Keniston 1965; Lasch 1979; Modell 1984, chap. 16; Sobo 1975) as characteristic of our culture: restlessness, instability, difficulty in making lasting commitments.

Social and historical trends, such as high mobility, rapid social change, open borders, and liberal moral norms, certainly contribute to this pattern and go beyond an individual's character. It is quite likely, however, that social trends interact here with internal factors and at times may be used by the restless individual to camouflage and rationalize personal motives for a driven lifestyle.

To what extent does the legend itself provide us with clues to the psychological roots of the inability "to come to shore"? The common element in its numerous versions (Frenzel 1963, 282–84) is the description of the protagonist as a captain of a phantom ship, doomed to roam the seas eternally. Many reasons are offered for this fate—a pact with the devil, blasphemy, murder, a plague—but the most commonly recurring theme is pride and defiance. "The Dutch captain . . . met with long-continued head winds at the Cape of Good Hope. He swore that he would not put back but would strive till the day of doom, if necessary, to double the Cape. He was taken at his word, and there he still beats but never succeeds in rounding Table Bay" (Shay 1951, 14).

This omnipotent defiance of nature brings to mind issues of narcissistic grandiosity, an association reinforced by the choice of the ship's name. In one of the legend's versions, immortalized by Wagner in his opera *The Flying Dutchman,* the captain is allowed to come to harbor once every seven years; if he can win a woman's love and fidelity, he may be freed from his curse (Menninger 1941). Object love is thus portrayed as the only counterforce that may stop the eternal wandering rooted in grandiose omnipotence.

In this essay, I explore through the example of a case study the determinants of restlessness and avoidance of commitment, with an emphasis upon issues of narcissism and object relations. The young man whose psychoanalytic treatment I present and discuss will here be named Peter.[2]

THE CASE

History

Peter initiated treatment at a psychoanalytic training clinic at the age of twenty-six. His life story starts from a highly traumatic childhood. His parents separated when Peter was about two years old; his mother deserted the family. The father, an industrial worker in a New England town, found himself unable to cope with the child and asked the state to take custody. Details of Peter's life up to the age of eleven are murky. Most of these years were spent in a series of foster families and orphanages. Peter has no continuous memory for that period, though some memory flashes did appear throughout the treatment, sounding like barely remembered dream fragments: fear and humiliation on the first day in a new orphanage, the awful taste of the food, sexual games among the boys, and some unclear incidents involving fire setting.

Peter also recalls a repetitive dream dating back to the orphanage period:

I have a big task. I have to throw masses of some substance away from me, into the air. I feel it will take a very long time, so I gather a much bigger mass and throw it. Then, suddenly, I feel great emptiness and depression.

Peter's continuous memory and continuous sense of self start close to age eleven. A woman claiming to be his mother starts visiting him in the

orphanage and bringing him gifts. She introduces a man as her new husband (her fourth husband, it turns out), and eventually he is taken to his mother and stepfather's house in New York City.

The new home, however, soon proves to be stressful and frustrating. The stepfather proves to be a strict, authoritarian, demanding man, determined to turn the "little savage" from the orphanage into a well-behaved school boy. He uses corporal punishment at times, but usually it is not needed, as a particularly threatening tone of voice becomes sufficient to frighten Peter into obedience.

For a while, Peter reluctantly corresponds with his real father. A few years later, he meets his real father, when the latter comes into the city with his buddies to watch a ball game. The meeting, in a noisy tavern, proves highly embarrassing; no more contact is ever initiated on either side.

Peter's relationship with his mother is also difficult. He resents her for not protecting him from her husband's authoritarian attitude. He cannot understand how she could be attracted to this man, who Peter himself finds repulsive. Gradually, however, he discovers that she has other relationships as well. Mother turns Peter into her confidant; on some occasions, she even introduces him to her boyfriends.

At around the age of fifteen, Peter goes on an extended vacation to Europe, to his mother's homeland. He falls in love with an older female relative and writes home asking to be allowed to stay with his girlfriend in Europe. His mother writes to the girl's parents, demanding that an end be put to the relationship and Peter be sent home. Enraged, he appeals for help to his stepfather, giving in his letter a detailed account of his mother's infidelities. The letter, however, is intercepted by the mother and never reaches her husband. The family insists on his leaving, and in an act of revenge he steals an expensive lighter from the girl's father and takes it back with him.

Some time after his return to New York, Peter becomes involved with the police. He is found to possess an illegal switchblade, is put on probation, but does not keep his appointments with the probation officer. Soon afterward he completely loses interest in school, drops out, and leaves home. He is quite poor, has to steal food, and becomes involved in the Greenwich Village street life—taking LSD and other drugs and drinking. He becomes a bartender by lying about his age. Later, he becomes the manager of a fancy nightclub.

At seventeen he moves in with a woman; at nineteen he becomes

father. The baby boy is given up for adoption two months after birth, mostly due to pressures from the woman's family, and the relationship eventually breaks up. Peter denies having any regrets about losing his son but mentions incidents of excitement when noticing little boys with his son's name and approximate age.

His career as a nightclub manager comes to an abrupt end when Peter becomes involved in a violent fight with a drunk customer, causing the customer some bodily damage. Frightened of prosecution or retribution, Peter abandons everything and goes on a year-long pilgrimage to the Far East. Though appalled by the poverty and frustrated by his loneliness in his travels, this trip becomes for him a prototype of spiritual rejuvenation.

Upon his return to the United States, he joins his mother and stepfather on a vacation trip. One night, while the stepfather is drunk and deep asleep, Peter's mother appears in his bedroom and seduces him. He enjoys the intercourse, but the following day becomes very scared: what if her husband finds out? They vow to each other to keep the event a secret. Peter actually suppresses it at the beginning of his therapy. When finally reporting it, he is highly defensive, disclaims any guilt, expresses hesitant regret, and emphasizes that the occurrence should not be judged by conventional standards in view of the fact that his mother did not bring him up.

Soon afterward, Peter meets a woman, named Audrey, who becomes the center of his emotional life in the following years. Following an initial period of happiness, their relationship develops into an endless sequence of separations and reunions.

After a brief abortive career as an independent businessman, Peter finds a semiprofessional job, which he gets by claiming to be a college graduate. He strictly guards the secret of his being a high-school dropout and feels justified in doing so in view of his actual success on the job. To augment his disguise, he starts using a new last name, as he already had at a few other points in the past, switching back and forth between his father's and his stepfather's names.

External success, however, cannot obliterate his inner feeling of despair. In his application to the clinic, he speaks of depression, feelings of inadequacy, and an inability to maintain relationships. He expresses a fear of "going off the deep end."

Treatment

There was a marked contrast between the expectations created by the history—in particular, by my knowledge of Peter's childhood—and his appearance and behavior during our first contacts. He was a tall, handsome, interesting-looking man; his style conveyed self-confidence, friendliness, and charm. He was quite verbal and articulate and proceeded with minimal questioning to tell me the main events of his life as he knew them. He appeared to be well-motivated. My main initial concern was his expectation for a fast, complete cure, related to an unrealistic idealization of me and the extent of my powers.

Peter was seen three times a week, on the couch. After a few months of treatment, he also joined a psychoanalytically oriented therapy group co-led by me and a female therapist.

In the fourth session, Peter reported the following dream:

> I am in my parent's place, having a long conversation with my mother. She suggests I should go and see my [step] father. I feel apprehensive. I walk in the corridor towards the bedroom where he is. It is night, but he responds as if it was daytime—maybe he asks me to go to the store or something like that. The sentence "time disorientation" keeps repeating itself in my head. My father stands surrounded by many plants. He has a smile on his face, but I know he is conniving. Behind his back he holds a long butcher knife, and he is going to stab me. I feel enormous pressure in my head, and I feel that if I let my father stab me the pressure will go away. But I can't—I wake up.

My sense was that this dream outlined the emerging transference in all its ambivalence and complexity. Intakes by two female psychologists led to his assignment to a male analyst. The prospect of treatment aroused intense emotions from the past, making him feel disoriented in time. My attempt to help him is highly dangerous, as it may repeat his stepfather's brutal attempts to turn him from a "wild" orphanage child to a "civilized" middle-class boy, destroying his existing coping mechanisms. My benevolent intentions may be only a disguise to my plan of murderous penetration, having the added connotation of a homosexual rape. And yet, while enormously scared of the attack, he yearns for it as well—as a means of achieving intimacy and gratification, as a way of solving his conflicts and tensions while maintaining his passivity. Fear overcomes the yearning, however, and he wakes up, foreshadowing withdrawal from the therapy.

The resistance expressed in this dream, which I chose to interpret cautiously, was manifested in many other ways from the start. Peter did not show up for the appointment following the session in which the incestuous incident with his mother was first mentioned. He did come to the session after that and started it by saying in an embarrassed tone, "I missed one, didn't I?" He explained the event as resulting from his confusion. Any attempts at interpretation were rejected, as if I was attributing deliberate intentions to him or suspecting him of lying. A subsequent attempt to interpret a missed session led to a furious attack on me.

It gradually became clearer that the deceptiveness that Peter feared I was attributing to him was, in fact, a pattern in his life. He frequently lied to employers and friends. He experienced irrational guilt feelings when telling friends about his travels in Asia or when entering supermarkets; the guilt feeling appeared to have been displaced from his lying to his friends about other matters (for example, his education) and from past instances of shoplifting.

Another issue was Peter's incessant talking. Pausing, or staying silent for more than a few seconds, was experienced by him as a waste of time, as an inability to gratify me, as an abandonment of his task, and as a source of embarrassment signifying lack of social grace (the shame of the orphanage child in good society became apparent).

Peter's dreams were replete with violence: a dog attacking a woman; a woman cutting his chest with a razor blade. Initially, he himself never played a violent role in them; the thought that the dreams were related to his own impulses crossed his mind but was soon dismissed, being incongruent with his defensively naive self-image as a peaceful individual, disgusted by the violence he observes around him. Following our first summer break, he reported the following dream:

I am driving on a big divided highway, with grass in the middle. On the opposite side, I see a car coming fast towards me and a big deer running along with it on the side, as if racing with the car. Suddenly the deer runs to cross the highway in front of the car, and the car crashes into it. A hard sound is heard, but the deer seems not to have been hurt too badly. It runs into the wood, but then the car suddenly gets off the road, chasing the deer, crashing through the plants and flowers on the side.

The dream was first mentioned in a group meeting and stimulated a valuable group discussion. Members of the group interpreted the deer as a self-representation and equated the deer's abrupt crossing with Peter's provocative behavior that invites violence from father figures. Further

discussion in subsequent individual sessions seemed to confirm this interpretation: Peter's associations led him to the angry encounters with his
stepfather and to his role in several crisis points in his life. One such
point was the fight in the nightclub, leading to his escape to the Far East.

As on several previous and subsequent occasions, bringing up the past
aroused intense anxiety in Peter. Most of the time he dismissed emerging
childhood memories as trivial and meaningless. At a later point, he said
explicitly that he had no wish to remember the past—it was too painful.
Eventually, he expressed the fear that overcoming his pervasive childhood amnesia would lead to his going crazy or committing suicide.

While his demeanor in individual sessions was usually cautious and
polite, except for the specific instances of angry outbursts at me, his
responses to the group were more continuously angry. He got especially
furious at a female group member whom he experienced as seductive
and emasculating, and his associations to her consistently led to his
mother and his girlfriend.

A constant complaint of Peter's was that the group was boring and
repetitive and that members failed to express their emotions openly. He
thrived on fights and dramatic confessions but failed to identify affective
disclosures and openness when they were conveyed in calmer, more
subtle ways. He made several dramatic confessions himself, eventually
culminating with the story of having intercourse with his mother. However, there was always a sense that he selected carefully which details to
emphasize and which to omit, attempting to maintain a public image of
strength and mastery.

Six weeks after the dream of the deer, he reported a sequence of two
dreams. In one, a heavy frying pan of cast iron, which belonged to him,
was broken or cracked and thrown into the garbage by Audrey, his
girlfriend, together with his sharp kitchen knife. In the other, while
riding his bicycle he ran over a naked woman who appeared to be dead.
Later, he noticed the woman had a small penis. In the last scene of the
dream, he found the woman's lost dog and, after some hesitation, brought
it back.

This dream sequence led us in many directions, some immediately
and others in months to come. Peter's immediate associations referred to
Audrey's recent refusal to have sex with him, to his sense of humiliation
and emasculation. Her attitude reminded him of his first day out of the
orphanage and the humiliation he felt when told by his parents to wash
the dishes. I had to point out myself, however, that his response in the

dream to the humiliation was murderous. For the first time, the violence in the dream was directly owned by him.

The image of the phallic woman reminded Peter of seeing his grandmother coming naked out of the shower and believing she had a penis. His fascination with the fantasy of the phallic woman emerged more extensively later, and its relationship to his own sexual perversions was explored further (Bak 1968).

Finally, the search for the lost dog, at the dream's conclusion, emerged as his own search for his lost self—for his lost childhood. The hesitation about "bringing it back" reflected his core resistance to the therapeutic process. It was related to the fear that what was broken could not ever be repaired.

The crisis in his relationship with Audrey, following the dream, illuminated the discontinuity in Peter's object relations. His view of Audrey easily switched from idealization to depreciation, from identification to rage. He could see her as an angel at one moment and as a devil five minutes later, but never as the confused, lost woman that she appeared actually to be. He felt addicted to her, unable to break loose, and enormously resentful about the dependence caused by his own neediness and by his fear that no other woman could ever want him.

Peter's homosexual impulses started to emerge during the same period. He mentioned homosexual experiences from previous years but also an intense fear of being attacked by homosexuals and a wish to be seen in a woman's company to discourage such an attack by affirming his heterosexual identity. The idea of sexual intimacy with a man and a woman simultaneously intrigued him greatly, and he was grateful to a friend who invited him to participate in such threesomes with himself and his girlfriend.

The day he described these adventures Peter also recalled a childhood memory, possibly a screen memory. He got lost in his mother's double bed while she and an unidentified lover were taking a bath together. He was stuck under the covers and got scared that he would never get out.

Peter's rich fantasy life, which he was willing to share only at later stages of treatment, abounded in sadomasochistic themes (for example, a wish to be urinated upon), in polymorphous bisexual impulses, and in voyeuristic wishes, frequently acted upon by staring at windows or attempting to look up girls' skirts in the park. He felt intensely ashamed about these wishes and acts, though rationalized his shame as resulting solely from social prohibitions. Sex with Audrey, and occasionally with other women, was enjoyable; but at times he enjoyed masturbation better, feeling more in control.

In the transference, a new issue emerged: Peter's fear of sharing any fantasies, questions, or criticisms regarding me, my behavior with him, and my private life. It turned out that the temperature in my office was too hot for him, but he was afraid to say so, feeling too vulnerable. He once criticized me in the group, and when I did not respond with a reassuring laugh, he became very scared. On this occasion, I brought up his initial dream, which foreshadowed the fear, and related it to his fantasy about my capacity to harm and destroy him. This fantasy supplied the missing link between his aggression and his submissiveness.

In the tenth month of treatment, Peter started expressing growing restlessness. His job, previously described as challenging and creative, now became limiting and boring. Treatment, which at some points in the past he felt to be very helpful, turned into just another frustrating routine that he had to follow. Overall, he started expressing the feeling that life in New York City was inherently ugly and destructive and that only a move to another place—less crowded, less polluted, less competitive—would bring real change into his life. This claustrophobic feeling kept appearing from that point on and culminated in his actual move, one year later, to another country.

On the first occasion in which his desire to move came up, I made the comment that this way of solving difficulties appeared to be his mother's way: in fact, this was the reason she had abandoned him. This remark angered Peter immensely. He declared that the connections I suggested were nonsensical. He did not like his mother and felt she played a minor role in his life; in no way did he believe he resembled her. Our further discussion led me to the interpretation that he saw himself as a "self-made person," born in adolescence and unconnected to the passive and helpless stages of his past.

In the following session, Peter reported two dreams. In the first, he met a man who had undergone a bodily transformation, acquiring a bluish green skin, smooth as if made out of rubber, with holes for eyes. He felt revulsion, as if he was supposed to kiss or hug the man. In the second, he made love to a girl he knew. When her boyfriend (or husband) suddenly appeared he knew he was in big trouble, as the man was in the Mafia.

The oedipal content, prominent in the second dream, was evident in the first one as well. Peter's stepfather had a skin condition, which Peter found quite revolting, especially when thinking about sex between his stepfather and mother. Peter's associations, however, led in an additional direction: Frankenheimer's horror film *Seconds,* in which people undergo plastic surgery in order to start new lives under assumed identities. This connotation reminded me of his constant preoccupation with the role he plays and the image he projects (most prominently in the group); of his two interchangeable names; and of a comment he had made a few months earlier: "I am most depressed in the morning, before I can put on the mask." The man with the rubber skin, I concluded, must be an aspect of himself as well, being both an object representation and a self representation (Berman 1983). I did not verbalize this thought, however. Soon afterward, the same man appeared in another dream, in which he attempted to murder Peter. After overcoming him, Peter passed by a mirror and noticed that his reflected face was the man's face.

In discussing his interpersonal relations, Peter started emphasizing his constant need to satisfy others and to guess and meet all their needs, to the point of forcing people to be helped by him. Their subsequent lack of gratitude frequently infuriated him. I commented on the grandiose quality of his "Superman" fantasy and the related resistance to the analytic situation, in which one admits weakness, requests help, gives up control, and owns one's neediness rather than projects it. A week later he expressed in the group his wish to shed all his defenses, like Jesus. That night he had another dream:

I am in an elevator at work, with two other employees—a man and a woman. We go down, I try to get out, but I have some bundles with which I fidget, and I have to zip my coat. I ask the man to hold the bundles for me, but meanwhile the door closes and the elevator goes up. I press the button for the tenth floor, but the elevator speeds up, buzzing. The woman is alarmed; I press the emergency stop button, but it's too late: the elevator goes through the sixteenth—top —floor and bursts through the roof into the air.

Peter's associations to this dream, which terrified him, were related to an instance of acrophobia and specifically to gliding, one of his hobbies, and to fears related to it. I sensed a fascination concomitant with the terror: the wish to defy gravity, to defy nature's and man's laws seemed to fit well in the fantasy of the self-made, self-propelled Superman, free from all human ties. (His fascination with gliding, rather than with engine-equipped airplanes, made sense.) On a transference level, I was probably the person who should hold his bundles (the burdens of the past?) for him but fails him.

A new theme emerged following the elevator dream. Peter bought a new, very expensive bicycle, clearly beyond his means. (A bicycle was one of the first gifts from his mother when she reappeared in his life.) He expressed great enthusiasm about the purchase, but our discussion revealed that several other expensive objects he had bought before—a motorcycle and a guitar—were as a rule decathected within a brief period and then sold or given away with great disappointment. A parallel cycle involved airplane models, which, it emerged, he loved to build but would always destroy soon afterward, finding them to be imperfect. This abortive creativity led him to destroy sculptures he had made, including a sculpture of his girlfriend when she was pregnant with his child ("It just got dusty"). My comment about abandoning the child himself led to his sad response, "Yes, it's always so; everything is so transient."

I kept interpreting his need to destroy and abandon everything he creates and everyone he cherishes. I started realizing that his chronic forgetfulness as to what happened in past sessions was of a similar nature; both his emotions and my words soon became dusty and were thrown into the garbage.

At one point, Peter mentioned noticing a vacant apartment in my building and said that he was thinking about renting it. About two weeks after experiencing this regressive fantasy, Peter started pulling away once more, developing a defensive isolation against any deeper feelings of involvement. A friend offered him a job in another state. He accepted the offer quite impulsively, although his prospective employer had manipulated him a few years earlier in a way that had caused Peter a considerable financial loss. I interpreted the decision as a self-destructive act related to irrational rebirth fantasies and to a wish to escape me, in line with his life-long flight from relationships. Peter, initially startled and disappointed by my reaction, started bringing up the details of his previous switch of jobs, when he pulled out impulsively from a business partnership and lost most of his investment. At the end of the session, he articulated some conditions he decided to set so as to "not sell himself cheap." The friend was unable to meet them, and the deal was nullified.

Following a second summer vacation, oral needs and dependency wishes became even more prominent. Peter talked about his insatiable appetite and later inquired whether I could not supply him with Lithium to overcome his moodiness. He expressed disappointment with my avoidance of giving advice. A week later, he had a dream:

I keep trying to clear my throat, which is irritated by thousands of small pieces of metal. I can't clear it. I realize that they come from a waxing machine operated nearby, which uses steel wool.

Following his account of the dream, he proceeded to voice his complaints about my analytic approach: lots of little details and no real answer. My attempt to relate this feeling to the dream aroused loud protestations about the absurd connections that I tried to establish. His anger prevented me from expanding my interpretation: what was sticking in his throat were both my words that he couldn't swallow (the dried-up milk) and his cry, his emotions, that he was unable to get out, keeping them suppressed and fragmented.

Peter's energy was again directed toward external change in his life. He decided to move to a new apartment and to stop living with Audrey, who infuriated him by having an affair. Following his separation from Audrey, Peter started dating other women. All of them, however, disillusioned him within a brief period. He ended up feeling contempt and disgust toward them. The only women he could admire, it seemed, were those he felt were unavailable.

Renewed wishes to terminate treatment took the form of hoping that I would say enough; in the lack of an inner sense of his own needs, my reassurance and approval—he appeared to be saying—could be sufficient. When I questioned him about possible angry feelings, he expressed a sense of frustration: I encourage him to express regressive wishes but would not accept them by guiding him as I would a child. He also, again, verbalized his frequent experience of any interpretation being an accusation and of the feeling that in encouraging him to remember the past, I am pressuring him to do the impossible. The relative safety of dealing with the known, the conscious, the rational, emerged more clearly than before as a source of resistance to analytic exploration. His argumentative style appeared to be a defense to a shaky sense of self; accepting another person's view might lead to a loss of his individuality.

At one point, Peter brought up in the group his disappointment with my being passive and not offering enough guidance. The group did not accept his version. Members started sharing their own frustration with his passivity, his emotioinal unavailability, his tendency to distort and to misrepresent. He rejected their comments but admitted in his next individual session that they made him rethink the issue. He also attempted to reassure me that he did not mean to put me down. When I questioned the need for such reassurance, his fear of rejection emerged again: he lived in constant fear of a dismissal note, "a pink slip." "A pink slip like your mother gave you?" I asked. Contrary to his usual reaction to transference interpretations, Peter did not argue. He expressed his fear of returning to thoughts of abandonment: Will they overwhelm him? Will he kill himself?

In the twenty-second month of treatment, an unusual session took place. It started with an extended silence, quite unusual for the compulsively talkative Peter. He then mentioned some rare moments of complete calm in his life and how much he valued this newly discovered capacity to relax. He proceeded to describe sensory distortions experienced by him while talking to me: his hands felt heavier; the office looked smaller; my voice sounded as if I was whispering in his ear, as if my face was next to his. It feels like being a baby at mother's breast, I suggested. While mentioning an impulse to "fight back" this interpretation, Peter calmly acknowledged its validity.

Two weeks later Peter accepted a new job offer, with much better conditions, from his business friend. The new offer involved relocating to another continent. Peter accepted the offer over the weekend, informing me of his decision only after finalizing the plan. While expressing gratitude to me, he said that "making it big" in the world was his greatest ambition and more important than any further self-exploration. I saw him for two more weeks, which were spent in the enthusiastic selling of all of his belongings, save his recently purchased fancy motorcycle, and in euphoric fantasies about his prospects. Some fears about his possible loneliness in his far-away location crossed his mind but were dismissed. He promised me and the group to keep us informed about his life.

In our last session, Peter mentioned an article he had read. It described people who feel empty inside. Women like this need to fill their vagina with a penis. Men may reassure themselves by compulsive eating. Is that —Peter wondered—why he was always hungry?

Treatment was terminated just before the end of its second year, thus approximately corresponding to the age of Peter's abandonment by his mother.

Discussion

In diagnostic terms, Peter's personality presents a complex, at times confusing picture. He has numerous neurotic symptoms, including phobias, hysterical-like amnesia, and compulsive behaviors. His mood swings take him from acute depressions to bursts of hypomanic enthusiasm. His sexual behavior includes incest, homosexuality, voyeurism, and sado-masochistic fantasies, side by side with an active heterosexual adaption. Instances of stealing and a constant dependence on lying in developing his career suggest psychopathy, and he could be seen as an imposter. However, the abundance of anxiety, guilt, and strong ego ideals presents another paradox.

It seems clear, however, that at the core of Peter's difficulties lies a severe disturbance of self integration and of object relations, related to the traumatic events of his childhood.

Kohut's (1971, 1977) description of the "vertical split" in the narcissistic personality fits the central characteristics of the case. We do indeed witness "an alternation between (a) states of grandiosity which deny the frustrated need for approval and (b) states of overt feelings of emptiness and low self-esteem" (Kohut 1971, 178).

Behind Peter's "pseudovitality," excitement, and intensity, we can discern "a deep sense of uncared-for worthlessness and rejection, an incessant hunger for response, a yearning for reassurance" (Kohut 1977, 5). His constant need for stimulation was particularly evident in group sessions, and its explorations did uncover an attempt to counteract a feeling of inner deadness. Kohut's belief that such patients, as children, "felt emotionally unresponded to and had to overcome their loneliness and depression through erotic and grandiose fantasies" (5) also appears appropriate in this case.

While more specific fears frequently appeared (for example, of castration, of violence), it is quite clear that Peter's central anxiety was a fear of disintegration, of "the dissolution of the self" (Kohut 1977, 102–4). This was his main fear of analysis: that remembering the past, especially the orphanage years and reliving the related affect, may lead to a collapse, to madness, to death.

The assertive, ambitious and powerful self-image is an attempt to fend off these painful, devastating memories. On a fantasy level, a central element of Peter's grandiosity is "antigravity" (Kohut 1972, 361). His repetitive childhood dream involves overcoming gravity, though at the end of the dream emptiness and depression (the reality of object loss) emerge. Of his dreams while in treatment, the clearest expression of this motive is in the elevator dream. Three of his major hobbies betray the same preoccupation: building airplane models (like Tom in Tolpin

1975, 217), motocycle racing, and gliding. The subsequent destruction of the models as "imperfect," as well as the self-destructive tendencies evident in his motorcycle and glider adventures, suggest a poor integration of the flying fantasy, a difficulty in progressing from the "Icarus" to the "Daedalus" pattern (Tolpin 1975; Katz 1968).

The origin of this grandiose fantasy was movingly conveyed by Peter when he once talked about a mother-ape who would never drop her infant. Peter has to fly, because he was dropped. The fantasy of the self-made person, a new personality "born in adolescence" (Berman 1981), replaces the real memory of the helpless, abandoned child (suppressed through extensive amnesia). The omnipotent Superman replaces the dependent, needy self. A set of falsifications, impostures [3], and name changes is utilized to augment the new persons and makes it possible "to use one self-image as a screen against another, more painful one" (Greenson 1958).

Being abandoned left its mark on Peter in both conscious and unconscious ways. "It is abnormal for parents to abandon their children", he says. He is aware of his rage at what was done to him but denies—blocks out of his memory, it seems—the fact that he abandons his own child. This abandonment is the most concrete expression of a repetition compulsion in which an attempt is made to master the trauma by a vengeful reversal of roles, from passive to active, from victim to victimizer (Freud 1920, 17). In abandoning women, friends, employers, and his anlayst, Peter generalizes this pattern. In the endless succession of acquired loved possessions, which for awhile become transitional objects (Winnicott 1953) then lost their value and are abandoned, the same rule applies.

It is clear that Peter's capacity for object constancy is limited. In view of his loss of his family around age two, this limitation is not surprising, especially if we accept the view of McDevitt and Mahler that libidinal object constancy only begins to be attained in the third year of life, during the fourth subphase of the separation-individuation process (Lax et al. 1986, 11).

The lack of object constancy extends to a general inability to retain inner contents, such as the physical (Peter reports having several bowel movements every day) or mental (memory disturbances). The constant hunger for new objects (expressed in Peter's openness and friendliness, so impressive on first contact) is compulsive, has the meaning of filling a void, and leads to the disappointing feeling of having "used people up."

A fantasy Peter verbalized was that the world does not exist except in his imagination, and places do not come into existence until he gets there. Indeed, many aspects of Peter's personality could serve as examples of the phenomenology of failed object constancy (Ray, in Lax et al. 1986).

Peter's "object-directed pursuits . . . [suffer] the burden of having to be undertaken in the service of defensively sought-after needs for the enhancement of self-esteem" (Kohut 1977, 41). At some moments, such as during his trip to India, he may display "archaic forms of idealization: ecstatic, trancelike, religious feelings" (Kohut 1971, 97). These moments do not last long and may culminate in disillusionment or in narcissistic rage (Kohut 1972). In Peter's world people are idealized and depreciated in turn, while ambivalence is rarely consciously experienced. The coexistence of opposing views about his parents, Audrey, or myself had to be demonstrated to Peter on various occasions, but he frequently would deny the existence of one side of his feelings. This labile pattern is discussed by Greenson (1958) as related to the adoption of "screen identity." Kernberg sees it as an aspect of splitting, of keeping apart introjections and identifications of opposite quality. Objects are seen as "all good" or "all bad," "with the concomitant possibility of complete, abrupt shifts from one extreme compartment to the other" (1975, 29). In its extreme, this shift leads Peter to a complete withdrawal from the object, as discussed before.

Abandonment around age two and the nine years of motherlessness were certainly central factors in Peter's development. He experienced a massive failure of his holding environment (Modell 1984). The events of his preadolescence, however, also played an important role in the formation of his personality. Being taken home by his mother around age eleven, although it may have ameliorated some of the earlier damage, also had destructive consequences. The complex relationship of his mother and her husband made the oedipal situation, belatedly concretized, into a burdensome experience for Peter. While we notice some attempts of resolution through identification with the stepfather (for example, in reporting the mother's infidelities), these attempts are thwarted both by the mother's seductiveness and intrusiveness as well as by the stepfather's need to belittle and humiliate Peter, inflicting further, excruciating narcissistic injuries upon Peter's vulnerable self. His experience of being fathered (both by his real father and by his stepfather) is predominantly hurtful and heavily burdened his capacity to trust his analyst.

At an intense moment of this family drama, Peter turned to his mother and won a full oedipal victory. It must be recognized, however, that having sex with his mother was more than the fulfillment of a normal oedipal wish. It was also a primitive reunion with a pre-oedipal mother, whose benign qualities may be the explanation to the fact that Peter did not become even more disturbed. The incest signified rebirth[4] and repossession, as well as the defiance of human law, just as soaring signifies the defiance of nature's law; it buttressed the grandiose segment of Peter's personality. At the same time, it aroused guilt and fear and contributed to Peter's constant anxiety that he might be caught and severely punished by some authorities.

Since the climactic secret event, Peter's involvement with his parents diminished, and he augmented his personal myth (Kris 1956) of himself, as "self-made," and unrelated to his past and to his family background. All of his subsequent relationships, however, bear the mark of his unresolved family drama, in both its preoedipal and oedipal stages. This includes his polymorphous sexuality, with its endless search for stimulation, sadomasochistic components, and sexualized merger needs (Kohut 1977, 127) directed toward both parents. The latter are most evident in his wish to make love to a couple and generally in his bisexuality.

The premature termination of treatment prevented full exploration of Peter's sexual practices and fantasies. There is good reason to assume, however, that the perverse aspects of Peter's sexuality can be understood within the framework offered by Stolorow: "For structurally deficient, developmentally arrested patients, the motivationally most urgent function of perverse activity is likely to pertain to an impelling need to restore or maintain the intactness of self and object representations which are threatened with dissolution" (1979, 41).

In the attempt to make sense out of Peter's life pattern, we are almost forced to consider the Kohut–Kernberg controversy. I noted before that Kernberg's description of splitting fits Peter well; moreover, many other defenses seen by Kernberg (1975, 29–34) as characteristics of borderline pathology also appear in Peter's case. We notice primitive idealization (of a Guru he met in India, at times of me), as well as early forms of projection, manifested in his fear of violence, homosexual attack, and so on. "The main purpose of projection here is to externalize the all-bad, aggressive self and object images, and the main consequence of this need is the development of dangerous, retaliatory objects against which the patient has to defend himself" (Kernberg 1975, 30–31). Denial, including "mutual denial" of independent and discontinuous areas of consciousness, as well as omnipotence and devaluation, also appear.

However, on the basis of the reinterpretation of the Kernberg–Kohut debate suggested by Lachmann and Stolorow (1976; also Stolorow and Lachmann 1978), I would argue that the defensive function of these primitive mechanisms in warding off conflictual drive derivatives (the aspect emphasized by Kernberg) is secondary in Peter's emotional life. In his case, these mechanisms are primarily the result of a major developmental arrest, as described by Kohut or by Balint (1968; "a basic fault"). Thus, in spite of my disagreement with certain aspects of Kohut's theoretical framework (particularly the separation of narcissistic development from the growth of object relations, while to my mind these are inseparable processes), I find Kohut's formulation more helpful in understanding Peter than Kernberg's viewpoint.

The case of Peter may also serve to demonstrate other weaknesses in Kernberg's scheme. In many ways he could fit the definitions of a borderline personality disorder; yet, the defenses operating throughout this treatment did not always fall into those seen by Kernberg as more primitive, and at times repression was clearly in evidence (for example, in aspects of childhood amnesia). This would support the views of the Kris Study Group (Abend, Porder, and Willick 1983) in this matter; namely, that a neat division of defenses into separate "borderline" and "neurotic" categories is oversimplified, and the two groups have much more in common.

We should remember the serious concern expressed by Calef and Weinschel (1979) about Kernberg's scheme being regressive, in that it harks back to a sort of Kraepelinian taxonomy. Even the use of the term *borderline* may at times signify a negative countertransference reaction, a defensive need of the therapist to distance himself or herself from the patient and thus lead to iatrogenic results (Brandschaft and Stolorow 1984). And theoretically, the exaggerated emphasis on the contrast of neurotic versus borderline may bring us back to the pre-Freudian emphasis on the contrast of normal versus neurotic, even if the word *neurotic* changed its emotional connotation in the process.

This debate has, of course, serious implications for technique. Kernberg's model leads him toward a strong tendency for interpretive confrontations of defensive distortions. My own experience makes me skeptical about the long-term value of such confrontations. When we try to destroy a pathological defense—for example, by insisting to call the two personalities of a multiple personality by the same name, as Kernberg recommends (Berman 1981)—we may drive the patient out of treatment. In the present case, my insistent interpretations of Peter's missed sessions as resistance were not effective at all. They aroused narcissistic rage (Kohut 1977, 90) and never promoted insight.

In the work with Peter, and with other severely disturbed individuals, I found more empathic strategies (such as those described by Balint, Winnicott, Kohut, and Modell) to be more useful. Various psychoanalytic models offer divergent formulations for the main function of the analyst's empathic responsiveness, and their comparison goes beyond the scope of the present paper. To mention just one dividing line, Winnicott would emphasize the option the patient has to use the analyst as an object, while Kohut would see the use of the analyst as a self object as more crucial.

My own view is that these are not two contrasting possibilities. (I am also skeptical about the possibility that some individuals have "real object relations" while others only relate to self objects—another overstated dichotomy that appears at times in Kohutian literature.) The same person may be experienced both as a needed separate object and as a self object, alternately or simultaneously. (In other words, the anaclitic and narcissistic functions of the object may coexist.) Accordingly, I tend to believe that "classical transference" and "self object transference" may also coexist, and I did experience elements of both in Peter's feelings toward me.

In evaluating the outcome of treatment, one can notice several significant changes. Some compensatory structures (Kohut 1977, 2–3) became functionally reliable. Peter became more sober in his experience of reality and less impulsive and self-destructive. He abandoned his most dangerous hobbies—motorcycle racing and gliding. He learned how to curb his unintegrated grandiose fantasies and thus to avoid being exploited. The use of denial, projection, and splitting has somewhat diminished. Both the individual and the group settings supplied him with benign objects and calmed some of his fear of destroying every object in his life.

Nevertheless, the timing and form of his termination prove that the central pattern of his personality did not change. The first steps toward therapeutic regression (Balint 1968) proved to be too threatening, and he counteracted them by mobilizing his grandiose ambitions: his quest for money and success. The voyage inwards was stopped; the magical rebirth fantasy was mobilized anew; and the restless wandering resumed once more.

NOTES

1. Only after choosing the title for this paper did I realize that there is already a "Flying Dutchman" in the history of psychoanalysis. H. D. (Hilda Doolittle), in her moving memoir *Tribute to Freud* (1974), tells the story of a patient of Freud whose hours were frequently adjacent to hers and who became the center of her own fantasy life for one period of her analysis. This was Dr. J. J. van der Leeuw, a Dutch industrialist and scholar, and also a pilot, whom Freud nicknamed "The Flying Dutchman." H. D. quotes Freud as saying, "The Flying Dutchman knew that at any given moment, in the air—his element—he was likely to fly too high, to fly too quickly" (6). Van der Leeuw crashed in Tanganyka in 1934.
2. This treatment was conducted during my training at New York University's Postdoctoral Program in Psychoanalysis and Psychotherapy. I am indebted to my supervisors and teachers, Emmanuel Ghent, M.D.; Ruth Jean Eisenbud, Ph.D.; Mark Grunes, Ph.D.; and the late Ernest Schachtel, J.D., for their help in understanding the case. I am also grateful to my group coleader, Laurice Glover, M.S.W. This case was first presented at the New York Center for Psychoanalytic Training.
3. Greenacre (1958) demonstrates that "the developmental history of the imposter reveals that the child had characteristically, from the beginning, a definite type of disturbance of evolution of object relationship" (101). "The imposter seems to be repeatedly seeking confirmation of his assumed identity to overcome his sense of helplessness or incompleteness" (103). In addition, in many cases "the parents were at odds, the mother frequently despising, reproaching, or attacking the father" (101), and she may have been experienced as a phallic mother (112). All of these points suit the case of Peter.
4. The equation of birth and intercourse is confirmed in yet another fashion. Peter expressed at times a fear of damaging the woman during sex: he claimed this fear developed as a result of Audrey's fragility. Only after termination, while rereading the intake reports on Peter, did I recall a fact that never came up again: his mother's uterus was damaged when she gave birth to him, and this is why she could not have other children. His awareness of this fact must be related to Peter's sense of uniqueness—he "broke the mold"—as well as his fear of the destructiveness of his emotions and impulses.

REFERENCES

Abend, S. M., M. S. Porder, and M. S. Willick. 1983. *Borderline patients: Psychoanalytic perspectives*. New York: International Universities Press.

Bak, R. 1968. The phallic woman: The ubiquitous fantasy in perversion. *Psychoanalytic Study of the Child* 23:15–36.

Balint, M. 1968. *The Basic fault: Therapeutic aspects of regression*. London: Tavistock.

Berman, E. 1981. Multiple personality: Psychoanalytic perspectives. *International Journal of Psycho-Analysis* 62:283–300.

———. 1983. "Collective figures" and the representational world. *Psychoanalytic Review* 70:553–57.

Brandschaft, B., and R. D. Stolorow. 1984. The borderline concept: Pathological character and introgenic myth? In *Empathy*, edited by J. Lichtenberg, vol. 2. Hillsdale, N.J.: Analytic Press.

Calef, V. and E. M. Weinschel. 1979. The new psychoanalysis and psychoanalytic revisionism. *Psychoanalytic Quarterly* 48:470–91.

Doolittle, H. 1974. *Tribute to Freud*. New York: McGraw-Hill.

Frenzel, E. 1963. *Stoffe der Weiltliteratur*. Stuttgart: Kroner.

Freud, S. [1920] 1955. Beyond the pleasure principle. *Standard edition*, vol. 18, 7–64. London: Hogarth.

Greenacre, P. 1958. The imposter. In *Emotional growth*, 93–112. New York: International Universities Press, 1971.

Greenson, R. 1958. On screen defenses, screen hunger, and screen identity. *Journal of the American Psychoanalytic Association* 6:242–62.

Katz, J. 1968. Dreams of flying: Omnipotency variances in ego development. *Israel Annals of Psychiatry and Related Disciplines* 6:162–72.

Keniston, K. 1965. *The uncommitted*. New York: Harcourt, Brace & World.

Kernberg, O. 1975. *Borderline conditions and pathological narcissism*. New York: Aronson.

Kohut, H. 1971. *The analysis of the self*. New York: International Universities Press.

———. 1972. Thoughts on narcissism and narcissistic rage. *Psychoanalytic Study of the Child* 27:360–400.

———. 1977. *Restoration of the self*. New York: Aronson.

Kris, E. 1956. The personal myth: A problem in psychoanalytic technique. *Journal of the American Psychoanalytic Association* 4:653–81.

Lachmann, F., and R. Stolorow. 1976. Idealization and grandiosity: Developmental considerations and treatment implications. *Psychoanalytic Quarterly* 45:565–87.

Lasch, C. 1979. *The culture of narcissism*. New York: W. W. Norton.

Lax, R. F., S. Bach, and J. A. Burland, eds. 1986. *Self and object constancy*. New York: Guilford.

Menninger, K. A. 1941. Eve and the Flying Dutchman. *Virginia Quarterly Review* 17:53–69.

Modell, A. H. 1984. *Psychoanalysis in a new context.* New York: International Universities Press.

Shay, F. 1951. *A sailor's treasure.* New York: W. W. Norton.

Sobo, S. 1975. Narcissism and social order. *Yale Review* 64:527–43.

Stolorow, R. 1979. Psychosexuality and the representational world. *International Journal of Psycho-Analysis* 60:39–45.

Stolorow, R., and F. Lachmann. 1978. The developmental prestages of defenses: Diagnostic and therapeutic implications. *Psychoanalyic Quarterly* 47:73–102.

Tolpin, M. 1975. The Daedalus experience: A developmental vicissitude of the grandiose fantasy. *Annual of Psychoanalysis* 2:213–28.

Winnicott, D. W. 1953. Transitional objects and transitional phenomena. *International Journal of Psycho-Analysis* 34:89–97.

2

THE SACRED AND THE MATERNAL OBJECT:
AN APPLICATION OF FAIRBAIRN'S
THEORY TO RELIGION

Harriet Lutzky, Ph.D.

The psychoanalytic approach to religion Freud evolved focuses principally on the notion of deity (Freud 1927) and on ritual practices (Freud 1907). Freud derived the concept of God, understood as a wish-fulfilling fantasy, from projection of the childhood image of the father, motivated by a continuing sense of the need for protection. He related religious ritual to obsessional mechanisms, deriving from the attempt to master drives—both sexual and antisocial impulses. Freud (1907) considered religion to be a universal obsessional neurosis and obsessional neurosis a private religion.

Since the nineteenth century, however, because of increased familiarity with non-Western religious traditions, scholars of religion have accorded increasing significance to religious *experience* (in contrast to the concept of God or to ritual behavior), most particularly to the experience of the sacred. The sacred has been analyzed by social scientists as well as by theologians, and many scholars consider that it is the presence of this factor, rather than belief in the existence of a deity, which is the defining characteristic of religion.

The existence of the sacred and its distinction from the profane seem to be universal. Its referents, however, vary from culture to culture. Sacredness may be an attribute of people, animals, objects, words, places, and times. But invariably, those phenomena designated as sacred are set apart from everyday life and evoke a qualitatively unique emotional response.

While theologians naturally believe the experience of the sacred to be a subjective response to an objectively sacred reality, secular social scientists, on the other hand, are not of one mind as to the origin and meaning of such experience.

A psychoanalytic approach to religion dealing with this emphasis on the sacred has not as yet been developed. In this essay, I propose that the psychoanalytic theory of W. R. D. Fairbairn (1944) provides conceptual tools for an object-relations analysis of the experience of sacredness. I suggest that the sacred and the relational stem from a common source and are divergent evolutions of the same basic phenomenon.

Fairbairn's concept of the internal object and the dynamics he attributed to this structure will be compared with the work of two scholars of religion. Emile Durkheim (1912), the French sociologist, took the radical position that the division of experience into the categories of sacred and profane is universal and inevitable and represents the most fundamental division the mind knows. Rudolf Otto (1917), the German theologian, analyzed the phenomenology of the sacred, which he, as well as Durkheim, believed to be the essential characteristic of religion. Although the work of these early twentieth-century scholars has been much discussed and criticized, they remain towering and influential figures in the study of religion. Durkheim's and Otto's analyses, taken together, show a striking congruence with Fairbairn's concept of the internal object world.

Integrating these three theories may permit us to develop an object-relations approach to religious phenomena, and perhaps at the same time to accomplish the converse as well—to discover within the sacred elements useful for psychoanalytic theory.

The perspective developed here is based on the assumption that religion is a human and, therefore, a natural phenomenon, which will ultimately be understood by means of psychological and sociological analyses.

THE NATURE OF THE SACRED AND OF THE INTERNAL OBJECT

The Sacred (Otto)

The distinguishing feature of the sacred is generally considered to be the fact that it is set apart. In Roman religion, access to the temple precinct (the *fanum*), within which the sacrum revealed itself, was restricted or prohibited. The *profanum,* in contrast, was the common, ordinary space outside the temple precinct, which could be freely approached (Colpe 1987).

The Hebrew word for sacred, *kadosh,* although of uncertain etymology, is said to imply separation or withdrawal; the Arabic word for sacred, *haram* (whence harem), contains the notion of prohibition (Smith 1914). The sacred is separated from and prohibited to ordinary use, protected from the everyday world of the profame.

The basic aim of religious rituals, which are largely systems of avoidance, interdictions, or taboos, is to uphold this primary law forbidding contact with the sacred: touching, looking, even uttering the very word. (Although within specific ritual conditions, the prohibition may be expressly transgressed.) Untouchability is the sign of the sacred.

Rudolf Otto's (1917) cross-cultural study of religion led him to the conviction that the irreducible factor in religion is not belief in a deity or in supernatural forces but rather the experience of the sacred. While he was not the first to hold this notion, his work gave it a prominent place in religious studies. As a theologian, Otto naturally believed that the experience of the sacred is a response to a transcendent reality—the "numinous" (which in his view cannot be reduced to psychological phenomena).

In Otto's analysis, the idea of God is seen as the rational aspect of religion because the categories of rational thought may be applied to it. The sacred, on the other hand, is seen as the nonrational aspect of religion, which cannot be thought about logically but that is, nonetheless, held to be the truth on which religion is based—its essence. Preconceptual, ineffable, the sacred can be expressed only symbolically, or be suggested by the emotion it arouses.

Otto analyzed the characteristics of the nonrational aspect of the object of religious emotion (the nonrational aspect of God, or the sacred), as well as the characteristics of the subjective emotional reaction to it. The object of sacred experience Otto calls the *mysterium tremendum*—the powerful mystery. Mysterious—because it is the "wholly other" *(das ganz Andere),* total, radical otherness—impossible to grasp, know, or to contact. And overwhelmingly powerful—because that is the nature of radical otherness, of that reality that precludes relationship. Though it is by definition alien and outside the limits of everyday reality, the mysterium tremendum presents itself nonetheless as encounter with an intense, heightened reality—paradoxically experienced as the true reality.

The subjective response to the mysterious tremendum is complex. The tremendum elicits a feeling of total dependency, which Otto calls "creative feeling," the awareness of having been created. This involves the sentiment of being nothing in relation to that power but, at the same time, of being one with it. The mysterium evokes an intensely ambivalent emotional reaction: both dread and fascination. On the one hand it elicits awe and terror; on the other, yearning and the desire to possess it. Encounter may evoke uncanniness or horror but also ecstasy. The wholly other is, in fact, the *mysterium tremendum et fascinans*. The ambivalently felt sacred has been described metaphorically as an electric charge that can either electrify or electrocute. Paradoxically—from a modern point of view—the sacred is both beneficent and dangerous, both pure and impure (or unclean).[1] Otto believed that in all probability the sacred originally involved only one aspect of this ambivalent reaction—that of dread.

While morality is a fundamental aspect of most religions, it is not, however, seen as intrinsic to the sacred. The subsequent introduction of the concepts "good" and "bad" has modified the notion of the sacred, which has come to refer mainly to the pure and good, while the everyday world of the profane (whose original meaning was not pejorative) has become associated with the impure, unclean, bad, and dangerous.

To summarize, in Otto's concept of the sacred, the emotional experience of a "wholly other" on which one feels totally dependent and whose awesome power is both terrifying and fascinating, first encountered on a preconceptual and premoral level, constitutes the universal experience of the sacred, underlying and defining all religion.

The Internal Object (Fairbairn)

Fairbairn's concept of the internal object can be used to understand the psychodynamics underlying Otto's concept of the "wholly other," the sacred. Fairbairn (1944) characterized the earliest object relationship as one of profound dependency. This relationship is of an ambivalent nature, as the mother occasions both good and bad experiences. Fairbairn postulated that the primary experience of the mother is split in two, as a way of coping with her emotionally inaccessible and frustrating aspects. The "good" maternal object derives from and represents the positive contact with the mother, resulting from her empathy and responsiveness. The "bad" maternal object derives from and represents her inaccessibility, her untouchability, and the frustration, rage, and anxiety that this engenders. This "otherness" of the mother resembles an encounter with nature—a power untouched by the expression of human need. Splitting is a defense against the anxiety—annihilation anxiety—aroused by the problem of relatedness, of finding support for the dependent ego. This first splitting is of the whole maternal object.

In Fairbairn's (1943, 1944) theory, in contrast to Melanie Klein's and D. W. Winnicott's, only the "bad" object is internalized (at first).[2] Internalization and repression of the split-off "bad" maternal object not only allow mastery of the terror of unrelatedness and the rage it stimulates but also, and most significantly, protect the relationship with the "good" mother—lived out in everyday reality—from those negative feelings.

The "bad" object (internalized and repressed) is then experienced in two ways (also split). On the one hand, it is felt to withhold contact (the rejecting object), and on the other, to hold out a never-to-be-fulfilled promise of contact (the exciting object). This dual "bad" internal object elicits terror and rage in response to its withholding quality and longing in response to its promise. (This second splitting is of the "bad" internal object.)

The internalization of the "good" maternal object as an ideal object is a secondary development, which Fairbairn (1943, 1944) calls the "moral defense," transforming "unconditional" badness into "conditional," moral badness. With the internalization of "goodness," the ego creates the reassuring sense that a better relation with the (good) object is indeed possible.

Fairbairn (1944) related the "bad," and consequently the splitting of experience, to inadequate mothering. He believed that the modification of the mother-child bond brought about by civilization has exposed the infant to trauma in the form of frustration of relational needs.[3] For this reason, he held splitting to be a universal, inevitable psychological phenomenon. When the relation to the mother is particularly problematic, the splitting of the maternal object is intensified, leading to psychopath-ology—splitting, or the schizoid position, being seen as the basis of all pathology.

In the hypothetical case where perfect maternal empathy were the norm, Fairbairn (1943) believed that psychology would become social psychology, the study of relations between people. The study of intrapsy-chic life (internalized split objects) would then be relevant only to psy-chopathology.

COMPARISON OF THE NATURE OF THE INTERNAL OBJECT AND OF THE SACRED

The thesis advanced here is that the inevitable absence of perfect mater-nal empathy creates the conditions for the first encounter with the "wholly other" in the "otherness" of the mother: an object of experience on which the subject feels totally dependent, but with which it cannot come into relation and which consequently elicits both dread (and rage) and fascination and longing.

The internal object (world) is proposed as the prototype of the sacred.

In their evolution also the sacred and the internal-object world resem-ble each other. In Otto's view, the later, secondary integration of moral-ity into the sacred changes the way it is experienced. In fact, the sense of good and bad attenuates sacred power, separating out the power of evil. Fairbairn's theory also envisions a secondary, "moral" transformation of the internal-object world, attenuating the power of the "bad" by introducing hope for a better relation.

On the question of representability, the sacred again resembles life in the internal-object world. The ineffability of encounter with the sacred suggests that the sacred has its roots in early psychic development. The archaic experience of the mother being preverbal, that aspect of it which is repressed is destined never to find expression in language.

The original form of expression of religious sentiment is, in fact, hypothesized to have been action (ritual acts, dance) rather than verbal-ization. This lends support to the notion that religion expresses (in part) experience lived at a preverbal level of psychic development.

Similarly, D. W. Winnicott (1954) felt that in order to treat problems originating in the preverbal period by psychoanalytic methods, the re-pressed preverbal experience would first need to be expressed in action, in the context of the patient's current life or of the analytic relation. The primitive experience, once relived, could then be symbolized and expressed verbally for the first time. Only then would analysis of the experience be possible.

The very *set-apartness* of the sacred (in ritual action, in the attribution of sacred value, in the organization of sacred time and space) might be considered the representation par excellence of the original (ineffable) experience that actually constitutes the sacred—the act of setting apart, reevoking, and expressing the "otherness," untouchability, inaccessibility, and unapproachability of the "bad" maternal object of Fairbairn's psychoanalytic theory—the "wholly other" of the phenomenology of religion.

THE DICHOTOMY BETWEEN SACRED AND PROFANE AND BETWEEN INTERNAL AND EXTERNAL OBJECTS

The Dichotomy between Sacred and Profane (Durkheim)

Durkheim's position on the relation between the sacred and the profane is the most radical one. He saw this universal dichotomy as the mind's most fundamental differentiation of experience, a division that splits the world—natural, psychological, and social—in two. The sacred and the profane are seen as two classes of experience whose essential nature and dynamics differ radically—the sacred having meaning only within this dichotomization of reality. To Durkheim, it is as if we have two consciousnesses or are in communication with two spheres of reality—separated from each other by a barrier—that, by definition, do not touch. This division has also been analyzed as an existential distinction between two modes of being in the world (Eliade 1957).

In Durkheim's view, mankind is dual, having within both an individual self rooted in the organism and a social self, which represents the highest values. It is this dichotomy between the individual and society that Durkheim believed to underlie the universal division of experience into the profane and the sacred.[4] Thus, while considering religion to be an illusion, Durkheim believed it nonetheless to be based upon and to express an underlying, social reality.

The Dichotomy between Internal and External Objects (Fairbairn)

Fairbairn's concept of the splitting of the object world, "the dichotomy of the object" (Fairbairn 1941, 35), can be used to understand Durkheim's dichotomy between the sacred and the profane. In his conceptualization of the constitution of mind, Fairbairn also postulated a radical division in experience described previously, with life being lived in two worlds—external reality and internal reality—simultaneously.

To cope with difficulties in the primary relationship, splitting occurs, not only in the experience of the maternal object but also in the ego relating to that object as well. The "ego is an integrated structure at the outset, and . . . it is only under the influence of stress which proves too great for the innate capacities of the ego to meet that disintegration occurs" (Fairbairn 1955, 147). Thus, in the conflict involved in maintaining both wholeness and relatedness, the originally unitary ego splits (Fairbairn 1944), part of it remaining attached to the internatlized object. (And this part of the ego splits again, with the split in the internal object.) As a result, the fundamental division between the internalized object world and the world of real objects is not limited to the experience of the mother alone but, being an aspect of the ego, characterizes all of psychic life.

Comparison of the Dichotomies of Internal/External Object and Sacred/Profane

The dichotomy Fairbairn proposed on the level of the individual psyche bears striking similarities to Durkheim's sacred/profane dichotomy on the level of society. Both the sacred and the internal object refer to the representation of the social (relational) within the personality.

Fairbairn's internal object represents the problematic aspect of relatedness. Religion also may be understood as a response to anxiety about relatedness. By adding an eternal dimension to existence, religion overcomes the anxiety aroused by the ultimate threat to related ness, the ultimate encounter with "otherness"—death (Berger 1969).

The splitting of the maternal object and the ego is proposed as the prototype of the dichotomy between sacred and profane.

This "basic fault," named by Michael Balint (1968) and analyzed by Fairbairn (Morse 1972), underlies all of psychic life. The universal experience of a sacred reality distinct from the profane would then be seen to translate into what Fairbairn has called the "universal (or basic) endopyschic situation," that of the splitting of the schizoid position.

THE ROLE OF THE SACRED AND THE INTERNAL OBJECT
IN STRUCTURE AND BONDING

The Role of the Sacred in Social Structure and in
the Social Bond (Durkheim)

In Durkheim's (1912) view, because of the individual's total dependence on community—without which no human life is possible—a higher value is attributed to society than to individual (profane) existence. The value of society to human life is expressed as sacredness. Thus, religion is seen as springing from and expressing the need for attachment—the attachment of the individual to the community. The sacred is understood as representing the social bond; it is the community divinized. God is seen as a symbolic representation of society.

The ambivalent aspect of the sacred would then represent, according to Durkheim, the mixed experience of society—which brings pain and suffering as well as comfort and security. Durkheim held that without the experience of the sacred, no social structure would be conceivable. For this reason, although he himself was a nonbeliever, Durkheim considered religion to be a permanent fact of human life, though he hoped its ideational content would evolve to become more secular.

One of Durkheim's major sources was the work of the nineteenth-century Scottish theologian and anthropologist W. Robertson Smith (1914) on pre-biblical Semitic religion. Smith considered the concept of the sacred to be in and of itself a relational one. For him, since sacredness is not a quality inherent in persons or things but rather is attributed to them, the concept necessarily refers to humanity's relations with such objects.

Smith believed that originally kinship was the major principle of religion. The religious bond and the social bond were the same, evolving from the same source—the family blood tie. The gods were seen as being integral parts of the kinship system and were though of as kin. It follows from Smith's work that the relationship to the mother, as the first kinship tie, should be seen as the primary religious tie. In fact, the early Semitic deities were often goddesses, Smith noted, and only later changed their sex.

In the view of both Smith and Durkheim, religion serves the function of the preservation of society through intensification first of the kinship bond—the original social structure—and then of the wider social bond, by pervading them with sacredness.

The Role of the Internal Object in Psychic Structure and in the Relational Bond (Fairbairn)

In Fairbairn's theory, the internal object is, in and of itself, psychic, or dynamic, structure. The processes of internalization and of splitting of the object and the ego build up the structure of the psyche.

The purpose of splitting and internalization is the protection of the relation to the "good" maternal object. The relation to the real, external mother is in this way freed of the burden of rage and anxiety generated by her limitations in empathy. It is only in the safety of the internalized relation to the "bad" object that the dread, rage, and longing are lived out.

To Fairbairn, if there were perfect maternal empathy, there would be no need to preserve the bond with the mother from the disturbing negative feelings, which in that case would not be aroused. Therefore, there would then be no splitting or internalization nor the constitution of a "bad" internal object world, but simply good relationships lived out in reality.

Comparison of the Role of the Internal Object and the Sacred in Psychic and Social Structure and in Bonding

The internal object serves the same function as does sacredness: the preservation of the relational bond. This is accomplished through creation of a psychic structure (internal object), on the one hand, sanctification of a social structure (kinship bond, society as a whole), on the other.

The protection of the good relation to the mother through the constitution of the internal object as described in psychoanalytic object-relations theory appears in the anthropological study of kinship as the sacredness of the blood tie to the mother, later to extend to the kinship system as a whole, including the gods who are an integral part of it (and who were probably often originally goddesses, projections of the internalized maternal object). On the level of sociological analysis, this appears as the divinization of society, described by Durkheim, where

God symbolizes community and religion serves to intensify the social bond.

Where Durkheim saw the sacred as an inevitable aspect of social structure, the position outlined here is that the sacred (in the form of the internal object) is an inevitable aspect of psychic structure as well, an "eternal," permanent structural feature of individual (as it is of communal) life.

The preservation of the bond with the mother by the constitution of the internal object as psychic structure is proposed as the prototype of the preservation of the social bond by the relation of the sacred to the social structure.

Thus, the "sacred" becomes a permanent (structural) feature of the human condition on the psychological as well as on the sociological level.

THE RELATION OF THE SACRED AND THE INTERNAL-OBJECT WORLD TO REALITY

The Modification of Reality in the Internal-Object World and in the World of the Sacred

In the absence of a hypothetically possible (but in reality impossible) perfectly empathic relation with the mother, splitting, in Fairbairn's (1944) theory, is inevitable—"the universal (or basic) endopsychic situation." The psychic splitting that, according to the present argument, constitutes the sacred, would thus be an inevitable and, consequently, a normal, rather than a pathological, phenomenon. The sacred is, therefore, postulated to lie on a continuum between a hypothetical, ideal psychic reality without splitting, on the one hand, and the schizoid pathology resulting from an exacerbation of splitting, on the other. This places religious phenomena (along with normal psychic life) on a continuum between (hypothetical) wholeness and pathological splitting.

The point of departure for the development of religion in Durkheim's theory, for the experience of the "wholly other" in Otto's theory, and for intrapsychic development in Fairbairn's theory is dependency. It is within the context of total dependency, whether conceived as dependency on society, on the mother, or on the numinous object, that reality is constituted.

There is a modification in the experience of reality in the encounter

with the "otherness" of the mother (Fairbairn 1940), as with the numinous "wholly other." But precisely which aspect of reality has in fact
been modified? The split Fairbairn described is, for example, qualitatively different from Klein's (1946) concept of a split between "good"
and "bad," which expresses the experience of reality as determined by
affective or drive states.

The sense of reality is held to be imparted most vividly by the sense
of touch of all the five senses. Perhaps this is true of touch in the
figurative sense as well (emotional contact). If so, the split between the
experiences of relatedness and unrelatedness to the mother, between
"touch" and "can't touch," between attachment and detachment would
lead to a disturbance of the vividness or intensity with which reality is
experienced. Detachment (splitting and internalization) would thus weaken
the sense of experience being real.

This modification of the sense of reality is effected by displacement of
affective intensity, from the profane to the heightened reality of the
sacred world, from the real external-object world to the world of internal objects. "The more empty life becomes, the richer and fuller becomes
God. The impoverishing of the real world and the enriching of the Deity
is one and the same act" (Feuerbach 1841, 33). Mankind is weakened
when power, vitality, and creativity are projected onto the gods (Fromm
1966).

The sacred is the true reality to a believer (Eliade 1957)—intense and
compelling. Authentic existence, the aim of the religious quest, is therefore to be sought in the domain of the sacred. Similarly, Fairbairn
(1952a) described that it is mainly those experiences that "click" with
the reality of the inner world that contain the vital spark and possess the
most true, intense, and compelling sense of reality. (It is in this way that
experience in the real (profane) world enters the domain of the internal
(sacred) world.)

The relation to the "good" mother of everyday (profane) reality
would then be the history of the vicissitudes of attachment—the emergence from union through self-other differentiation to a new mature
relation with the other(s), apprehended within the context of his or her
own reality. The relation to the "bad" mother of internal (sacred) reality
would be the history of the vicissitudes of *detachment*—from "otherness" and unrelatedness to illusory relatedness to a self-object (like a
god)—intense and compelling.

The modification of the sense of reality (loss of intensity) associated with ego splitting would thus seem to be an inevitable aspect of the human condition. This alteration of reality, associated with the experience of the sacred, is of greater significance than the illusion of the existence of a deity, the split affecting all psychological functioning—the whole relation to the world.

Splitting—held to constitute both the internal object and the sacred —diminishes the intensity of the experience of (external, profane) reality. If splitting is, in fact, inevitable, then this modification (loss) in reality must be inherent in the human condition.

The Distortion of Reality in Schizoid Pathology and Its Similarity to the Phenomenology of the Sacred

For Fairbairn, psychopathology stems from and expresses an exacerbation of the ego splitting of the schizoid position—"the basic endopsychic situation" (Fairbairn 1944, 106), caused by greater than ordinary difficulties in the primary relation to the object. Schizoid pathology, like "normal" splitting and internalization of the object, has qualitative similarities with life lived in relation to the sacred (though in pathology these features may be more extreme).

Detachment from the world and preoccupation with another, higher reality has positive value in many religious traditions, in which otherworldliness may even be a goal. And preoccupation with another (inner) reality is the major characteristic of the schizoid attitude (Fairbairn 1940).

The omnipotence of the schizoid position is expressed in religion by identification with the grandeur (tremendum) of the sacred. This grandeur alternates with the contrasting sense of nothingness, so well known in the analysis of psychopathology. This alternance suggests the construction of the self taking place between the poles of the grandiose self and the idealized other, analyzed by Kohut (1971), who was influenced by Fairbairn (Robbins 1980).

The attitude of mystery and secrecy that characterizes the schizoid personality (Fairbairn 1940) corresponds to an essential aspect of religion—some religious rites being known simply as mysteries. And Otto defined the sacred as a powerful mystery—the mysterium tremendum.

The awe and sense of the uncanny experienced in contact with the sacred, as described by Otto, were identified by H. S. Sullivan (1953) as characteristic of reactions to the threat of intense primitive anxiety (associated with the not-me), with dissociation, and with schizoid phenomena. In Freud's (1919) discussion of the etymology of the term *uncanny*—both *heimlich* and *unheimlich* (familiar and unfamiliar)—we see the two aspects of the maternal object dealt with in Fairbairn's theory: home and not-home, relatedness and "otherness," the "thou" and "it" of Martin Buber's (1923) existential theology.

Under the sway of the internal-object world, life is lived (as if) in mythical time—"circular . . . , reversible and recoverable" (Eliade 1957, 70). The reliving of past problems was related by Freud (1920) to the phenomenon of the repetition compulsion, which he derived from the death instinct. But in Fairbairn's (1951) theory, the problematic aspect of relatedness is fixed in psychic structure (the "bad" maternal object), and it is considered to be for this structural reason, rather than because of a compulsion to repeat, that the past continually colors present experience—the (ineffable) relationship to the internal object being lived out over and over in present reality. The primary-process quality of sacred time—an eternal present—attests to its archaic psychic origins.

Qualitative similarities exist between the phenomenology of the sacred and the phenomenology of schizoid pathology.

Breaching the Wall Protecting the Internal Object and the Sacred

Closedness, characteristic of the sacred world, is the main characteristic Fairbairn (1958) attributed to his internal-object world. In pathology, the internal world is an extremely closed, totally absorbing one. Originally instituted as defenses against the stress of lack of contact, splitting and internalization may paradoxically constitute a barrier against the possibility of real contact—a psychic wall.

Similarly, the walled temple precinct, home of the sacred, may be entered under ritual conditions only. While ritual passage between profane and sacred is possible, the difficulty involved—often requiring symbolic death and rebirth—bears witness to the profound nature of the split.

Fairbairn (1958) stated that it is an *"aim of psychoanalytic treatment to effect breaches of the closed system which constitutes the patient's inner world, and thus to make this world accessible to the influence of outer reality"* (380, italics in original). Further, he believed that it was, in fact, the quality of openness itself that distinguished Freud's reality principle and that it was only in an open system that inner and outer reality could be "brought into relation" (381).

In psychoanalytic treatment, "what mediates the 'curing' or 'saving' process . . . is the development of the patient's relationship to the analyst" (Fairbairn 1955, 156). H. Guntrip (1961), Fairbairn's disciple, expressed the religious corollary of this statement: "Religion has always stood for the saving power of the good object-relationship" (256).

To Fairbairn (1958), "the greatest of all sources of resistance—is the maintenance of the patient's internal world as a closed system" (380). Resistance to change in analysis might be seen as a defense of the wall separating the "sacred" precinct from the "profane." The force of the resistance to change would be similar to the force of the resistance to breaking a taboo and approaching the sacred.

The well-known difficulty in modifying schizoid pathology by psychoanalytic treatment has its parallel in the phenomenology of religion: "The sacred is the uniquely unalterable" (Max Weber 1922, 9).

Winnicott (1963) perceived the positive side of the internalized, untouchable, ineffable, and immutable part of the self: "At the centre of each person is an incommunicado element, and *this is sacred* and most worthy of preservation" (187, italics added).

The closedness of the internal object world is proposed as the prototype of the inviolability of the sacred. Breaching the psychic/sacred wall and overcoming resistance/taboo require mediation—of ritual (social sanction), of a good object relation.

AN OBJECT-RELATIONS/DURKHEIM APPROACH TO THE STUDY OF RELIGION

While Durkheim's theory of religion has been influential, his insistence on the radical dichotomy of the concepts sacred and profane has not been generally accepted. In particular, the social basis he gave the concept of the sacred is rejected by many scholars, who suggest that he underestimated the role of individual psychology in religion.

The present application of Fairbairn's psychoanalytic theory to the sacred (as analyzed by Otto) is explicitly intended to elucidate those factors in individual psychic life that underlie not only the phenomenology of the sacred itself but also the dichotomy of sacred and profane. It is also an attempt to lend support to Durkheim's view of the role of the sacred in preserving the social bond, of the sacred and the social as two sides of the same coin (Durkheim 1912).

The theories of the sacred developed by Durkheim and Otto have thus paved the way for development of a psychoanalytic object-relations approach to the sacred, based on Fairbairn's work. I propose that integration of object-relations theory with Durkheim's sociological theory of religion might continue to be a fruitful way to study religious phenomena.

A POTENTIAL CONTRIBUTION OF THE STUDY OF THE SACRED TO OBJECT-RELATIONS THEORY

The study of the sacred may have its own contribution to make to object-relations theory. The sacred domain of experience expressed in religion and lived out in the normal relational world of the individual suffuses experience with an intense, qualitatively unique feeling-tone that cannot be adequately analyzed by Freud's concept of psychosexuality.

Whereas Freudian psychoanalysis roots psychodynamics in passion, deriving ultimately from bodily experiences of pleasure/unpleasure and of drive, object-relations theory, in contrast, it is curiously affectless, its concepts generally behavioral or cognitive, for example: attachment, dependency, symbiosis, identification, relatedness, harmony.

In Freudian theory, where the point of departure is the body, the dominant emotional force is a psychological derivative of bodily states —psychosexuality. By the same token, a theory whose point of departure is social—that is, object relations—might draw on the study of social (religious) phenomena—in this case, the experience of the sacred, —to identify another major psychic force. The quality and intensity of affect revealed by the study of the sacred seems specific to the dynamics of attachment/detachment. This affectivity, linked to the internal object world and analogous to the experience of the sacred, might be seen as a sort of *psychosacrality*.

THE "FUTURE OF AN ILLUSION" FROM AN OBJECT-RELATIONS PERSPECTIVE

Freud (1927) believed that to achieve full maturity, humanity would have to give up its wish-fulfilling belief in the existence of an illusory deity and that religion was destined to be overcome by reason and by courage in facing reality.

The argument developed here, however, implies that religion, understood as the emotional experience of the sacred (Otto, Durkheim),—with or without illusory ideation (that is, the concept of deity), but necessarily including modification of the sense of reality—would appear to be a permanent feature of the human condition when analyzed from the (secular) perspective of Fairbairn's object-relations psychoanalytic theory, just as it appears to be when analyzed from Durkheim's (secular) sociological perspective.

CONCLUSION

The sacred—born from attachment and especially from the sense of its fragility, stemming from kinship and the social bond and serving to secure them—is hypothesized to have its source in the need to protect the primary bond with the mother.

SUMMARY

This paper presents an object-relations interpretation of the experience of the sacred.

W. R. D. Fairbairn's concept of the dichotomy of the object is compared with the dichotomy between sacred and profane, as discussed by E. Durkheim. It is proposed that the distinction between sacred and profane emerges from the dual nature of the primary experience of the maternal object.

The relation to the internal object is compared with the encounter with the sacred, described by R. Otto. The internal object is proposed as a prototype for the sacred.

The similar role of the internal object and of the sacred in preserving the relational bond is discussed, as well as the modification in the sense of reality associated with each.

The encounter with the sacred, rather than being seen as an illusion to be overcome, is here seen as an irreducible fact of the human condition. It is further suggested that analysis of the sacred may increase our understanding of the emotional quality of internal object relations.

This paper is seen as a step in the development of a combined object-relations/Durkheim approach to religious phenomena.

NOTES

1. The ambivalent quality of the sacred itself, both holy and unclean, was first pointed out by W. Robertson Smith, who influenced both Durkheim and Freud on this point.
2. The argument in this article is based on Fairbairn's 1944 description of the internal world, in which the "bad object" is considered to be internalized first (in contrast to the descriptions in the 1941 and 1951 versions), and the "good object" internalized only secondarily.

   I should add that, in my opinion, it is always "bad" objects that are internalized in the first instance, since it is difficult to find any adequate motive for the internalization of objects which are satisfying and "good." Thus it would be a pointless procedure on the part of the infant to internalize the breast of a mother with whom he already had a perfect relationship in the absence of such internalization, and whose milk proved sufficient to satisfy his incorporative needs. According to this line of thought it is only in so far as his mother's breast fails to satisfy his physical and emotional needs and thus becomes a bad object that it becomes necessary for the infant to internalize it. It is only later that good objects are internalized to defend the child's ego against bad objects which have been internalized already; and the super-ego is a "good object" of this nature. (Fairbairn 1944, p. 93)

3. The citing of this notion of Fairbairn's is not to be taken as supporting arguments for return to a hypothetical idealized "precivilization" mother-child bond. On the contrary, the full import of this view of Fairbairn's has yet to be analyzed.
4. It is Durkheim's stress on this fundamental and universal dichotomy of experience that is relevant to the discussion here, rather than the issue that he considers to underlie the dichotomy.

REFERENCES

Balint, M. 1968. *The basic fault*. London: Tavistock.

Berger, P. 1969. *The sacred canopy*. New York: Anchor.

Buber, M. [1923] 1970. *I and thou*, (3d ed., trans. W. Kaufmann. Edinburgh: T. & T. Clark.

Colpe, C. 1987. The sacred and the profane, tran. R. M. Stockman. In *Encyclopedia of Religions,* edited by M. Eliade, 511–26. Chicago: University of Chicago Press.

Durkheim, E. [1912] 1976. *The elementary forms of the religious life*, (2d ed., trans. J. W. Swain. London: Allen and Unwin.

Eliade, M. [1957] 1959. *The sacred and the profane,* trans. W. R. Trask. New York: Harcourt Brace Jovanovich.

Fairbairn, W. R. D. Unless another reference is given, article is from *Psychoanalytic studies of the personality (PSP).* London: Rutledge & Kegan Paul.

————. 1927. Notes on the religious phantasies of a female patient. In *PSP,* 183–96.

————. 1940. Schizoid factors in the personality. In *PSP,* 3–27.

————. 1941. A revised psychopathology of the psychoses and psychoneuroses. In *PSP,* 28–58.

————. 1943. The repression and the return of bad objects (with special reference to the "war neuroses"). In *PSP,* 59–81.

————. 1944. Endopsychic structure considered in terms of object-relationships. In *PSP,* 82–136.

————. 1951. A synopsis of the author's views regarding the structure of the personality. In *PSP,* 162–79.

————. 1952a. *PSP.*

————. 1952b. Theoretical and experimental aspects of psychoanalysis. *British Journal of Medical Psychology* 25:122–27.

————. 1955. Observations in defense of the object-relations theory of the personality. *British Journal of Medical Psychology* 28:144–56.

————. 1958. On the nature and aims of psycho-analytical treatment. *International Journal of Psycho-Analysis* 39:374–85.

Feuerbach, L. [1841] 1957. *The essence of Christianity,* trans. George Eliot, ed. E. G. Waring and F. W. Strothman. New York: Frederick Ungar.

Fromm, E. 1966. *You shall be as gods.* Greenwich, Conn.: Fawcett.

Freud, S. [1907] 1959b. Obsessive acts and religious practices. In *Collected papers,* vol. 2, 25–35. New York: Basic Books.

————. [1919] 1959c. The uncanny. In *Collected papers,* vol. 4, 368–407. New York: Basic Books.

————. [1920] 1959. *Beyond the pleasure principle.* New York: Bantam.

————. [1927] 1961. *The future of an illusion.* New York: W. W. Norton.

Guntrip, H. 1961. *Personality and human interaction.* London: Hogarth.

Klein, M. 1946. Notes on some schizoid mechanisms. In *Envy and Gratitude,* 1–24. New York: Delta, 1975.

Kohut, H. 1971. *The analysis of the self.* New York: International Universities Press.

Marx, K. [1844] 1975. Contribution to the critique of Hegel's philosophy of law. In Karl Marx and Frederick Engels, *On religion.* Moscow: Progress Publishers.

Morse, S. J. 1972. Structure and reconstruction: A critical comparison of Michael Balint and D. W. Winnicott. *International Journal of Psycho-Analysis* 53:487–500.

Otto, R. [1917] 1950. *The ideas of the holy,* 2d ed., trans. J. W. Harvey. London: Oxford University Press.

Robbins, M. 1980. Current controversy in object-relations theory as outgrowth of a schism between Klein and Fairbairn. *International Journal of Psycho-Analysis* 66:477–91.

Smith, W. R. 1914. *The religion of the Semites,* 2d ed. London: Adam and Charles Black.

Sullivan, H. S. 1953. *The interpersonal theory of psychiatry.* New York: W. W. Norton.

Weber, M. [1922] 1963. *The sociology of religion,* trans. Ephraim Fischoff.

Winnicott, D. W. 1954. Metapsychological and clinical aspects of regression within the psycho-analytic set-up. In *Through pediatrics to psycho-analysis,* 278–94. London: Hogarth, 1975.

———. 1963. Communicating and not communicating leading to a study of certain opposites. In *The maturational processes and the facilitating environment,* 179–92. London: Hogarth, 1965.

3

A PERSPECTIVE ON AMERICAN
INTERPERSONAL RELATIONS

Benjamin Wolstein, Ph.D.

There are, in my view, two sorts of critical themes from which the major contributions of the American school of interpersonal relations evolve: first, the relation of psychology and metapsychology in the structure of psychoanalytic knowledge; and second, the relation between the psychoanalyst and the patient in the experience of psychoanalytic therapy. It is, no doubt, possible to consider the Austrian school of ego psychology and the British school of object relations,—in fact, any approach to psychoanalysis—from these same two points of view. However, the American interpersonalists introduced a special clinical quality of openness to new experience from both psychoanalysts and patients, which represents a radical shift away from the Austrian and the British schools in both theory and practice.

In theory, for example, the American interpersonalists did not simply extend and transcend the significant features of the instinctual-libidinal perspective of classical metapsychology. They did accomplish that, of course, and more. They found it possible to detach the analysis of transference from that singular metapsychology and even, for the first time, to work with the manifestations of transference in a pluralistic perspective for interpreting them. The detachment of the empirics of transference from the interpretives of instinct and libido, self-consciously wrought, and its attachment to the diverse perspectives of both psychoanalysts and patients, openly welcomed, were truly radical innovations. Radical, that is, in the original sense of the term: taking the therapeutic inquiry down to its psychic roots in human experience, as distinct from stopping at the biosocial limits of the environment in which the therapeutic inquiry is being conducted. Radical, also, in making psychoanalysis do that which its name indicates: analysis of the psyche. It brought psychoanalysis back, so to say, to its self.

This theoretical move, jolted the American psychoanalysts out of their therapeutic slumbers. It made a powerful difference in how they thought about the interactive ways they practiced, about the wider varieties of patients they learned to treat as a result, and about the diverse interpretive perspectives they now saw more clearly among themselves and also, of course, between themselves and their patients during actual psychoanalytic therapy. Not to know the interpretive meaning of transference before the live transference becomes roundly manifest to its agent is, as such, not so radical a change. To cope with that sort of clinical ignorance, among other things, traditional psychoanalysts had long since learned to project a studied attitude of interpersonal neutrality. The mirror, the surgeon, the catalyst—these metaphors served them well in this circumstance. But to accept openly and to welcome wholeheartedly the patient's own effort at interpretation, even if it was clearly unrelated or ran deeply counter to the psychoanalyst's perspective, produced a sharp contrast to earlier clinical practice. Moreover, not to treat it as prima-facie resistance took them into unexplored and uncharted territory. It made the therapeutic interaction into a qualitatively more real experience without precedent in classical psychoanalytic inquiry. They and both their metapsychologies were in it together.

Adopting the pluralism of perspectives on metapsychology as a therapeutic guideline during psychoanalytic inquiry is unique to the American school. Without pluralism, there are no discrete individuals to interpret or speculate about in metapsychology. Individuality, here, is just another point of view—no flesh of hope and despair, no blood of love and hate. That, in turn, leads to a lifeless nihilism about human values in psychoanalysis, following which any one deconstructed belief is as good and as true as any other, and according to which there is, finally, no reason to believe in anything at all. The pluralistic approach to beliefs and values was not imposed from without; nor was it predictable from within. It quite naturally and steadily grew out of the increasing clinical psychoanalytic practice with patients who were reared and immersed in a pluralistic culture, itself made up of participatory cultures from all parts of the world. The pluralistic approach, taken seriously by psychoanalysts and patients, brought the indigenously American democratic ethos into their metapsychologies of therapeutic inquiry. It transformed the mood and temper of their psychoanalytic interaction.

It seemed that interpersonal psychoanalysts took their main cues and leads from Breuer's undogmatic work with Anna O. rather than from Freud's doctrinaire work with Dora. The interpersonalists began to hear the communication of their patients unfold in new ways. They found it easier than their classical predecessors to listen to patients develop their own understandings and misunderstandings of what went wrong in their lives, without having to interpose a set of automatic instinctual-libidinal interpretations that came from another time, another place, another culture of life experience. The fate of their cultural circumstance released the interpersonal psychoanalysts from the authoritarian grip of an iconic perspective. It claimed, of course, to interpret the problems of their patients from a universal and absolute point of view. The interpersonalists found the claim a bit extravagant. It was not validated by their own changing culture. As one directly serendipitous result, they also found it possible to make far closer experiential contact with their patients, who, interestingly enough, felt freer to do the same with their psychoanalysts. Metapsychology became pluralistic receded, as such, into the therapeutic background, while interpretation was no longer the only empirical method permitted in psychoanalysis.

Freed from the therapeutic burden of making singular interpretive judgments, the American school turned its attention to other issues. During clinical psychoanalytic inquiry, it sought a new respect for the individual striving, feeling, and thought, both conscious and unconscious, brought to the therapeutic inquiry by both therapist and patient. This new freedom of experience in metapsychology meant that psychoanalysts and patients were for the first time free to express themselves more spontaneously, flexibly, and directly, whether or not their evolving interpretive ideas coincided with any perspective previously established in psychoanalysis. Bringing a new sense of freedom into the atmosphere of psychoanalytic inquiry, it suggested not only that interpersonal psychoanalysts, following Freud, could make mistakes in interpretation, which is the awareness of countertransference, but that following Ferenczi, they could even admit having made them to patients, which begins the undisguised analysis of countertransference. This new sense of freedom of inquiry was, accompanied by a noticeable reduction in tensions between autonomy and dependency, especially about having to stick like glue to interpretive metaphors not drawn from, nor in accord with, the analysis of their own experience. And probably as a direct result, those tensions were reduced for their patients as well.

Perhaps more importantly, this new freedom of interpretive inquiry fostered the closer intuitive quality of their understanding of the lives of their patients, in addition to their own. They became more subtle, their inquiry more refined. Now released from the bonds of a hermeneutic tradition they did not produce, to follow the lead of their own creative imagination wherever it pointed—even beyond the schema of the instinctual-libidinal metaphor—they did not have to trim down their own imaginative insights to fit the Procrustean bed of a singular doctrine not of their own making, one that bore little relation to their own unconscious psychic experience.

It is clear that the American interpersonalists never practiced exclusionary dogmatics. Instead, they built psychoanalysis—its empirics, systematics, and interpretives,—into a more openly inclusive discipline. This increased regard for the intuitive leads and hunches coming from their own unconscious psychic experiences expanded their clinical horizons indefinitely. For those leads and hunches allowed them to establish their own individual metapsychologies. This new self-regard opened the interpersonalists further to the emanations of their own direct experience and to a new regard for whatever leads and hunches their patients brought forth from their unconscious psychic experiences. Only after they removed their classical linchpin from the working structure of psychoanalysis and loosened the relation between psychology and metapsychology could they proceed with the clinical study of transference as well as other concepts from still other perspectives on metapsychology.

In practice as well, of course, new perspectives resulted from the cultural and interpersonal assimilation of psychoanalysis to the American scene. Central to the rise of interpersonal psychoanalysis was the unreserved acceptance of the direct psychic connection between psychoanalyst and patient. Regardless of their obvious individual differences in clinical procedure, and perhaps even because of them, the American interpersonalists knew that connection existed. Doubtless aware of their strong individual differences, they still knew they could all develop powerful therapeutic relationships with patients, more easily with some than with others, in spite of the differences among themselves and between them and their patients. To account for this ubiquitous finding, they put the cultural emphasis of their perspective aside for a while, took the interpersonal emphasis far more seriously, and pushed the clinical interpersonal program to its psychic limit.

In this sharpened interpersonal focus, the practice of psychoanalysis came down, finally, to a two-person relationship—a relationship, in short, of two whole persons and whatever was between them. That is an emphasis oceans apart from the object relations of the British school, which, by internal definition, pushed the subjective side of both the psychoanalyst and the patient beyond the boundaries of the therapeutic field. The American school of interpersonal relations, by way of contrast, taught and practiced a therapy of inclusion. Instead of a one-sided metapsychology of the object and its pre-oedipal phases of development, the interpersonalists relied for therapeutic guidance on the subject in all phases of development as well. That is, they emphasized the psychic connection arising between psychoanalyst and patient in the experiential field of therapy as a special instance of the general interpersonal view of what goes on between persons.

This psychic connection is more than a cognitive connection, or an affective connection, though it does at some point, in some still undiscovered way, always become both affective and cognitive. It is larger than both, however, in that it somehow connects the patient and therapist through all the conscious, preconscious, and unconscious psychic experiences they bring to their shared effort. It provided the often diaphanous, always qualitative medium the two create for carrying on the therapeutic exchange; so it is, as such, inevitably more than the sum of their individual experiences. They may break it down into discrete entities for quantitative analysis, into transference, resistance, anxiety, and countertransference, counterresistance, counteranxiety, and the two individually centered selves. Yet the qualitative medium of their psychic connection is, finally, unquantifiable and irreducible. They may only sense and feel it rather than think and express it. Ordinarily coparticipating in it, they unselfconsciously generate a field of transference and countertransference, and so on, in which there is desire to explore and know and understand both self and other. In fact, when the desire is already there, it is primarily self-motivated yet mutually enhanced from both sides of their unique dyad.

The experiential field of therapy evolves around the principe of interaction. The interaction of individual and environment, when applied to psychoanalyst and patient in their shared field of therapy, means that each individual becomes the immediate psychological environment for the other in that field. That is to say, the psychoanalyst becomes the immediate psychological environment for the patient; the patient the immediate psychological environment for the psychoanalyst. Their psychic connection evolves, in turn, through the dialectic they develop of self and other. Note my use of *dialectic* rather than *adaptation* here: as they are each transforming themselves, so are they each being transformed by the other in their dialectical interaction.

The principle of adaptation does not imply a two-way process. It rather suggests that the individual adapting to the environment is transformed, without the dynamic counterpoint of the environment adapting to the individual also being transformed. The individual, we often say, adapts to the environment; the environment, we rarely say, adapts to the individual. For psychoanalysts working with the adaptive point of view, the burden fell on their patients to adapt to the average, expectable standards of their environment, namely those psychoanalysts. Expressly for adaptive purposes, therefore, did patients undergo the necessary shrinkage of their uniquely individual interests, which they kept in accord with the environment. Patients were, under those conditions, themselves transformed. That is the main reason, I think, why psychoanalysts are called "shrinks."

Nor, during clinical inquiry, was the principle of adaptation ordinarily conceived as a two-way dynamic process that psychoanalysts and patients create with one another. Consider, further, what happens when this principle is brought unmodified into the field of therapy. Then, the self-defined mirror psychoanalysts, taking the attitude of neutrality to the limit, become the uninvolved psychological environment to which patients have to adapt through transference. Also, on the prearranged principle of neutrality, patients adapt without making any explicit reference to countertransference or, having done so, without expecting any coparticipant consideration of it in return. The interaction may, in this circumstance, be construed as being adaptive for patients only and not for their psychoanalysts. At the risk of both becoming adept at interpersonal artifice and psychic remoteness, moreover, does the interaction stay in neutral very long.

Though unexpected from a theoretical point of view, yet inevitable as a matter of clinical fact, patients who seek to adapt soon discover some undisclosed aspects of the immediate therapeutic environment, engendered by the personality of their psychoanalysts. It is inevitable, in my view, because it is true in the nature of things. Patients, when adapting, ordinarily encounter through intuitive observation certain qualities and patterns of their psychoanalysts, some temporarily revealed from awareness for a particular patient, others deeply repressed for reasons that have little to do with that, or any other, particular patient. And here, Freud's early injunction to the contrary notwithstanding, patients may move into a direct and detailed consideration of aspects of countertransference, no matter how psychoanalysts may then choose to proceed with it or with the intuitive capacity of their patients to make such observations. Those psychoanalysts who continue to insist on the stance of neutrality, especially if they assume it as a mannerism or attitudinized gesture, will soon see patients going around it, under it, through it, searching for some inkling of how their psychoanalysts are adapting to them from behind the facade that they are not. In any event, however, the therapeutic inquiry no longer makes sense from an adaptive point of view going one way; it has suddenly become dynamic and dialectical, its focus unalterably interpersonal to the core.

The metaphor of neutrality, in this circumstance, appears from behind the shadows of the blank screen in its full sense and meaning. What it stands for, as metaphor, becomes clearer to see: the engaged therapeutic experience now in progress. Along with the whole complex of military metaphors that classical psychoanalysts enjoyed using, that of neutrality no longer has a privileged status in interpersonal psychoanalytic procedure. Post-Freudian understanding of the developments in therapeutic interaction, like those being discussed here, cannot support the continued and unquestioned use by all psychoanalysts of Freud's highly personalized metaphors, especially because later clinical observation has made them optional at best. They are, in my view, idiosyncratic to Freud's private psychology, both aggressive and defensive by turns. And the interpretive somersaults undertaken since to make that complex of military metaphors mean what it wasn't intended to mean also do not qualify it for continued acceptance in the future. "Caveat emptor!" is the best anyone can now say. Not all post-Freudians see the experience of psychoanalytic therapy through the spectacles of the same metaphors. In fact, no two psychoanalysts, no two patients, no two dyads are exactly the same. Nor do they all share the common field of their inquiry and experience it as a military battlefield on which, to put it starkly, the point of the classical psychoanalyst's conquering resistance is to achieve an interpretive victory over the patient's neurosis, with the attitude of neutrality but another weapon for doing battle with the enemy. Therefore, not only is this metaphor not mandatory but also it is truly a manner of personal sense and feeling the particular psychoanalyst may have in the therapeutic moment, with no prescriptive value extending beyond that moment, except for those who prefer it. There is, obviously, no one way set for all psychoanalysts, self-described as neutral or not, using military metaphors or not, to deal with countertransference when it actually occurs or when patients become interested in observing its effect. The attitude of neutrality, like some great army generals, did not die. Except for an occasional effort to redefine and revive it, it simply faded away.

Psychoanalysis, as developed by the American interpersonal school, is an exploratory inquiry into the relatedness and experience arising in the therapeutic field between any two coparticipants. Note the term *experience*. It refers to whatever quale or quantum they may observe to occur between them. For that is, in essence, the interpersonal approach fully applied to clinical psychoanalytic inquiry. It covers all the felt and thought relations between persons, whether imagined in quality or discrete in quantity. It explores the world of psychic experience without prior reservation. The appeal to experience is central to the thought and practice of the American school, no less than it is to the science, art, and philosophy of the American culture at large. Thus, the American school fully accepts the natural unfolding of any interpersonal activity experienced by psychoanalysts and patients, on the principle that there is more to the psyche than its reactive objective side. That more is, namely, its spontaneity, intuitive insight, and creative imagination, its self-generated origin, sense of self, and first-personal reality. This active subjective side of the psyche comes into far greater therapeutic play in the interactional context than it does in a more remote position based on the reactive objective side and coolly neutralized against the long-standing fears of countertransference. These two sides of the psyche supplement and complete one another. Either side repressed may, of course, be derepressed. Neither disappears.

American interpersonalists use more methods than the interpretation of transference. Their method of preference is, rather, a function of the clinical material at hand. In addition to interpretation, they seek an open inquiry into the dynamic experience arising within the context of interpersonal relatedness between them and their patients. Hence we find the focus on the close and detailed exploration of resistance by the method of relatedness. That is, in essence, what the approach from the perspectives of ego, object, or interpersonal relations entails. Differences in metapsychology aside, these perspectives converge on the same sector of personality, using the method of relatedness directly applied to clinical psychoanalytic inquiry. The interpersonalists created the method of re-latedness, primarily for studying resistance, and sighted the method of experience, primarily for studying anxiety, in addition, of course, to using the traditional method of interpretation, primarily for studying transference. It is in the close and detailed study of relatedness, however, that the American interpersonal school found its clinical *raison d'être,* encouraging the strongest empirical study of the natural course of inter-active security operations any two coparticipants—both observing, both observed—can do. Such therapeutic activity was considered workable, not merely because it freed the psychoanalytic procedure from the stilted formalism of traditional neutrality. It was considered acceptable, not merely because it reflected the generally individual and interactive tem-per of the American cultural experience. These procedural and cultural factors, while certainly critical were not the finally decisive ones. This new movement toward freer interpersonal activity during clinical psy-choanalytic inquiry had still another source, which, I think, sustained the American interpersonal point of view through its changing emphases from many different sources. This new freedom found its supportive cornerstone in the fact that there is more to the psyche than its reactive objective side as manifest, for example, in the adaptive point of view and the attitude of neutrality—that is, its active subjective side as manifest, for example, in spontaneity, intuitive insight, and creative imagination. The active subjective side of the psyche comes into far greater therapeu-tic play in a liberated interactional context, open to two-way activity from both psyches in the interpersonal field, than it does in a coolly neutralized position surrounded by mirrors to counter the fear of coun-tertransference becoming observable to patients and interpretable by them.

To be interactive, psychoanalysts cannot assume an authoritarian stance—except, perhaps, in private fantasy—nor do they avoid trans-formation through clinical inquiry with their patients—nor, indeed, with their personal analysts—nor do they arrogate to themselves special avenues of psychic knowledge that are closed to patients simply by virtue of their socially defined role as patients. True, psychoanalysts may al-ready have had the good fortune of a deep-going and self-regenerative personal analysis, from which they received a first-hand knowledge of the distortive relations among conscious, preconscious, and unconscious psychic experience. That sort of methodological expertness comes from accumulated practice experience, however, not from a substantive distinction in psychic being between the two coparticipants, based on some absolute difference inherent in their socially conditioned roles.

Both psychoanalysts and patients, I am suggesting, possess a human psyche in the same terms, conditions, and capacities—such as transference, resistance, anxiety, a unique sense of self, unconscious psychic experience, and so on—and that fact makes psychoanalytic inquiry possible. With no common denominator in psychic being, they would, of course, find it impossible. We are, as Sullivan put it, all more simply human than otherwise; and, I might add, trying to become even more so. Those human-psychic capacities are, in some sense, universal. Yet, how psychoanalysts and patients experience the qualities of those capacities across time and place undoubtedly varies in uniquely individual ways. They differ in part because of their inborn temperament and its psychic gift, in part because of their first-personal sense of self and its psychic point of origin, and in part because of their acquired social and cultural patterning and its interpersonal anomalies. Thus, it is fair to conclude that they express their common psychic capacities in uniquely individual ways.

This shared ground of all clinical psychoanalytic inquiry is acknowledged without reservation in organized psychoanalytic knowledge, if not as unreservedly in organized psychoanalytic associations. It is because they share this common ground that psychoanalysts and patients are coparticipants in psychoanalytic inquiry. Now that countertransference, counterresistance, counteranxiety, and the psychoanalyst's unique sense of self may clearly be considered inalienable factors in any psychoanalytic inquiry and now that, equally clearly, they are always in dynamic interaction with transference, resistance, anxiety, and the patient's unique sense of self, it is also clear that the two participants, in effect, become coparticipants. They are, as we might say, each other's psychoanalyst and each other's patient during various phases of the work, to the extent that they are both capable and desirous of it, and in the manner to which the unique dyad they evolve is open to it, with the cooperation of the other or on their own. Their socially assigned roles are, at such points, irrelevant to the dynamic psychology of their continuing inquiry. The only encumbrances they now face are in themselves. Further exploration is a matter of personal interest and individual choice. The structure of psychoanalytic inquiry, as now constituted, both admits it and supports it.

Hence, the principle of interaction and the principle of individual differences are inextricably tied; neither holds up without the other. The dynamic activities that psychoanalysts and patients each undertake with the other bring to the foreground of the therapeutic field their acknowledged general diversity among themselves, as particular groups and as particular dyads. No two psychoanalysts, no two patients, no two dyads can be identical. The wide diversity among psychoanalysts and patients —perhaps, since the 1960s, more openly accepted by all schools of psychoanalysis—already was implicit in the new cultural and interpersonal metapsychologies of Fromm, Horney, Sullivan, and Thompson, who collaborated in the late 1930s. They produced strong perspectives that were deeply affected by the values of economic and cultural change in the 1930s, translated into social security, rather than the nineteenth-century values of evolutionary biology, translated into Social Darwinism.

Adler, Jung, Ferenczi, Rank, and others had already shown that successful psychoanalytic therapy could be done without a blind and sticky adherence to Freud's instinctual-libidinal perspective in every detail in every case. In effect, therefore, both transference and resistance could be untied from that singular interpretive point of view and be treated as well, if not better, from other points of view. To show how that same disengagement of empirics from interpretives could also succeed in the context of American culture remains, of course, the enduring contribution of the interpersonal relationists. Fromm, Horney, Sullivan, and Thompson were among the first to reach that standpoint for the study of psychoanalysis in the United States and the first to undertake the extraordinary labors in theory and practice to bring about that new convergence of the two. Not only were they not dissuaded from this task, on one side, by Freud's originally dour and pessimistic pressure against exporting his Viennese creation to America, they also were compelled, on the other, to enlarge and modify the philosophies of science and pragmatism embedded in the psychologies of James, Mead, and Dewey. Toward this new American school gravitated the foremost researchers in this psychoanalytic point of view, in which they nested the empirics and systematics of therapeutic inquiry.

There are other basic themes they found in the American life experience that contribute to the mood and striving of interpersonal relations as metapsychology. In addition to the principles of interaction and diversity already discussed above, they found the futurism of a frontier psychology; the changeability of personality and culture; the ultimate value of the individual; the appeal to direct experience for making and remaking personal beliefs, values, and ideals and to creative intelligence for their establishment in each case, therefore, of the uniqueness of each psychic self. From all of these characteristics derive the pluralism in interpretive metapsychology, the separation of religious belief from political conduct, and the difference between religious experience and institutionalized religion—which, in turn, give firm support to the empirical and systematic workings of psychoanalytic inquiry, no matter how diverse its interpretives.

The enduring attraction of Freud the man, as well as his clinical vision, lies in his uncompromising struggle (agree with it or not) to root the theory of the hypnoid state, later termed the theory of unconscious psychic experience, in the guts and genitals of nineteenth-century Darwinian biology. The central aim of his effort, I suggest, derives from this same enlightened impulse, also characteristic of American interpersonalism yet worked out in another *Zeitgeist:* namely, to separate absolute dogmatics from science and superstitious belief from empirical and systematic inquiry in the psychoanalytic domain. In his hands, however, that new evolutionary biology and the very intricately authoritarian perspective he cultivated around it became sealed off from other possibly useful, certainly creative perspectives, particularly those of Adler, Jung, Ferenczi, and Rank in his generation, not to mention those of Fromm, Horney, Sullivan, and Thompson in the next. Moreover, in the hands of his coworkers and followers, both abroad and in the United States his instinctual-libidinal perspective took on the aura and cast of interpretive dogmatism—comparable, in the narrow sense, to a religious dogma— that brought classical Freudism to the very dead end both he and they had so desperately sought to avoid. That is, either you fully believed it or you were fully out of it. The coming of psychoanalysis to America, seen from this point of view, sparked a revival of the original scientific striving that fostered the development of clinical psychoanalytic inquiry in the first place—with new values, new energies, new groups of patients. Such was the unexpected, clearly unintended result of disentangling the empirics and systematics from classical interpretives that brooked no alternative and not from any special animus against the Freudian canon as such. How else to join those empirics and systematics to still other perspectives quite foreign to it in mood, in temper, in culture?

This is the reason—in my view, the crucial reason—why the American school of interpersonal relations was founded. To call attention to the particularly American origins of this school is, simply, to call attention to a historical and cultural fact. It is not, as some might say, a matter of flag-waving chauvenism, any more than calling attention to the Austro-Hungarian origins of the id and id-ego school undercuts its relevance beyond that time and place. It is a fact that the school of interpersonal relations came into being on those shores. Its enduring contribution to the structure of psychoanalytic knowledge, among other things, rests on this very fact: it brought the clinical practice of psychoanalytic therapy into a strong conceptual accord with the American ethos of cultural pluralism, without incurring any loss of exploratory power in clinical depth. If anything, the opposite was true for both psychoanalysts and patients untouched by Freud's singular metapsychology: this novel way to hook up the empirics and systematics of psychoanalysis with a viable and credible interpretive pluralism actually made it possible to map that exploration toward greater psychic depth and intensity. The theory of unconscious psychic experience, I am proposing, is no more the exclusive possession of classical Freudism than, in its earlier statement as the hypnoid state, it was exclusively possessed by Breuer, not to mention Bernheim, Charcot, Janet, and other major hypnotherapists of that time,—all of which bodes well for the freer and fuller development of psychoanalysis everywhere.

4

VARIETIES OF SYMBIOTIC MANIFESTATIONS

Norbert Freedman, Ph.D.

What has been the fate of symbiosis over the past four decades? Symbiosis came to the attention of psychoanalysts during the late 1940s, primarily as a concept borrowed from biology—largely through the writings of Theresa Benedek (1949). During the 1950s, the emphasis initially was on the psychopathology of early infancy, notably Mahler's (1952) work on autistic and symbiotic psychoses. Yet, Mahler soon also recognized a normal, developmental phase in early child development. It was not until the 1970s that symbiosis, as a developmental phenomenon, became fully integrated as a component subphase of the separation-individuation sequence. This, of course, resulted from the work of Mahler, Pine, and Bergman (1975). However, in the 1980s the idea of symbiosis as a normal developmental phase has come under increased attack (Stern 1985; Pine 1986), especially in light of the new infancy-observation studies. Nonetheless, what we have witnessed in the 1980s is a reaffirmation of the pervasive unconscious fantasy of symbiosis, of the fantasy for merger or boundarylessness as important clinical phenomena among adults that is not only descriptive but explanatory as well. And this is so regardless of its precise correspondence to any known developmental data. It is toward this interpretation of symbiosis —as a phenomenon of adult psychopathology—that this essay was originally directed.

Pine's (1979) paper "On the Pathology of the Separation-Individua-

The chapter was originally written in 1963 and revised for presentation at the October 1967 monthly scientific meeting of the Institute for Psychoanalytic Theory and Research. It could not be published at that time because it contained confidential case material. Today, these considerations no longer apply. Its publication at this time calls for a recontextualization of the psychoanalytic concept of symbiosis from a historical perspective.

tion Process as Manifested in Later Clinical Work: An Attempt at Delineation" is an important reference paper and is related to this chapter. In this excellent and sophisticated paper, Pine cautions against the danger of overextension of the concept as well as its potential under-utilization. The most general common denominator of symbiosis as a psychoanalytic concept is that it refers to the mental representation of an inner state—a construction, not a behavioral state of oneness. Pine further suggests a greater sequence of relatively more or less differentiated states of merger or boundarylessness of the undifferentiated self vis-à-vis an undifferentiated object. Such a relativistic view is not inconsistent with Stern's (1985) recent assertion of the recurrence of developmental tasks throughout the life cycle. There are three other considerations that govern the use of the notion of symbiosis in the study of the clinical process among adults: its delineation, its explanatory value, and its application to psychoanalytic practice.

Symbiosis is a psychological state of consciousness and must be distinguished from nonsymbiotic or pseudosymbiotic phenomena. Thus, the criteria for symbiosis are not simply linguistic ("I feel so empty and wish to be one with you") nor behavioral (clinging or dependency), but its existence is inferred from a matrix of cognitive, affective, or drive-related phenomena—that is, symbiosis as a clinical state is an inference from a matrix of psychological attributes.

Symbiosis in the adult patient is an explanatory concept. It is a motivational or even drive-related state. Patients yearn for a merger, or they may dread it. It is a state that can undergo regression, denial, or disavowal. In fact, in current clinical discourse, symbiosis is often treated as an id drive.

Finally, symbiotic phenomena in adults, as a graded series of more or less differentiated experiences of merger, provide a framework for a more sophisticated approach to psychoanalytic diagnosis. In this sense, the view is consistent with the recent work of Grand and coauthors (1988) on levels of integrative failure. From this vantage point, symbiotic phenomena as a graded sequence vary from being totally pervasive to being focal and circumscribed and may be indicative of a patient's mental organization around issues of body ego, self/object, or object-relation organization.

All in all, today we are confronted with a lively discussion concerning the utility of the concept of symbiosis, its delineation, its motivational significance, and its relevance to the psychoanalytic description of psychopathology. These issues were sensed in the early 1960s but have been fully articulated in the 1980s.

INTRODUCTION

In introducing his concept of narcissism, Freud (1914), in one ingenious stroke, perceived an essential common denominator in a series of widely divergent clinical manifestations: schizophrenia or paraphrenia, organic disease, hypochondriasis, being in love, and even femininity were brought together under a conceptual umbrella. While this stroke has yielded a significant advance to our theory of human motivation, it nonetheless has led psychoanalytic thinkers and clinicians over the past four decades to disentangle the specifics from the general. Whereas all the above phenomena do partake of narcissism, they appear in widely different constellations. In fact, the term *narcissistic fixation,* in certain circles, has taken on such a pessimistic prognostic meaning perhaps because of this very overgeneralization.

I believe an analogous situation has arisen with respect to the concept of symbiosis. When Mahler (1967), Benedek (1949), and others in the 1940s and 1950s introduced the term into psychoanalysis, an important advance was achieved, for they were in a position (in spite of widely different definitions of the phenomena) to show a concomitant to the later phase of orality (six to twelve months) in terms of a very particular relationship between the self and the object world. Since the ego state described represented a very early developmental process, it lent itself to description of pathological regression and fixation.

This chapter focuses on symbiotic representations in adulthood. Symbiosis refers to an extrapolation from what Mahler (1967) has called the dual unity between mother and infant on the preverbal level and the representation of this relationship in adulthood. But symbiosis in infancy is not a single state, nor are its representations in adulthood derivatives of a single state. As a single state, symbiosis emphasizes the regressive features of the patient and leads to prognostic pessimism; yet it may be possible to discriminate qualities of symbiosis. Thus symbiosis needs to be charted in terms of kinds of symbiotic manifestations. It is the nature of progress in scientific theory that first a phenomenon and concept are identified, then we begin to specify its constituents and attributes and, finally, define its boundaries.

One of the tasks needed to identify the constituents of symbiosis is to recognize the broad scope of the term and to consider symbiosis not as a single state but as reflecting a sequence of developmental events. There is a considerable range of the emergent experiences between mother and child in the second six months of life. The phase notion is only a shorthand description of a series of developmental events of ego functions and object relationships having an arbitrary beginning and end point. Similarly, there is considerable variation in symbiotic phenomena in adulthood. In the present essay, I ask if there is a pattern in adult representations that stands in some isomorphic relationship to the patterns of early mother/infant unity. The relationship between childhood experiences and adult symbiosis may be patterned, or it may be a quantitative one. Pollock (1964) suggests a quantitative hypothesis: namely, the earlier the fixation, the more total the adult symbiosis—that is, the less the amount of available autonomy or differentiation. Whether adult symbiosis is best described along such a quantitative dimension or in terms of patterned and structural concepts will be described later. Such extrapolation should not yield a picture of symbiosis but the identification of symbiotic patterns.

A second task, if one is to define the constituents of symbiotic manifestations, revolves around just what classes of clinical phenomena are to be used in the definition. As an extrapolation of the original mother/child dual unity, the most prominent description in the literature deals with behavioral transactions between two participants, or symbiants. This refers to those partnerships marked by strong-weak bonding, using such terms as *mutualism* and the *parasite-host relationship*. The behavioral characteristics of such symbiotic transactions are clinging, touching, passivity, and dependency, as well as provocative maneuvers aimed at preserving the union. There is little question that "symbiosis" may partake of these kinds of transactions; if they are not noticeable in the patient's daily functioning, they usually emerge in the transference relationship. Yet, there are many kinds of interpersonal, mutual, or exploitative bonds that derive their motivational source from later developmental experiences; and these, as will be indicated, should be regarded as nonsymbiotic. Conversely, there may be many symbiotic experiences that lack a readily identifiable external—that is, interpersonal—expression.

Symbiotic *experiences* have also been assigned a specific pattern of instinctual discharge. Symbiotic experiences and relationships are often marked by diffuse and indiscriminate libidinalization. This overlibidinalization has been contrasted to the unneutralized aggression in so-called autistic states; yet all clinical descriptions of such discharge patterns point to corresponding representations of significant objects, and these representations may be said to exert a regulatory impact on the mode of instinctual expression.

The requisite clinical data, those most consistent with a psychoanalytic model on which descriptions of symbiosis rest, are phenomenological—that is, experiential data dealing with internalized representations of self and object, which are used in the resolution of reality contacts. The hallmarks of symbiotic representations are first, experiences of fusion in which the boundaries of the self are, in an amorphous way, fused with those of the object, and second, the experience of envelopment in which the patient feels himself or herself enclosed and contained within the object. Symbiotic manifestations may differ in terms of kinds of fusion experiences accompanied by certain patterns of libidinalization and interpersonal transactions. It is the patterning of subjective representations of self and object, described along developmental states, that should aid in the more discriminating analysis of symbiosis.

Before returning to this theme, it is appropriate to highlight the theoretical interpretation given to symbiosis in the literature as it contrasts to the position taken here. In considering the recent literature on symbiosis, one is struck by the wide range of interpretation to which the term is subject. Symbiotic phenomena in adulthood are seen as (1) derivatives (regressions or fixations) of an infantile psychosis, (2) as derivatives of a normal developmental phase leading in the case of regression or fixation to the stunting of growth and differentiation, (3) as a mode of pathological fixation that may occur at any point in human development, and (4) as a particular mode of interpersonal coexistence, regardless of any temporal fixation point. One of the broadest interpretations of symbiotic phenomenon has recently been offered by Pollock (1964). He speaks of symbiotic neurosis as a mode of mutualism and contiguous coexistence. One important issue by which the boundaries of the term symbiosis can be distinguished is by identifying the degree of phase specificity—that is, to what extent is the adult symbiotic symptom regarded as a derivative of a very particular developmental state, or to what extend may it be inherent in any ongoing transaction? To extend the term, as does Pollock, while logically tenable, is to rob it of specificity of meaning.

The second distinguishing feature for the theories of symbiosis has already been alluded to. This refers to the degree to which transactions, libidinal expressions, or phenomenological data are emphasized in defining the phenomenon. If interpersonal criteria are used, they can be extended to apply to any human relationship where two people need each other and coexist for some mutual benefit. I believe this view, first introduced by Benedek (1949) as "emotional symbiosis" and followed by Pollock (1964), is a kind of literal translation of the concept as used in biology and specifically ecology. In biology, it refers to the vital coexistence between two organisms living in close proximity for their mutual benefit. The emphasis here is on interaction and contiguity. Its translation into psychology disregards the known human capacity for internalization and symbolization. The patient's need for coexistence may not be directly observable. The literal biological view of symbiosis contrasts with the psychological one, which is phase specific and which limits the phenomenon to those internalizations that refer to that stage of human development during which contiguous existence is necessary for survival.

Let me return now to the major theme: the need to delineate the constituents and boundaries of symbiotic manifestations. My observations of symbiotic manifestation in adulthood are guided by these considerations: they deal with representations of the patient's self and object; these representations are derivatives of actual developmental states in infancy; and they may be patterned either in terms of developmental states or in terms of concomitant interpersonal and libidinal expression.

With these thoughts in mind, four different patterns of symbiotic phenomena will be delineated. The four patterns to be described will be identified in terms of the experienced position of the self vis-à-vis the object. Only the first three of these four should be identified as symbiotic, but this may be debatable. Excerpts from case material will be presented to gleen examples illustrating the patterns. I have thus not given heed to Hartmann's (1958) advice that case material is only confusing in attempting to clarify theoretical concepts. He is probably right. Therefore, I only hope that the reader can see the material as I intended it to be seen.

PATTERN ONE: THE POSITION OF SUBJECTIVE IDENTITY

Subjective identity refers to a state of experienced fusion with the maternal object, especially marked by a blurring of boundaries. The patient showing this pattern is a thirty-eight-year-old nursery-school teacher. She had been married at about eighteen, divorced at nineteen, and ever since finds it impossible to establish a new heterosexual relationship. She lives a fairly lonely existence but does have a few girlfriends with whom she goes to parties in a seemingly hopeless attempt to find a man. "It all looks so unfamiliar. I'm strange. As I enter a party, I am looking for an immediate glance that tells me we have a total communication. I long for something familiar, something warm out there." Occasionally, after a party is over, she is picked up by a man and overwhelmed by what almost amounts to a sexual assault. She is being injured. (She has masturbatory practices in which she injures herself.) When she has intercourse, she feels "completely dissolved in his arms. I do not know where he begins or where I end. I don't know anymore where I am." She experiences sensations that are not specific to any part of the body but seem to cover the entire surface of the skin. When the man turns around and closes his eyes, she is full of rage. She feels completely overcome by sensations that she cannot articulate.

The feelings of fusion became intensified after the recent death of her mother. *She felt that not only had her mother died but that she also had died.* She felt she was old and about to die. She experienced gastrointestinal symptoms that were characteristic of her mother's illness. "My body is the same as hers." Nonetheless, she is still performing some of the perfunctory tasks that she must "to stay alive." She still "drags herself to her job." These so-called autonomous functions are performed because they are accompanied by a feeling that she is doing it as though she were her mother. Half of her is with her dead mother; the other half is alive, with the illusion that her mother is still with her.

In treatment, the patient was readily receptive to any interpretations that suggested not only her tendency but also her wish to merge and to lose herself completely in the other person. She used to alternately expose herself (wearing a very low-cut dress) or sit in a crouched position, waiting for me "to envelop her." Any intervention, such as my refusal to give her a match or to allow her to bring chocolate milk containers into the sessions, was experienced as cold, brutal, and incomprehensible. In our work, the patient gradually allowed herself an experience of greater separateness. This was clearly reflected in her concept of time. At the height of the fusion experience, any momentary feeling seemed like an eternity. She could not conceive, however, of herself existing in the future. Recently she said, "I couldn't think of the future.

Previously, I could never buy a winter coat in the fall because I could not believe that it would ever be January or it would ever become cold." Similarly, she could not plan a vacation for June during the wintertime. The anticipatory function, according to Hartmann (1958), is one of the important functions in the development of secondary autonomy. The sense of time may be used as an indication of varying degrees of self-object differentiation. It is worth noting the possible connection between a sense of time and sleep experiences in childhood. (The patient had prolonged exposure, until well into her teens, of sleeping in the same bed with her mother.)

I have termed this the position of identity because the case material is permeated with experiences in which the patient feels identical with the mother, without any "as-if" qualifications. The motto is, "I am the object." We can observe the presence of phenomenological, libidinal-aggressive, and interpersonal indices of symbiotic fusion. In terms of self-representations, the patient's position vis-à-vis the object is not only one of envelopment (in picking up small children "I tend to hug and smother them") but more prominently of fusion and diffusion of body boundaries, especially in states of heightened excitation. Concomitant libidinal states are described when she reports that sexual arousal is felt orally and all over her skin.

There is an important structural aspect in this case. It is noteworthy that merging representations are not defended against. She will accept interpretations that she feels merged, that she feels like mother, that she wants to be enclosed in a warm and protected place, and, in fact, that she strives toward such a state. She is threatened by any questions that challenge that such a state is, in fact, desirable. Fusion, for her, is an ideal that has the function of preventing further individuation. Individuation, for her, elicits fears of a confused state. As she gradually developed a greater capacity for anticipation, there were concomitant shifts in eating patterns and toward more localized sexual sensations. I shall later develop the theme that the altered self-representation and anticipatory functions have a regulating effect on libidinal and aggressive expression.

PATTERN TWO: THE DOUBLE-ASPECT POSITION

In this pattern, the patient experiences himself or herself as being enveloped by the object but at the same time also feels independent of it. The experience of envelopment, however, undergoes strong denial. Patients characterized by the double-aspect position show, in their adaptive functioning, a great deal of effective and efficient performance. The symbiotic representations are not easily discernible and come to the fore only in moments of crisis.

It is difficult within these few pages to document the gap that can be noted in the behavior of the executive, the chairman, the young scientist —behavior marked both by effective, creative performance and yet by panic and paralysis when these persons are confronted with the possibility of weakness or fusion. The young executive woman, who had not spoken to her family for years, drew an emblem on a notepad showing three circles enclosed in the body of an eagle. This reminded her of herself and her two sisters. When she showed it to me, I remarked, perhaps not too wisely, "You are all together now." This comment set off a series of instances of regressive behavior.

It requires what appear to be only minor incidents to precipitate fusion-signifying panic. In a young scientist, such a reaction revolved around smoking. Smoking a cigarette was an action his father disapproved of. It could initiate a spiral of anxiety reactions, which culminated in his barricading himself in his room, closing all doors against attack. He felt, "I am weak, my body is that of a woman. My body is enclosed in this room, I cannot breathe anymore. The room is suffocating. If I can only get peace." When he is in this state, he tries to get out of his room but is overcome by an acute phobia about walking in the open streets of New York City. It is noteworthy that patients exhibiting the double-aspect pattern often seem to have well-developed phobic reactions.

The biographical substrate in this case is sharply different from that of the first pattern. There is also a sleeping problem. While his father was away from home for prolonged time periods, he lived alone with his mother. Mother frequently would call him to bed with her to "warm her up" but after an hour or two would push him away and send him back to his room. Mother had frequent depressed periods of prolonged noncommunication with severe neglect of the household. It was particularly in these periods of noncommunication that she called him into bed with her. There is again an interesting phenomenon in the conception of time. After he had achieved a previous accomplishment, it no longer existed for him. "Nothing I have done in the past seems to really have been. I am afraid that anything I do now will also disappear. As I look back, there has never been continuity to my life." One is reminded of Erikson (1959), who defines the ego as the sense of continuity of one's biography. Whereas in the first pattern, time and the patient's actions in the past had to be obliterated.

In these cases, we can again observe representations of merging, but the emphasis is on being enveloped and being contained within rather than being totally fused. While this is still a primitive experience of self and object, it does reveal a relatively clearer demarcation of boundaries. There is, furthermore, an important structural difference. The envelopment fantasies undergo denial and are coexistent with highly differentiated functions. In any given transaction, the patient may show a high degree of quasi autonomy together with features of regressive experiences. The cleavage has led me to term this pattern the *double-aspect position*. An interpersonal criterion would never have revealed these symbiotic features. There is little evidence in these patients of clinging behavior. The symbiotic manifestations are revealed only in preconscious data or are triggered off by minor daily events leading to a panic state.

These observations also stress the important distinction between the wish for symbiosis (characterized by the identity pattern) and the defense against the wish for symbiosis. The patient in the double-aspect position dreads union. The motto is I must be *in* the object. While the wish for enclosure is defended against, it may be that it is a defense against more primitive fusion experiences. The degree of defensiveness may also dictate the patient's affective state. A constant depressive resignation characterizes the mood of the identity pattern, with the patient feeling helpless and disbelieving that the wish for a state of fusion can be gratified. But in the double-aspect position, there is a tenacious and often efficient clinging to reality with the abrupt emergence of phobic reactions.

Several characteristic ego functions and libidinal states may be related to the envelopment representations. The characteristic conception of time has already been described. Sexual experiences were marked by anesthesia, and when sexual feelings did occur, they provoked panic. The patient's perception of the physical features of his mother, often associated with experiences of rage, are vague and blurred. Finally, certain qualities of the early mother-infant relationship may be inferred from the case material. There appear to be differences in the two patterns. Whereas in the first pattern the suffocating and overstimulating relationship (sleeping together up to adulthood) seems to facilitate fixation on fusion, an inconstancy element appears to be the mark of the double-aspect position (sleeping and ejecting from bed).

Little attention has been given to the degree of autonomous and synthetic achievement (science, art, and so on) in patients showing the double-aspect position. The case material suggests that in large measure this attainment derives from a relatively indiscriminate internalization of the parental ego ideal. These functions have the characteristics of an overdifferentiated self-image as described by Lewis (1958). The uneven development of quasi autonomy, side by side with envelopment fantasies, may be related to such vacillating infantile object experiences.

PATTERN THREE: THE POSITION OF PARALLELISM

The phenomenology of this pattern is best expressed by the image of Siamese twins living side by side. In the two cases in which I have observed this pattern, there was also a cycloid picture marked by significant shifts in affect from depression to elation.

The patient is a twenty-nine-year-old single girl, a painter, who has a steady woman companion of her mother's age. This friend drives her to wherever she wishes to go (including to the analytic session). The patient takes her friend along on casual dates, for example, having cocktails with a boyfriend. When this woman friend is busy, and this does not happen very often, there are other girlfriends to call upon to serve a similar function. The behavioral union is reflected in subjective experiences. She will say, "We are in fact like Siamese twins. Our arms are tied together; we cannot be apart." It is a side-by-side representation. Her heterosexual experiences have a similar characteristic. While she has had a number of more turbulent relationships in which she has had experiences of being enveloped (and this emphasizes that the different patterns of symbiotic experiences are far from pure and are constantly subject to the vicissitudes of regressive and progressive forces), there is always one male partner whom she sees on an ongoing basis. They rarely have sexual relations; but when they do go to bed, she just likes to lie next to him and to touch him but wishes to avoid penetration.

There is, however, an intrinsically unstable quality about these twin-ship patterns. The oscillation of twinship experiences, vis-à-vis her female companion, and affective shifts can be traced within a twenty-four hour period. Let us start on a particular morning. She experiences a rebuff (for example, the boyfriend fails to call) and becomes seriously depressed with suicidal thoughts. She calls her female companion. She will find quick relief in unburdening herself. They will plan an evening party together. In the course of the party, the patient becomes exceptionally charming and vivacious, especially toward influential guests. She asks her female friend to leave. As the party continues, she becomes more and more elated. She truly experiences being the mistress of the house. In this state, there is a pseudoautonomy. She initiates professional contacts. She makes plans for summer vacation. She feels on top of the world, but a slight rebuff elicits new panic leading to severe depression, again with suicidal thoughts. She seeks to reestablish contact with her companion. Within twenty-four hours, the symbiotic partner has joined, been ejected, and rejoined.

We can observe a pattern of parallelism in this patient in two senses: First, her contiguous bind to both her boyfriend and her female companion. Second, perhaps more important in the cycloid pattern, the parallelism is revealed if one takes the entire twenty-four hour period as a symbolic expression of a biographical crisis regarding her mother's separation from her father and subsequent remarriage to another man. For the hectic pace does represent, in condensed form, the mother's behavior at the time of separation vis-à-vis her daughter.

It is of interest that the patient has her own characteristic conception of time. Instead of the denial of the future or denial of the past, we can observe that all critical experiences are compressed within a twenty-four-hour period. Past and future are not denied but are on the periphery of awareness. She will come into the session saying, "I have experienced so much I do not think I can cram it into this session. Time moves so fast. A hundred things occur in a single moment." Again, a sleeping pattern is important in this case, in that the patient, up to the age of eleven, was exposed to sleeping in the same room alone with her father with whom she lived after his divorce.

I have also observed, in another patient, the association between the symbolic representation of parallelism and an affective cycle involving depression and elation condensed into a short time span. In this patient, the twinship ideation was beautifully described in a day fantasy. "I thought of the first day of Chanukah. The *shamus* (associated with father) was burning down quickly, flickering up, flickering down; and the flames struggled, extinguished, and died. The other candle (identified with the patient himself) followed in the same course. There was no choice. It flickered up and down, and it had to go out the same way and vanished."

It is of interest to consider these foregoing observations in the light of Lewin's (1950) interpretations of elation. Lewin stressed that the greatest fusion experiences take place in the elated state. In the present observations, the greatest experiences of fusion were noted in the identity position, in which the patient also showed marked depressive features. Lewin does not stress the representation of parallelism. One wonders whether there are intrinsic connections between the cycloid affective pattern and the representations of parallelism.

To summarize thus far: In the identity pattern, the self-object representations emphasized fusion; in the double-aspect position, the emphasis was on being enveloped; and the model for the parallelism pattern is that of contiguity, symbolically expressed by the image of Siamese twins. The quality of vital interconnection is reminiscent of Greenacre's (1958) conception of focal symbiosis in which a particular body part is used to mark the connection.

Various adaptive characteristics mark the pattern of parallelism. There is first the characteristic mode of defense. In the double-aspect position, we have noted a denial of the wish for union; in the parallelism, there is frequently an affirmation of this wish. Another aspect of this pattern is the variability of symbiotic representations, including, as we have seen, feelings of being enveloped and instances of fusion. The affective cycle also reveals, as expected, a variety of expressions of orality, such as nail biting, cursing, and drinking. The great variability and instability of this pattern may also reflect the patient's continual attempt to leave the symbiotic orbit; for as we have seen, she embraces the symbiotic partner, leaves her, and rejoins her.

In what specific way can the pattern of parallelism be said to be symbiotic? Boundaries between self and object representations are relatively clear. The union image of "I" and "she" can be used adaptively: they both run the house together before a crisis tears them apart. These observations certainly speak for a lesser intensity of symbiosis. Yet the union is a matter of perceived existence and survival. Threat of dissolution can call forth intense homicidal or suicidal feelings. The partners act as though they were unable to exist apart. The survival quality of the merging representations, although not previously mentioned, was also a characteristic of the other two symbiotic patterns.

PATTERN FOUR: THE INTERACTION POSITION

The fourth pattern exemplifies a fusion experience in a patient who otherwise shows a well-defined representation of self in her interaction with the object world. She is a social worker, a most effective one, dedicated to her work. Her central character problem is one of clinging and passivity, particularly toward authority figures. She feels intensely anxious in her occasional dealings with the male head of the agency, especially since she fears reprisal from her female supervisor. She is talented and would like to try sculpting but cannot allow herself to do this for fear that her mother, who had artistic aspirations herself, may be offended by her success. She has long and loyal friendships with women, but these well-sublimated homosexual experiences act as a constant inhibitor whenever she tries to flirt with a man. The patient's dependent and clinging social behavior, her fear of competition with women, and her restriction in carrying out projects of her own might point to a kind of "symbiotic clinging." The case, in fact, shows many features similar to those of the case presented by Pollock (1964).

In the course of analysis, the hypothesis was supported that the clinging behavior in this woman represented a homosexual regression as a defense against oedipal wishes. She would not allow herself to look into a man's eyes if a woman was present. When she did establish a relationship with a man, she developed acute anxieties about facing the women in her friend's hometown. (She viewed them as a "bunch of hyenas.") In her sexual relationships, she apparently was able to experience a vaginal orgasm but only if the following transformation took place: "I feel I'm entering the body of a man. I feel protected by him; I am him looking at my vagina." (This experience elicited childhood memories in which her mother showed an inordinate interest in the cleanliness of the patient's vagina during various bathroom scenes). After intercourse, she regained her sense of personal identity but now felt bitterness and resentment toward the man.

The clinging social behavior, the loyal and sublimated homosexual relationships with women, and the transformation of identity and sexual experiences are, as indicated, defenses against oedipal wishes. Fusion and envelopment experiences here are defenses, but not so much against autism or unneutralized rage as in pattern two but against heterosexual wishes. These fusion experiences should not be regarded as symbiotic: First of all they are transitory; they are used adaptively, almost as a

matter of choice in the service of obtaining sexual pleasure. Most important, they do not involve the theme of survival—that is, there is no crisis
of existence. A further criterion for an experience to be classified as
symbiotic is that not only must there be representations of merging but
these representations must be viewed as essential for survival or existence.

DISCUSSION

Let me start the discussion of these observations with a confession: in
choosing a name for the four patterns of symbiotic manifestations, I was
intrigued, perhaps seduced, by the theories of the relationship between
mind and body in philosophy. These theories vary in terms of the relative
degree of unity and separateness attributed to mind and body. Thus,
there is the theory of identity; the double-aspect theory (in which the
identity is still retained and different aspects emphasized); the theory of
psychophysical parallelism, where both are bound by a single common
force; and the theory of interactionism. I used the word seduced because
I know that such attractive classifications may become a trap. I do
believe, however, that the present proposal may be a fruitful classification.

Since the topic under discussion is symbiosis, we must not lose sight
of the common denominator underlying all patterns. In fact, I believe
that the identification of the foregoing patterns allows us to better define
the phenomenon of symbiosis, particularly as it appears in adult patients. Namely psychological symbiosis refers to those lasting representations that have the characteristic of object fusion, envelopment, and
parallelism, and which must be sustained because of their perceived
survival and existence value to the patient. The patient, in each of the
first three patterns, feels that he or she cannot exist without the object.
By including the criterion of survival, we are maintaining a biological as
well as a psychological conception of symbiosis. All of the symbiotic
patterns deal with the problem of separation, each representing a different mode of negotiating separation. In this sense, all symbiosis involves
an existential problem.

As one reflects upon these observed patterns, one wonders whether
they represent a single quantitative scale of progressive differentiation or
whether they represent discrete qualitative categories. In part, the former
may be true, for as we move from the identity position to patterns of

parallelism and interaction, we observe also that the images of union and merging become less intense, less total and pervasive in the patient's life, and less disruptive to his or her daily functioning. Thus, the awareness of the wish for merging in the double-aspect position can be far more disorganizing and trigger off an acute psychosis than the experience of identity in the first pattern. The concept of development patterns implies the coalescing of different processes and events at a particular stage. The notion of discrete levels would seem to be more appropriate than that of a gradient. The following is an outline of some of the processes that I believe make up the discrete patterns of symbiosis.

The first and most obvious is that of the *clarity of self and object boundaries*. Here we have the clear progression from pattern one to Pattern four. Next, there is the degree of *defensiveness*. For any symbiotic manifestation we can ask, Is the merging wish dreaded (as in patterns two and four) or does it represent a wished-for state (as it may be in patterns one and three)? Defensiveness may give us important clues about the structural position of the symbiotic manifestation. I suspect that the defensive structure in which the symbiotic ideas emerge may indicate whether we are dealing with a fixation or a regressive phenomenon. This decision has obvious practical applications to treatment and guides decisions regarding intervention.

A further process determining the qualitative pattern or structure of a symbiotic manifestation is the *constancy of its emergence*. Certainly, the symbiotic experiences are more constant from session to session or within a single session as we move from pattern three to pattern one. The hypothesis itself suggests that this constancy may be related to the mother-infant relationship in the patient's biography. In the identity position, there was a quality of continuous overstimulation and smothering. In the second and third case, the pattern was one of seduction and ejection. Greenacre (1958), in particular, has emphasized that one of the conditions contributing to symbiosis is a lack of responsiveness to the usual and natural rhythmic fluctuations observed in the first few months of life. In this sense, a smothering and overstimulating relationship may be thought of as one that produces a state of overconstancy. Furthermore, constancy may also be intimately related to the nature of affective fluctuations. For example, the degree of chronic depression was more characteristic of the first pattern, and the degree of cycloid shifts was a characteristic of the third pattern.

Implicit in what I have said is the idea that for each pattern having a certain representation of self and object, there may be concomitant patterns of defense, libidinal expression, and biographical events. This appears to be the case in the six cases I have studied. I have no idea whether it will hold true, but the patterns do represent hypotheses of the interrelationships between phenomenological aspects of symbiosis and other dynamic processes that can be checked empirically.

One may raise the further question, What is gained by such a description of the patient's phenomenology? More specifically, one cannot help but be impressed, as one considers the case material, that each pattern has its own libidinal concomitant and, specifically, its particular type of orality. A description of the four patterns in these terms is equally feasible.

In terms of sexual disturbances, the material offers evidence in support of Handelsman's (1965) contention of an association between ego defect signifying symbiotic merging and sexual disturbances. Moreover, one can extend and specify this contention in the following manner: in pattern one, the position of identity and sexual fusion seemed to be complete, synesthetic, and involving the entire skin surface; in pattern two, the double-aspect position, sexuality appeared to be marked by anesthesia; in pattern three, the position of parallelism, sexuality was promiscuous and emphasized touching—that is, experiences of contiguity; in pattern four, the interaction position, we seemed to be dealing with a homosexual defense against heterosexuality.

Similarly, with respect to orality, we can see in the data an association between different kinds of orality and ego defects. The patient in pattern one seemed to be bent on continuous introjection of sustenance marked by oral passivity. Pattern three shows an alternating introjection and ejection with oral sadism in evidence. This oscillation has an adaptive as well as a discharge function. Escalona (1963) has stressed the double aspect of orality in infancy: when an infant takes in something with his or her mouth, he or she is not only gratifying a need and thus reducing awareness of external stimulation but may also be using the mouth as a sense organ in an adaptive way. The infant learns to identify the touch and taste of the thing "out there."

Let us return then to the question of the gain that may be derived from charting the regressive patterns of symbiosis. We have good documentation of the close concomitant of the various ego defects and various libidinal states. The message that ego psychology has to offer is to correlate the economic processes with ego states. That, to be sure, is one task. But correlation, no matter how exact, does not mean identity. The emerging adaptive functions, as the organism learns to cope with his or her environment, may have a regulatory impact on the libidinal processes as well. The adaptive and need-gratifying functions not only coexist but the former may also determine the latter. This possibility gives us a significant handle for technique in therapy.

The point was further supported by my observations on the sense of time among these patients. Three of the patterns, as will be recalled, showed different qualities in the perception of the patient's life span. In pattern one, the future time appeared to be inconceivable; in pattern two, the past appeared to be obliterated; in pattern three, both future and past had to be condensed into the now—that is, to a single twenty-four-hour period. Time is meaningless unless we consider the events and actions represented in it. We can then ask the patient: "When are you going to buy a new coat?" or "What are your plans for vacations?" or "How could you alter your place?" Such direct communication can then have an important impact upon significant areas of object relationships and bring out the critical psychosexual conflicts.

In conclusion, I have some comments on the basic mechanisms leading to the patterns of symbiotic functioning. They all deal, as I mentioned, with different modes of negotiating separation. The psychoanalytic model for separation was provided for us in Freud's *Mourning and Melancholia* (1917)—that is, we separate by taking into the ego a part of the person who leaves us or who signals he or she may leave us. Then comes the question, How well can we use adaptively what we have taken? I wonder whether the controversy regarding the various kinds of internalization (introjection, incorporation, or identification) may deal not with different mechanisms but with the degree of adequacy of integrating whatever has been internalized at a particular level. It may be floating about as a foreign body and then it would be called an introject, as was observed in pattern one. Here, the patient said at one point, "I cannot understand where this craving for warmth comes from." Or, it may be used in a quasi-adaptive manner, as in pattern three, when both the patient and her companion felt that they were the keeper of the house.

The more integrated the internalization, the more, as Freud has pointed out, can the ego grow through identification—that is, the more can it partake of life by taking in. Symbiotic representations are essentially nonintegrated internalizations, and they force individuals to look constantly for objects that will sustain them. The therapeutic task is to gradually shift the patterns of symbiotic representations in the direction of internalization that can be used adaptively.

REFERENCES

Benedek, T. 1949. The psychosomatic implications of the primary unit: Mother-child. *American Journal of Orthopsychiatry* 19:642–54.

Erikson, E. 1959. *Identity and the life cycle.* Psychological Issues, monograph 1. New York: International Universities Press.

Escalona, S. K. 1963. Patterns of infantile experience and the development process. *Psychoanalytic Study of the Child* 18:197–244.

Freud, S. [1914] 1957. On narcissism: An introduction. In *Standard edition,* vol. 14, 237–58. London: Hogarth Press. 1988.

———. [1917] 1957. Mourning and Melancholia. In *Standard Edition,* vol. 14, 237–58. London: Hogarth Press.

Grand, S., N. Freedman, K. Feiner, and S. Kiersky. 1988. Notes on the progressive and regressive shifts in levels of integrative failure: A preliminary report on the classification of severe psychopathology. In *Psychoanalysis and contemporary thought* 11, no. 4.

Greenacre, P. 1958. Early physical determinants in the development of the sense of identity. *Journal of the American Psychoanalytic Association* 6:612–27.

Handelsman, I. 1965. The effects of early object relationships on sexual development: Autistic and symbiotic modes of adaptation. *Psychoanalytic Study of the Child* 20:367–83.

Hartmann, H. 1958. Ego psychology and the problem of adaptation. In *Journal of the American Psychoanalytic Association,* monograph series 1. New York: International Universities Press.

Lewin, B. D. 1950. Addendum to the theory of the oral triad. In *Psychoanalysis of elation.* New York: W. W. Norton.

Lewis, H. B. 1958. Over-differentiation and under-individuation of the self. *Psychoanalysis and the Psychoanalytic Review* 45:3–24.

Mahler, M. S. 1952. On childhood psychosis and schizophrenia: Autistic and symbiotic infantile psychoses. *Psychoanalytic Study of the Child* 7:286–305.

———. 1967. On human symbiosis and the vicissitudes of individuation. *Journal of the American Psychoanalytic Association* 15:740–63.

Mahler, M. S., F. Pine, and A. Bergman. 1975. *The psychological birth of the human infant.* New York: Basic Books.

Pine, F. 1979. On the pathology of the separation-individuation process as manifested in later clinical work: An attempt at delineation. *International Journal of Psychoanalysis* 60, part 2:225–41.

————. 1986. The "symbiotic phase" in light of current infancy research. *Bulletin of the Menninger Clinic* 50, no. 6: 564–69.

Pollock, G. H. 1964. On symbiosis and symbiotic neurosis. *International Journal of Psychoanalysis* 45, part 1: 1–30.

Stern, D. N. 1985. *The interpersonal world of the infant.* New York: Basic Books.

5

PARTICIPANT-OBSERVATION, PERSPECTIVISM, AND COUNTERTRANSFERENCE

Irwin Hirsch, Ph.D., and Lewis Aron, Ph.D.

The theory of instinctual drives is the cornerstone of Freud's meta-psychology, and Freud's fundamental conceptualizations are formulated with drive theory as an underlying assumption. Implicit in drive theory is a view of the person as a biologically closed system seeking to discharge energy in order to maintain homeostasis. From the perspective of classical psychoanalytic theory, the fundamental unit of study is the individual; therefore, all that is interpersonal ultimately must be traced back to the vicissitudes of drive and defense, to the intrapsychic, and to the realm of a "one-person" psychology (Aron in press, a).

For Freud, what needs to be uncovered are the patient's dynamics that are conceptualized as existing inside the patient's mind. These dynamics are driven by instinctual forces inside the patient. The classic psychoanalytic method is designed to allow the spontaneous unfolding of intrapsychic dynamics, including the spontaneous emergence of the transference, which is thought to be "endogenously determined" (Arlow 1980, 193). The psychoanalytic situation is thought to represent a standard experimental set of conditions whose purpose is to minimize external stimuli so as to allow the spontaneous unfolding, from within, of derivatives of drive and defense. From within this model, reality is viewed as absolute, and it is the analyst's function to elucidate the truth about the workings of the patient's mind. Consequently, who the analyst is as a person is of lesser importance (Cooper 1987). It is the content, precision, and timing of interpretations as they reconstruct the past that are critical. From within this positivist view of psychoanalysis as objective science, the analyst as a unique individual should not matter, if he or she is analyzing correctly. Countertransference, in this classical model, necessarily represents the interferences in the method inadvertently created by the limitations of the analyst's scientific objectivity.

The single greatest shift in psychoanalytic thinking for critics of classical theory has been the evolution from its origins as a "one-person psychology" to a "two-person psychology," or field-theory paradigm. The thrust of much theoretical revision within psychoanalysis has been to rework psychoanalytic conceptions so as to accommodate a contextual view of people and of "mind." Across a wide range of theorists and various schools, a view of psychoanalysis has emerged that views people as capable of being studied only within the context of their interpersonal relations. In the analytic situation, this means that they can only be studied within the context of their relation to their psychoanalyst. From the perspective of a relational, or "two-person psychology," who the analyst is and his or her personal contributions to the analytic process are central to the psychoanalytic investigation. The analytic method cannot be considered as isolated from the personal variables and immediate affective experience of the individual analyst. From this point of view, countertransference is not an occasional lapse that intermittently requires investigation and elimination, but rather a continual and central element of the investigation. The analyst as a person and his or her shifting affective experience is both a central component of the analytic research method and a central variable in what is being investigated.

Once it is accepted that there are two people in the analytic situation, each of whom shapes and affects their relationship with each other, then it is clear that the psychology of one of the participants cannot be studied independently of the psychology of the other. The classical stress on the importance of transference as the vehicle for psychoanalytic understanding might lead one to think that classical analysts had recognized that the individual patient needed to be studied within the context of his or her relationship to the analyst, but this involves a serious misunderstanding of the historical notion of transference. For most classical analysts, transference represents the patient's distortion of current interpersonal experience on the basis of displacements from the past. Thus, the analyst is thought not to contribute to the spontaneous unfolding of the patient's transference and remains neutral, anonymous, and as much as possible a blank screen that refrains from contaminating the analytic situation. This model implies that the analyst represents both "rationality" and "reality" while the patient "regresses" in the transference, thus distorting and misperceiving interpersonal reality. The analyst, from his or her objective perspective, rationally interprets the patient's irrational, child-hood-based distortions. Schwaber (1983) has argued against this notion of transference as distortion because of its embeddedness in a "hierarchi-cally ordered two-reality view" (383). Similarly, Gill (1983) following Levenson (1972) has suggested that a perspectivist view replace this objectivist view.

Psychoanalysts who have shifted to some version of a two-person, relational or interpersonal psychology have consequently shifted from a positivist, objectivist view of reality to a "perspectivist" or "relativistic" view. Perspectivism represents an epistemological view in which inter-personal reality is considered relative to the perspective of each partici-pant in an interaction (Gill 1983, 501). Hoffman (1983) described this epistemological shift in terms of a change in models from an "asocial" to a "social conception of the analytic situation" (395). From a relativ-istic or perspective view of interpersonal reality, each participant in any interaction always has a "relevant" or "plausible" and in some sense "valid" perspective on the relationship. Meaning is not objective, it depends entirely on context (Levenson 1972). Perspectivism implies "the recognition that within the organized totality of the other person's world, his perceptions and behavior are coherent and appropriate" (p. 77). Rather than viewing transference in the analytic situation as a distortion of misrepresentation of interpersonal reality, a perspectivist thinks of the patient as having a relevant and plausible perception of that reality. The analyst is no longer thought of as representing reason, rationality, and reality, while the patient represents irrationality, distortion, and illusion. From a perspectivist, social, or relational view of the psychoanalytic situation, there are two psychologies at play with two relevant perspec-tives on what is occurring between them. The analyst's perspective—that is, the analyst's character and immediate psychology—becomes viewed as an alternative perspective to that of the patient, rather than a more accurate perspective to be interpreted to the patient.

Many of the contributions of contemporary psychoanalytic theorists may be regarded as elaborations from various theoretical starting points of a two-person psychology. Theorists from a wide variety of different schools of psychoanalysis have attempted in their own ways, out of their own traditions, and in their own theoretical languages to articulate the consequences for psychoanalysis of the shift from a one-person, largely or exclusively intrapsychic psychoanalysts, to a two-person, relational, or interpersonal view. (For a comprehensive discussion supporting the need for both a one-person and two-person psychology, see Ghent 1989.) This may be seen, for example, in the post-Kohutian development of "intersubjective" theory (Atwood and Stolorow 1984; Stolorow, Brandchaft, and Atwood 1987), in which Kohut's emphasis on psychoanalysis as a method defined by introspection and empathy is broadened and deepened to mean that psychoanalysis always takes place within the intersubjective field created by the subjective perspectives of patient and analyst. Similarly, what Cooper (1987) has referred to as the "modernist" model of transference, in contrast to the classical "historical" model of transference, emphasizes the interactive nature of transference responses with important interpersonal and intersubjective components. Hoffman (1983) described a movement toward a social and relativistic position within psychoanalysis, "a kind of informal school of thought which cuts across the standard lines of Freudian, Kleinian, and Sullivanian schools" (407). I believe that this movement represents the most important development in the history of the conceptualization of psychoanalysis. It is the most radical aspect of what Greenberg and Mitchell (1983) and Mitchell (1988) described as the "relational model," referring to this new paradigm in psychoanalysis. This relational, interpersonal, field-theory model of psychoanalysis was first anticipated by Ferenczi in the 1920s and was first fully elaborated on and developed by Sullivan in the 1940s. In a parallel development, Ferenczi's influence was extended in Britain, particularly by his student Balint (1949, 1968) and other object-relations theorists who elaborated on psychoanalysis as a "two-person psychology." Ferenczi's notions of "mutual analysis" and countertransference interpretations implied a fully two-person model of the analytic situation. Sullivan's articulation of the participant-observation model represented a full development of the two-person model in principle if not in practice. It remained for post-Sullivanian interpersonal and relational theorists to develop fully the implications of the participant-observation model for the psychoanalytic situation.

Just as perspectivism and relativism follow from the adoption of a two-person psychology, so too the study of countertransference experience as potentially useful data logically follows from participant-observation as a psychoanalytic model. It is inherent in a model in which the physical science base is relativity theory and the principle of uncertainty. Harry Stack Sullivan (Perry 1982), not formally analytically trained and largely a self-educated intellectual, reflected the prevailing culture of his time and place—Chicago—during and post World War I. This was apparently the setting for Sullivan's possible schizophrenic break as well as for his personal and conceptual rejuvenation. A farm boy from the East, Sullivan was exposed for the first time to a middle American, urban, immigrant city. In contrast with the long-standing traditions and values in Freud's conservative, turn-of-the-century Vienna, Chicago was disorganized, chaotic, and lacked tradition. For Freud, science was hard science, and the researcher sought absolute and indisputable truth. He studied from objective distance, controlled most of the variables, and, if operating properly, was not affected by his own person or his own biases. To think otherwise would undermine the validity of the findings and raise the specter of anarchy. Grey (1979) refers to Freud's research approach as reflecting the principle of isolates. "The most reliable way to acquire information about a phenomenon is to examine it in a vacuo, in a test tube in its purist and most simple form" (473). Freud's approach grew out of his cultural milieu. Living in a new and developing society (and new to himself), Sullivan resonated with the theories of relativity and uncertainty and field theory, all of which throw into question the notion of absolute truth in the basic sciences, much less the social sciences. The scientist as personal researcher interacts with the data under study. Everything is contextual. What one sees is at least somewhat dependent upon who one is and where and when one looks. The observer and the idiosyncratic conditions of observation are inevitably reflected in the findings. The researcher-observer is part of the observed. Absolute truth is elusive.

In addition to the trends in the physical sciences, Sullivan as a developing thinker was influenced by, and much interested in, the nascent social sciences. Freud, though far more formally educated than Sullivan, had no opportunity for such exposure. Anthropology and sociology were new American disciplines, directly relevant to the new urban world. The prevailing philosophy—pragmatism—lined up well with uncertainty and relativity. The social scientist was called upon to be of practical value to a society in some turmoil. Pure, in contrast with applied, research was a bit esoteric for this unsophisticated culture. The charge was for the researcher to affect his subjects and not simply study them. Practical outcome had more value than the discovery of universal principles. Large or small group interactions (or even dyads) are to a large extent each unique and encompass their own particular forces of interaction. What produces an effect in one field may not be duplicable in another. Sullivan, a bit later, became interested in another new discipline: social psychology. Field theory was a dominant early force in social psychology, and its object of study was interactions within a field. The interactive focus was consistent with Sullivan's emerging scientific orientation. It provided a sharp contrast to Freud's natural-science emphasis: the isolation and pure study of one variable. The study of interactions on the one hand and the study of the solitary subject on the other leads to contrasting psychoanalytic philosophies.

Clear, easily repeatable and neat technique have never been the hallmark of interpersonal psychoanalysis. There is far too much uncertainty, relativity, subjectivity, and uncontrolled forces. This apparent systemic deficiency, however, can be turned to advantage in analytic technique. This is precisely what Sullivan, Clara Thompson, Erich Fromm and Freida Fromm-Reichmann tried to initiate in their shift of psychoanalysis from a purely intrapersonal subject matter to an interpersonal focus. Interpersonal psychoanalysis studies the intrapsychic as it is manifest in the analytic dyad, while classical psychoanalysis tries to isolate and study the individual in vacuo (Barnett 1980a; Greenberg and Mitchell 1983). Objectivity and notions of absolute truth are possible when the analyst is a natural scientist studying the data (the patient) from outside the dyadic system. This view emphasizes diagnoses of the patient and evaluations of suitability for analysis in which the analyst evaluates and judges the patient as an "object" from an external perspective. If the analyst is viewed as a coparticipant (Wolstein 1975) inside the system, then he or she too must be the object of study for he or she inevitably influences the data being investigated (the patient). From an interpersonal or relational viewpoint, rather than diagnose the patient, the analyst attempts to evaluate not the individual but the state of the relationship evolving between the patient and the analyst. In this way the analyst recognizes his or her embeddedness as a participant in the very field that he or she is simultaneously observing. In this interpersonal model—participant-observation—the study of countertransference is inherent in the system.

This notion has never generated popular appeal within the American psychoanalytic community, and until quite recently only a small minority of trained analysts have worked within this framework. One reason for this, not directly relevant to the main theme of this essay, is the notion that when the dyad is studied the individual gets lost. Thus, interpersonal psychoanalysis has been viewed by many classically trained analysts as constituting a superficial focus and a study of social relations and not an individual, depth psychology. It is often said that the internal life of the patient gets short shrift. This has been the subject of much accusation and defense, and the best interpersonal record is that the inner world of the patient is studied but in the context of the dyadic field.

The artificial dichotomy created by the terms *internal world* and *external world* obscures the recognition of the complex and circular interactions that are continually at play between the person and his or her interpersonal situation. By conceptualizing an internal world that seems to exist in spite of external reality and that is maintained independent of the ongoing events in the person's present life, psychoanalysts have mistakenly overlooked the many ways in which people maintain their internal worlds through their ongoing social interactions. Wachtel (1987), following Sullivan and Horney, proposed a "cyclical psychodynamic" view in which early psychodynamic patterns are seen to persist *not* despite changing external conditions, but precisely because the person's patterns of experiencing and interacting with others tends to recreate the old interpersonal conditions again and again. People's problems and dynamics are not seen as something inside them that "emerge" or "unfold" in the analytic situation. Instead, dynamics are viewed as self-perpetuating patterns of transactions that are maintained and perpetuated in the present by the ways in which interpersonal expectations and consequences generate each other. The internalized self is based upon past interpersonal experience and lived-out in all current interactions (Barnett 1980b). There is no more logical and sensible way to study the inner world of the individual than by studying it in the context of interaction with the external world. The recent infant observation research of Stern (1985) supports the long-held minority argument that social interaction is the primary determinant of development every step of the way. The individual cannot be studied apart from the social context. Winnicott (1965) said something similar when he spoke of there being no such thing as an infant, but only infant and mother pairs. Similarly, Balint had been arguing from as far back as the 1940s that much of what was being studied in the psychoanalytic situation could only make sense from the perspective of a two-person psychology.

A second reason for the lack of wide appeal for the participant-observation model is directly related to its (by definition) more subjective, less systematic procedure. In the classical theory of therapy, objectivity and neutrality are felt to be reasonably reachable ideals. By operating from outside of the patient's system, one can ostensibly achieve clarity without getting caught-up in the patient's world. To most analysts this position has been clearly preferable. It presumes to be a cleaner method that keeps the patient and the analyst each in his or her own separate tracks. It is assumed that the patient's perceptions of the analyst are usually projections and/or distortions. The analyst, unless he or she is not working properly, does not have to be concerned about how he or she is influencing or affecting the patient. It is allegedly not happening. There is only one person to examine, the patient, who is projecting his or her inner world on to a relatively blank screen. The patient's transference, dynamics, and inner world are thought to emerge and unfold from within, if only the analyst does not contaminate the field or disrupt the process. Again, we see how the artificial split between the internal and external world obscures the recognition of their continual, mutual, and cyclical interaction and interconnectedness.

A third reason for the recoil from participant-observations is directly related to countertransference (Epstein and Feiner 1979). The participant-observation model acknowledges mutual influence. The analyst observes but is also an unwitting participant. Patient and analyst are coparticipants (Wolstein 1975) in the analytic process. Contrary to some criticism of this orientation, the analyst does not consciously *try* to participate or to influence the patient or even to be more verbally active than the classical analyst. Just as in classical technique, the analyst attempts primarily to listen, inquire, make observations, and interpret. How quiet or active the analyst is, is an individual variable for analysts of all persuasions. The participant-observation analyst is primarily an observer but one who recognizes that the observer inevitably becomes part of the observed. It is not as if this is a virtue to strive for but simply a human given. Analysts must become skillful at participating with the patient in an interpersonal interaction, while still maintaining a perspective on the entire analytic field, including their own participation in the field. A balance needs to be created between participation and observation, with the recognition that the act of observation is itself a form of participation and that the effects of participation must be subject to ongoing examination. As Bromberg (1984) has argued, the implications of participant-observation are not that the analyst needs to be more active or more "interactional" than in the classical stance. Participant-observation is not a "prescription" for a certain type of behavior on the analyst's part (Greenberg 1986), but is rather a "description" or recognition of the inevitability of participation and of the need to observe the effects of this participation on the analytic process.

When not ignored, the analyst's psychology becomes an essential part of analytic data. As many contemporary authors have noted (Searles 1965; Racker 1968; Langs 1976; Gill 1982; Levenson 1983), the patient is quite capable of picking up the analyst's errors, attitudes, values, feelings, anxieties, and personal characteristics. The philosophy behind the participant-observation model is such that it invites the patient to address these observations. Aron (1991) has discussed this in terms of the centrality in the clinical situation of examining the patient's experience of the analyst's subjectivity. Parenthetically, though Sullivan developed the participant-observation model, he personally avoided examination of the transference-countertransference interaction in the here and now. It was Ferenczi, among early psychoanalytic pioneers, who first acknowledged the need for the analyst to invite the patient's observations regarding the analyst's participation in the treatment. According to Gill, a major advocate of encouraging patients to point out the analyst's unconscious participation, the analyst must view these observations as at least plausible, not simply as projections or distortions. The analyst is made aware of often uncomfortable countertransference enactments and attempts to use this to deepen the understanding of the patient's patterns of interaction. In the traditional model, transference is understood as a distortion of the current relationship with the analyst based on displacements from the past. Patients' observations regarding the analyst are viewed as manifest content that need to be analyzed in terms of the inner dynamics of the patient's mind. If the patient's perceptions of the analyst's interactions were deemed accurate and not seen as distorting, then the orthodox position would view this as a result of excessive analytic engagement—a countertransference problem. For analysts who emphasize a relational approach, there is little anonymity (Singer 1977). Relational and interpersonal analysts recognize that they are always revealing aspects of themselves to their patients. There is much appeal in the relative blank-screen model, for it can be used to reduce the anxiety of exposure and provide the analyst with a sense of more rigorous, scientific boundaries. Such boundaries help quell fears of acting-out and provide a shield of safety behind which the analyst may operate with a feeling of greater comfort and precision. But the participant-observation model when taken to its logical conclusion implies a fully two-person point of view. There are always two plausible perspectives of the interpersonal process in the analytic situation. This demands what Hoffman (1983) has referred to as a "radical" critique of the blank-screen concept.

There is increasing evidence that the participant-observation model is gaining wider acceptance in the psychoanalytic mainstream in the United States. Much significant current writing on countertransference, though often not labeled as countertransference literature, has been penned by classically trained analysts. Cooper (1985), past president of The American Psychoanalytic Association, describes an increasing convergence between historically disparate psychoanalytic models. He states, "A portion of the growth of psychoanalytic theory can be seen as the effort to incorporate, often without acknowledgment, the valid aspects of the critique of oppositional schools. Recently, for example, Sullivan's work has increasingly reappeared in mainstream psychoanalysis, not always with attribution" (11). Hirsch (1985) has directly addressed the issue of the rediscovery of the participant-observation model and of the ubiquitous presence of countertransference in the psychoanalytic relationship. Probably for the first time, the *Journal of the American Psychoanalytic Association* has devoted a significant portion of an edition (1986) to the subject of countertransference. In one of these articles, Blum (1986), past editor of that journal, states, "Present-day interest in a two-person, analytic field of forces and the analyst as participant observer has many ramifications. One of these ramifications has been the vast broadening of the concept of countertransference to take into account the entire emotional set of conscious and unconscious reactions that analysts may have to a patient" (34). Illustrative of the neglect of the interpersonal tradition is that Blum does not refer to Sullivan's work or other interpersonal literature. Cooper discusses this neglect as largely a function of Freud's dominance and the degree of organizational disruption over the early deviations of Alfred Adler and Carl Jung. Freud's attitude forced other significant ideas into "oppositional" schools where they could not interact with the main directions of psychoanalytic development. Cooper sees this as just now beginning to shift—that is, formerly "oppositional" schools (for example, interpersonal) are starting to be acknowledged as contributors to what is considered mainstream psychoanalysis. Hirsch has suggested that the classical veering toward a more field-theoretical, participant-observation approach has come about largely through Freudian analysts, like Blum, introducing or reintroducing other conceptions without recognizing that they represent already developed thinking and an already published body of literature. When introduced from within, these ideas are more acceptable; as a result, as Cooper notes, the formerly "oppositional" schools may then perhaps be acknowledged. Loewald (1986), in that same *JAPA* volume devoted to the examination of countertransference, notes that countertransference as a concept was particularly difficult for Freud to integrate, partially because he analyzed himself. More specifically, Freud never viewed psychoanalysis as a mutual relationship. The notion of mutuality is inherent in the participant-observation model as well as in conceiving of countertransference experience as inevitable and potentially useful. It should not be surprising that the shift in psychoanalytic theory from an exclusively one-person psychology to include field theory would occur following Freud, since Freud's theory was an outgrowth of his own self-analytic experience. Among other reasons for its development, Freud's one-person psychology was literally an outgrowth of his one-person self-analysis (Aron in press, b).

The manner in which the American psychoanalytic mainstream is becoming increasingly interested in countertransference and concepts of the self and is converging with the participant-observation model is based more on personal and political matters than on scientific advance. Classical analysts have been gradually assimilating the contributions of the British and South American object-relations groups (Winnicott 1947; Little 1951; Heimann 1950; Racker 1968) and the more recent developments of Kohut (1977, 1984) and the self-psychologists. Though not everyone would agree, I believe that most object-relations analysts and self-psychologists (particularly those who adhere to the more recent, post-Kohutian developments in self-psychology) are closer to interpersonal than to classical thinking in their theories of development, their notions of the self, and in their acknowledgment of the analyst's strong participation in the analytic process. Although their notions about the specifics of development and the exact nature of analytic participation may be quite different from that of the interpersonalists, both reject the blank-screen and natural-science methods of investigation and both see countertransference as having a potentially productive role in technique. Most of the leading contributors of these schools were trained originally as classical analysts or had mixed training. By and large they all maintain a tie to Freudian theory through at least an allegiance to the language of drive theory, even though they may indeed reject drive theory entirely (Greenberg and Mitchell 1983). Their early training, their psychoanalytic language, and the entrée they have to mainstream psychoanalytic journals have led to influence and acknowledgment not shared by analysts of the interpersonal school. (For a thorough critique of the similarities and differences between interpersonal theory and self-psychology, see Bromberg 1989 and Ghent 1989. For a comprehensive and selective integration of relational theories, which includes the interpersonal, self-psychological, and object-relational schools, see Mitchell 1988.)

I believe that these trends, in part, have influenced perhaps the most powerful new voices of participant-observation. We refer to a group of liberal classical analysts who, except for Gill (1983, 1984) are unaware of, or have not acknowledged, their harmony with the participant-observation model and the centrality of countertransference, per se, in their thinking. Recent contributions of Schafer (1983) and Spence (1982) are most widely known, though less-known authors (Tower 1956; Bird 1972; McLaughlin 1981; Jacobs 1986) have contributed significantly. Schafer and Spence take the notion of participant-observation to an extreme that Sullivan and a number of interpersonal writers (Levenson 1983) addressed but have never spelled out as thoroughly. They, as well as Jacobs (1986), are saying that literally every aspect of what analysts do is affected by the analyst as person. This includes the choice of the theory the analyst uses in formulating the patient's dynamics and the understanding of the patient's allegedly veridical life history. According to Schafer, analysts' psychoanalytic theories are their "story lines." Theories make sense to analysts based on who they are, who their analysts were, and who their teachers were. When an analyst interprets analytic material, he or she is placing it in a framework that belongs to his or her own being and into a theory that makes personal sense to him or her. Different analysts, with the same patient, will develop different recountings of history and offer different interpretations based upon disparate theories. There is not an objective theory, an objective history, or an objective interpretation. Everything can be seen as based on the transference-countertransference integration, an interaction between the person of the analyst, his or her belief system, and the object of study—the patient. Participant-observation is total.

Spence speaks to much the same issue, emphasizing efforts at historical reconstruction and explanatory interpretations. He states that given that early history is not truly available for recall and certainly not verifiable in the analytic dyad, analysts help patients construct fictional narratives that satisfy requirements of "making sense." These narratives may be based on theoretical biases, personal idiosyncrasies of the analyst, and so on. Nonetheless, if they generate a good explanatory account they can provide historical coherence and be helpful to the patient. He is, of course, saying that analysts, based on their own countertransference inclinations, unwittingly participate with patients in making up stories. These stories may have only minimal relation to the elusive truth. The observer is intimately a part of what is observed. This notion is also central in Jacobs's (1986) documentation of how generally accepted technique can serve as a guise for countertransference enactments. We must add, however, that while these theoretical formulations move in the direction of participant-observation and seem to imply a perspectivist position, the clinical contributions of many of these classical authors do not demonstrate this shift. Schafer, for example, indicates that in spite of his narrative, hermeneutic orientation, his technique remains within the Freudian method. It seems to us that an acceptance of the participant-observation model and of relativism and perspectivism implies a radical change in the understanding of such fundamental clinical concepts as transference, countertransference, interpretation, and resistance. It remains puzzling to us how Schafer can indicate that the analyst constructs plausible storylines, rather than uncovers *the* truth, and yet can claim that he interprets transference as distortion of interpersonal reality.

McLaughlin (1981), also from within the classical school, objects to the terms transference and countertransference as too biased in the direction of the patient as primary distorter. He believes that transference is the better term for what occurs with both patient and analyst, since he views both parties in this mutual process as reflecting their own subjective or psychic reality. It is not necessarily the patient who does it first (transference) and provokes the analyst (countertransference). Along somewhat similar lines, Tower (1956) and Bird (1972), in two widely cited articles, speak of a countertransference neurosis in conjunction with transference neurosis. What they observe, in what they call the eye of the storm of transference neurosis, is a shared countertransference neurosis. In the midst of the most intense analytic moments, the analyst is just as lost in subjectivity and repetition as is the patient.

Hoffman (1983) summarizes what is the logical extreme of the participant-observation model and the ubiquity of countertransference. He integrates the work of leading thinkers from varying analytic schools (Gill, Levenson, Racker, Sandler, and Searles) and refers to it as the "radical social paradigm." Hirsch (1987) has referred to this group as the "observing-participants," borrowing the term from Fromm (1964) and Wolstein (1964), who elaborated upon it. The emphasis is on participation, with *observing* as the modifying adverb. From the perspective of these authors, the analyst inevitably becomes thoroughly enmeshed in the interactional world of the patient. This is not by premeditated intent but occurs as a natural process during the normal analyzing functions of observation. The analyst, in spite of attempts otherwise, lends him or herself to the influence of the patient and over time becomes drawn into the patient's characteristic interpersonal patterns. These patterns most likely conform to the patient's early significant interactions with family members and to the patient's current ways of forming relationships with others. Each individual analyst brings his or her own unique personality and theory to the situation and will not engage in precisely the same way as any other analyst. According to the point stressed by these thinkers, however, the analyst will enter the patient's interactional field in some way that resembles those of significant early others. This is similar to what Bird and Tower describe in their concept of countertransference neurosis, though it does not necessarily reflect only one intense period in the analysis. The analyst is trying to be an observer but has unwittingly become a coparticipant (Wolstein 1975). In Levenson's (1972) language, the analyst had been "transformed"; in Sandler's (1976) words, the analyst had been "nudged into role responsiveness." Contemporary Kleinian and other object-relations school analysts tend to use the language of projective identification to indicate the many ways in which the patient evokes particular feelings and responses from the analyst. Casement (1985) provides captivating and well-detailed clinical examples of a variety of forms of interactive communication in which childhood events are re-created through an interplay of projective identification, countertransference, and role-responsiveness. It is usually the patient who conveys this to the analyst in a direct or disguised manner. In Hoffman's (1983) and in Searles's (1979) terms, the patient interprets the analyst's countertransference and wakes the analyst up to what is happening between them.

Gill (1982), in particular, stresses how crucial it is to listen for the patient's observations about the participation of the analyst. He makes the strongest case for the ubiquity of analytic influence and the effects on the process when the analyst remains unaware. According to Gill, if the analyst is not helped to become aware of his or her unwitting participation, two serious dangers occur. The first is the loss of the ability to make explicit and to analyze the patient-analyst interaction. The second is the likelihood that the analyst will influence the patient without this being clear to either participant and that what might have potentially evolved into analytic change could merely dissolve into a transference cure. Gill has been criticized for implying that the patient, like the customer, is always right. Indeed, adopting a perspective position, he does believe, as do others who emphasize the validity of the patient's psychic reality (Schwaber 1983), that all of the patient's perceptions are plausible and that the analyst does not have the corner on objective reality. From this perspective, both parties participate with their subjective selves, and the patient cannot be assumed to be projecting or distorting.

One of the values of working from this theory of therapy lies in the way observations may be made from direct and potent experience in the immediacy of the analytic exchange. As is implied in the notion of a transference neurosis, what is addressed is the essential life patterns of the patient as they are actually being lived-out with the unwitting observing-participant analyst. The patient repeats early experience and tries to shape his or her current relationships to conform to this. When the analyst is sensitive to the patient's countertransference interpretations, he or she can more readily focus upon these transference-countertransference enactments at the point of urgency. The patient is more easily able to see how the analytic interaction lines up with other significant patterns of engagement and how consistent are his or her patterns of living. The emerging clarity and explicitness of the analytic relationship in conjunction with the awareness of how this parallels both historical and current extratransference patterns combines the value of insight, on the one hand, and formation of a new relationship or corrective experience on the other. What I value in the concept of the transference neurosis is its emphasis on affective immediacy, the centrality of the here-and-now interaction, and the intense experience of interpersonal involvement. Where this position differs from the traditional use of the term is that I do not assume that the transference neurosis is in the mind of the patient. I view the analyst as mutually (if not equally) caught up in the transference-countertransference neurosis, a view which is in the spirit of Bird (1972) and Tower (1956). The central interpersonal dynamics are actualized between patient and analyst, and each of them has a unique and plausible perspective on that interaction. A relational or interpersonal model views transference as a particular, idiosyncratic, or unique way of viewing the interpersonal situation, but not as a distortion or misperception that is unrelated to the current interpersonal events occurring between patient and analyst. The internal world is never maintained in isolation from present external interpersonal relations.

Sullivan's introduction of the participant-observer model has been pushed to its logical extreme by analysts from within and outside of the school he initiated. Analysts from a wide variety of "schools," including contemporary Freudians, interpersonalists, object-relations theorists, self psychologists, and Kleinians, despite significant theoretical and technical differences, each in their own language and with their own slant have moved in the direction of a two-person psychology at least as a complement to the traditional one-person view. Adopting an increasingly relational or interpersonal perspective, they are more likely to acknowledge the contributions of the analyst's personality to the analytic process. The clinical advantage is that by acknowledging the inevitability of participation, analysts are more likely to recognize its occurrence clinically and attend to the effects of their participation in the analytic situation.

REFERENCES

Arlow, J. A. 1980. The genesis of the interpretation. In *Psychoanalytic explorations of technique: Discourse on the theory of therapy,* edited by H. P. Blum, 193–206. New York: International Universities Press.

Aron, L. 1991. The patient's experience of the analyst's subjectivity. *Psychoanalytic Dialogues* 1(1).

———. In press, a. One-person and two-person psychologies and the method of psychoanalysis. *Psychoanalytic Psychology.*

———. In press, b. Free association and changing models of mind. *Journal of the American Academy of Psychoanalysis.*

Atwood, G., and R. Stolorow. 1984. *Structures of subjectivity: Explorations in psychoanalytic phenomenology.* Hillsdale, N.J.: Analytic Press.

Balint, M. 1949. Changing therapeutic aims and techniques in psychoanalysis. In M. Balint, *Primary love and psychoanalytic technique,* 221–35. London: Hogarth Press, 1952.

———. 1968. *The basic fault: Therapeutic aspects of regression.* New York: Bruner/Mazel.

Barnett, J. 1980a. Self and character. *Journal of the American Academy of Psychoanalysis* 8:337–52.

———. 1980b. Interpersonal process, cognition, and the analysis of character. *Contemporary Psychoanalysis* 16:397–416.

Bird, B. 1972. Notes on transference: Universal phenomena and hardest part of analysis. *Journal of the American Psychoanalytic Association* 20:267–301.

Blum, H. 1986. Countertransference and the theory of technique: Discussion. *Journal of the American Psychoanalytic Association* 34:309–27.

Bromberg, P. 1984. On the occurrence of the Isakower phenomenon. *Contemporary Psychoanalyses* 4:600–24.

———. 1989. Interpersonal psychoanalysis and self-psychology: A clinical comparison. In *Self-Psychology: Comparisons and contrasts,* edited by D. Dietrich and S. Dietrich. Hillsdale, N.J.: Analytic Press.

Casement, P. 1985. *On Learning from the patient.* London and New York: Routledge.

Cooper, A. M. 1985. A historic review of psychoanalytic paradigms. *Models of the mind,* edited by A. Rothstein. New York: International Universities Press.

———. 1987. Changes in psychoanalytic ideas: Transference interpretation. *Journal of the American Psychoanalytic Association* 35:77–98.

Epstein, L., and A. Feiner 1979. *Countertransference.* New York: Jason Aronson.

Fromm, E. 1964. *The heart of man.* New York: Harper & Row.

Ghent, E. 1989. Credo: The dialectics of one-person and two-person psychologies. *Contemporary Psychoanalysis* 25:169–211.

Gill, M. M. 1982. *Analysis of transference, vol. 1.* New York: International Universities Press.

———. 1983. The interpersonal paradigm and the degree of the therapist's involvement. *Contemporary Psychoanalysis* 19:200–37.

———. 1984. Psychoanalysis and psychotherapy: A revision. *International Review of Psychoanalysis* 11:161–79.

Greenberg, J. 1986. Theoretical models and the analyst's neutrality. *Contemporary Psychoanalysis* 22:87–106.

Greenberg, J., and S. Mitchell. 1983. *Object relations in psychoanalytic theory.* Cambridge: Harvard University Press.

Grey, A. 1979. Countertransference and parataxis. *Contemporary Psychoanalysis* 15:472–83.

Heimann, P. 1950. On countertransference. *International Journal of Psychoanalysis* 31:81–84.

Hirsch, I. 1985. The rediscovery of the advantages of the participant-observation model. *Psychoanalysis and Contemporary Thought* 8:441–59.

———. 1987. Varying modes of analytic participation. *Journal of the American Academy of Psychoanalysis* 15:205–22.

Hoffman, I. 1983. The patient as interpreter of the analyst's experience. *Contemporary Psychoanalysis* 19:389–422.

Jacobs, T. 1986. On countertransference enactments. *Journal of the American Psychoanalytic Association* 34:289–307.

Kohut, H. 1977. *The restoration of the self.* New York: International Universities Press.

———. 1984. *How does analysis cure?* Chicago: University of Chicago Press.

Langs, R. 1976. *The therapeutic interaction, vol. 2.* New York: Jason Aronson.

Levenson, E. 1972. *The fallacy of understanding.* New York: Basic Books.

———. 1983. *The ambiguity of change.* New York: Basic Books.

Little, M. 1951. Countertransference and the patient's response to it. *International Journal of Psychoanalysis* 32:32–40.

Loewald, H. 1986. Transference-countertransference. *Journal of the American Psychoanalytic Association* 34:275–87.

McLaughlin, J. 1981. Transference, psychic reality and countertransference. *Psychoanalytic Quarterly* 50:639–64.

Mitchell, S. 1988. *Relational concepts in psychoanalysis.* Cambridge: Harvard University Press.

Perry, H. S. 1982. *Psychiatrist of America.* Cambridge: Harvard University Press.

Racker, H. 1968. *Transference and countertransference.* New York: International Universities Press.

Sandler, J. 1976. Countertransference and role-responsiveness. *International Review of Psychoanalysis* 3:43–47.

Schafer, R. 1983. *The analytic attitude.* New York: Basic Books.

Schwaber, E. 1983. Psychoanalytic listening and psychic reality. *International Review of Psychoanalysis* 10:379–92.

Searles, H. S. 1965. *Collected papers on schizophrenia and related subjects.* New York: International Universities Press.

———. 1979. *Countertransference and related subjects.* New York: International Universities Press.

Singer, E. 1977. The fiction of analytic anonymity. In *The human dimension in psychoanalytic practice,* edited by K. Frank. New York: Grune and Stratton.

Spence, D. 1982. *Narrative truth and historical truth.* New York: W. W. Norton.

Stern, D. 1985. *The interpersonal world of the infant.* New York: Basic Books.

Stolorow, R. D., B. Brandchaft, and G. E. Atwood. 1987. *Psychoanalytic treatment: An intersubjective approach.* Hillsdale, N.J.: Analytic Press.

Tower, L. 1956. Countertransference. *Journal of the American Psychoanalytic Association* 4:224–55.

Wachtel, P. 1987. *Action and insight.* New York: Guilford Press.

Winnicott, D. W. 1947. Hate in the countertransference. *International Journal of Psychoanalysis* 30:69–74.

———. 1965. *The maturational process and the facilitating environment.* New York: International Universities Press.

Wolstein, B. 1964. *Transference.* New York: Grune & Stratton.

———. 1975. Countertransference: The psychoanalyst's shared experience and inquiry with his patient. *Journal of the American Academy of Psychoanalysis* 3:77–89.

6

INTERPERSONAL PSYCHOANALYSIS: AN ELUSIVE AND MYSTERIOUS CONSTRUCT

Marcia Pollak, Ph.D.

This chapter reflects an interest in the evolution of theory and practice in interpersonal psychoanalysis since the profound contributions of Harry Stack Sullivan were made. It attempts to do the following: to present some of the underlying principles of theory and practice of interpersonal psychoanalysis, including points of controversy and harmony; to consider some research findings that relate to two diverging strands in theory and practice; and, lastly, to present some of my views on the subject.

Both the chapter title as a whole and its second half are oxymorons. These are defined as a combination of contradictory or incongruous words. Perhaps the most famous oxymoron appears in *Romeo and Juliet:* "Parting is such sweet sorrow." Another is the phrase "cruel kindness." A *construct* is an arrangement in logical order of concepts, ideas, or instruments under specific conditions. Its purpose is to explain and interpret by presenting us with a picture whereby we see and understand what might contain disparate elements. So a construct should be neither "elusive" nor "mysterious," and the phrase "elusive and mysterious construct" is, therefore, an oxymoron.

Yet the oxymoron is an ancient figure of speech that has survived because it conveys compactly and dramatically certain truths about our world and its ways. As this chapter tries to demonstrate, interpersonal psychoanalysis, an acknowledged construct, is both elusive and mysterious, and we cloud our vision and distort our methods when we lapse into thinking otherwise.

The elusiveness and mystery of this construct is evident in that it sometimes does not appear in prominent surveys of various schools of psychoanalysis. It is not visible yet it exists, like a collar button dropped on the floor and not to be found. The construct is not mentioned once in Eagle's (1984) book *Recent Developments in Psychoanalysis,* declared by Holt to be the "best survey of the current status of psychoanalytic theory that I have seen." In it, there is just one reference to the term "interpersonal theory" (not interpersonal psychoanalysis): "although Guntrip has described object relations theory as the British parallel to Sullivanian interpersonal theory," which is followed by Eagle's analysis of the theory of Fairbairn. In the rest of Eagle's book, there are six references to Sullivan, who is mentioned only in passing as Eagle analyzes the theories of Freud, Fairbairn, and Kohut. For example, "in this regard, Kohut's work takes it place alongside the formulations of Sullivan, Erikson, Jacobson, G. S. Klein, and Gedo" (71).

This chapter cannot present a comprehensive historical overview tracing the development of the various principles of interpersonal psychoanalysis. Such a task is too ambitious for now. What is worthy of mention is that the principles did not begin with Sullivan, who is recognized generally as their most significant representative and originator. The literature unjustly deemphasizes many who have contributed important concepts. For example, as early as 1935, Jung said during a lecture to the Zurich Medical Society:

The demand that the analyst must be analyzed culminates in the idea of a dialectical procedure, where the therapist enters into relationship with another psychic system both as questioner and answerer. No longer is he (the analyst) the superior wise man, judge and counsellor; he is a fellow participant who finds himself involved in the dialectical process just as deeply as the so-called patient. (1935, 8)

Jung's remarks are the early melodies of interpersonal psychoanalysis. These remarks contrast with Freud's description of the analyst's role: "The doctor should be opaque to his patients and, like a mirror, should show them nothing but what is shown to him" (1912, 118). Here, whether the analyst-guide walks ahead of you or with you is precisely what is at issue between Jung and Freud (Trungpa 1973).

Of interest in more current literature (Masson 1984) is Freud's abandonment of his "education theory" in favor of the oedipus theory as he was developing his monumental body of work. How mysterious and elusive that one of the foundations of the interpersonal model—namely, that the neurosis is the product of adult interpersonal activity with children—was Freud's initial conception. He later reoriented his theories such that neurosis is interpreted as the product of childhood fantasies about adults. Thus he moved away from accounting for the part played by the family and other formative social influences in shaping the individual. Here emerges one of the more important distinctions between classical and interpersonal theory: classical theory would be more likely to explore what lies beneath reality; interpersonal theory what happened and what can be observed.

Late in 1985, Edgar Levenson, a prominent spokesperson of interpersonal psychoanalysis, delivered an informal talk on the interpersonal model. According to Levenson, the interpersonal (Sullivanian) model states that neurosis is caused by an absence of awareness of that which can be observed, not by repressed or by internal fantasies. Persons do not grasp and operate in reality in the field of interpersonal relations. Through the process of selective inattention, developed partially in response to mystification (contradictory levels of communication by important family members), persons early on learn to screen out anxiety. Because of this they also do not develop an ability to communicate their problems in words. Through the analytic process, they learn how anxiety in the early years moved them to attend selectively in social situations in the present.

This model maintains that fantasies and dreams are imaginary constructions of reality. For instance, when the patient dreams about the analyst undisguised, this may be an awareness of something important in the self of the analyst rather than an indication that the patient is distorting the analyst because of the transferential implications. To put it another way, in the interpersonal model, the patient's dream of the analyst often represents a realistic appraisal of the situation between them or of the analyst in some way to be discovered by them.

As a group, interpersonalists would tend to focus on reality; therefore, they do not seek to foster a transference neurosis and do not search for reenactment of repressed experience in the transference. Rather, they work to bring to their patient's attention his or her relation to important people in his or her life. This does not mean that the analyst discourages the patient's reactions to the analyst. Transference and countertransference are different sides of the playing field in which the two participants meet. Countertransferential experience provides the analyst with important data to use in the work. However, a caveat from Levenson warns that the therapist should not express wild, intuitive, corrective emotional experiences with the patient. The form of the participation is rigorously determined and contained by the material presented by the patient in the therapy. Grandiosity and self-indulgence are not encouraged. (Levenson 1985, 65)

Some discussion on how to discriminate judiciously between this "rigorous determination" and these "self-indulgent" modes of expression appears later.

As a group, analysts of the interpersonal persuasion agree they are greatly interested in the pragmatics of language. Sullivan believed that unconscious thoughts and feelings are unformulated experience, and Donnel Stern (1983) has elaborated impressively on this conceptualization.

The analytic process frames unformulated experiences into words. Thus language reworks, transforms, and conceptualizes. It does not so much comment on experience as make it available for comment. Language is the major modality that conceptualizes unformulated, unconscious, and conscious experience; and, of course, it can distort these as well.

Up until this point of this essay, interpersonalists, as a group, are more or less in harmony on these dimensions of theory and practice. Their principles are neither elusive nor mysterious. However, interpersonalists may be divided into two divergent groups when they consider the source of basic anxiety and its relation to the process of psychoanalysis. The first group is the Sullivan one. Its adherents believe that, very early on, the self-system, a major part of the personality, develops in order to avoid anxiety at all costs. The intolerable pain of anxiety has its origin in the infant's perception of its mother's disapproval. In order to judge whether interventions are appropriate, the analyst calibrates, with exquisite empathy, the patient's anxiety level. The analyst then tries to determine when the anxiety level has become too high, such that the patient is unable to tolerate the analyst's interventions. The second interpersonal group follows what may be called the Frommian approach. This group affirms that the experience of anxiety signals change and separation from embeddedness. In this group, it is understood that anxiety can originate in the early conflicts between the developing self, with its potentials for individuality, and the need to relate and conform to the mother and other persons in the family. The Frommian analyst is not as likely to withhold interventions because of concern about the patient's anxiety level (Fromm 1947).

An acceptance of Sullivan's theory of personality development in relation to the concept of anxiety and activity directs the way the interpersonal analyst works. The theory states that the personality develops in order to avoid anxiety. During the state of deep sleep there is a total absence of anxiety, thus euphoria exists during deep sleep. Sullivan assumes that during this state of inactivity the infant is in a total euphoria and also exists in an absolutely communal (symbiotic) relationship with its "physicochemical universe," which is dependent upon the mother's own sense of security, anxiety, and well-being. Security is freedom from anxiety. As the infant develops, its overriding concern is to seek security, and this need continues throughout life. Learning in infancy is motivated by behaving in ways that seek to avoid anxiety. To quote Sullivan:

> the infant learns to chart his course by mild forbidding gestures, or by mild states of concern or disapproval (on the part of the mother) . . . the infant plays . . . the old game of getting hotter or colder, in charting a selection of behavioral units which are not attended by an increase in anxiety. (1953, 159)

Thus, according to Sullivan, early development is a gradual process of separation and individuation. Early on, the self-system emerges—it is the organization of experience within the personality that develops to avoid anxiety. In this framework, anxiety about anxiety is at the core of psychopathology.

An analyst who embraces this view of personality development keeps in mind at all times the patient's anxiety level. As a good mother is empathically attuned to the infant's level of security and emotional well-being, the analyst is careful to intuit the patient's level of anxiety in order to determine when and when not to intervene and how. For example, this careful determination might be the reason for the analyst to use the impersonal pronoun, *one,* instead of the more intimate and possibly anxiety-producing, *you.* (The analyst might say to the patient, "One might be angry with one's mother," instead of "you might be angry with your mother.")

Sullivan developed his position working with an unusually anxious population—namely, schizophrenics, the category of mental illness at that time excluded from treatment by the Freudians. Sullivan did not work with infants. However, observational studies of infants during the 1950s tended to confirm the conclusions he reached theoretically. Now, forty years later, an examination of current infant research no longer supports the idea that an infant's overriding concern is to seek security and freedom from anxiety. As Levenson (1972) cogently states, it has been the fate of many of the contributions by theorists to become anachronistic and irrelevant because the times have passed them by.

Yet the theories continue to develop. Daniel Stern (1985) has presented an original, possibly revolutionary, contribution to personality development. His research supports the thesis that there is no symbioticlike phase during infancy. Different and successive phases of self form beginning at birth. He claims that from birth to two months, the sense of a "core self" develops; from seven to fifteen months the sense of an "intersubjective self"; and from eighteen to thirty months the "verbal sense of self." For some time it has been known that beginning at two months, infants undergo a dramatic change—they smile, make eye contact, and coo. But this is Stern's second stage of self-development—the "core self." The first phase from birth to two months, the "emergent self," is the phase that contains strategies of inordinate importance for an understanding of development.

Stern's research compels us to reconsider, reevaluate, and certainly respect the infant's subjective social life during its first two months. Newborns regularly are in a state of "alert inactivity" (1985, 37). Although they are physically quiet and appear inactive, they are alert and are clearly taking in the external occurrences of their environment. This state of alert inactivity nonetheless manifests at least three observable behaviors under voluntary muscular control that can be performed by the infant beginning at birth: head turning, sucking, and looking. A number of studies reveal that infants come into the world with "attentional (potential information-gathering) strategies that have their own maturational unfolding" (Field et al. 1982, 179). Infants experience persons as unique forms from the state. Two-day-old infants can discriminate and imitate smiles, frowning, and surprise expressions.

From the start, infants mainly experience reality—not fantasy. According to Stern,

their subjective experience suffers no distortion by virtue of wishes or defenses, but only those made inevitable by perceptual or cognitive immaturity or overgeneralization ... the capacity for defensive distortions of reality is a later-developing capacity, requiring more cognition processes than are initially available ... reality experience *precedes* fantasy distortions in development. (1985, 225)

It should be noted that Stern's discussion of "fantasy distortion" is not the same as fantasy.

Stern's conclusion suggests a thoughtful reevaluation of classical theory as well as of the theories of scientists and philosophers that address the origin and nature of thought. Freud did say that the infant's hallucinatory need-satisfaction is the ancestor to thought. In 1959, Schachtel wondered about this idea of Freud's and went on to posit that there was not just one ancestor to thought but two ancestors. The second ancestor to thought, according to Schachtel, is the distinctly human capacity, relatively autonomous, to be interested in objects. As mentioned earlier in this chapter, the interest in objects can be observed in the two-day-old infant.

Research reveals that somewhere between the second and sixth months of life, an experiential sense of self develops, which Stern calls the "sense of a core self." Now interpersonal experience can operate in the domain of core-relatedness; infants sense that they and the mother are separate, different beings, with separate and different emotional states and histories. Here, Stern continues, a symbioticlike phase is not present. And, he continues, the crucial, developmental experience of uniting with another being takes place only after there exists a sense of both a core self and a core other.

Union experiences are thus viewed as the successful result of actively organizing the experience of self-being-with-another, rather than as the product of a passive failure of the ability to differentiate a self from other. (1985, 10)

Accepting this view means that a union or merger with the other is preceded by the separateness of the other from self and not by symbiosis. For symbiosis in this context stands for the inability to differentiate self from other, an event that would be subjectively experienced by the infant as a form of dual unity with the other. What is at issue here? At issue is whether the earliest stage of human existence is one of aloneness or togetherness. If it is aloneness, the infant must have a core self before the infant can strive actively for union. Human connectedness, which requires antecedent separateness, is the end point, not the starting point, of a complex course of active development that involves an interweaving of predesigned and acquired behaviors. Stern's research findings demand that the infant be recognized as capable of much more activity upon birth than has previously been ascribed to the neonate. In this regard, Schachtel was way ahead of his time, when he wondered:

Everything is new to the newborn child . . . it is the period of human life which is richest in experience. His . . . discoveries go far beyond any discovery that the most adventurous and daring explorer will ever make in his adult life. (1959, 292)

Schachtel goes on to opine that the beginning of adulthood is often an ending of wondering. All is familiar and conventional; curiosity is dead.

It is clear that current infant research supports the Frommian principles of personality development that affirm the potential of a unique and healthy individual self almost from the start, after which family and society force the person to insulate the "true core" with various defensive styles. In contrast, Sullivan conceives of the personality as developed totally from interactions with others. Individuality does not exist. The self is an amalgam of defenses against anxiety. Fromm postulates an innate humanness that society and family may frustrate. Early on, the self exists, then, in order to develop its potentials.

The Sullivanian and the Frommian models are now walking down separate roads. A Sullivanian might focus more on helping a patient understand how security operations interfere with effective living; a Frommian might want to transform the personality by breaking through the false self and defense systems to reach the true core, the true self. The Sullivanian patient is more likely to develop sharper semiotic and social skills; the Frommian patient is more likely to become aware of unconscious strivings and to understand their relation to societal influence.

These two roads meet by their agreement that cure through psychoanalysis does not necessarily alleviate symptoms that come and go. However, the groups part again in addressing the nature of cure. According to Sullivan, cure occurs when the patient's knowledge of self matches the knowledge of the patient by significant people in the patient's world (1953). So self-deception is gone. Cure and change in the patient is the achievement of clear and distinct self-knowledge. This reminds me of the thoughts of the Buddhist Trungpa (1973):

the idea of having an operation and fundamentally changing yourself is completely unrealistic. No one can really change your personality absolutely. . . . The existing material, that which is already there, must be used. . . . Your whole make-up and personality characteristics must be recognized, accepted, and then you might find some inspiration. (64)

The Frommian group views cure differently. The analyst is more likely to respond fully to the potential—the inherent possibilities—of the person before the analyst. As Tauber (1979) poetically says, "[the analyst] can convey important human truths to the patient; in other words . . . he can transmit to his patient a vision of what life could be" (213).

It is hoped that this description of the divergence and the convergence of these two strands in interpersonal psychoanalysis results in less elusiveness and mystery. Now I wish to present some of my observations and views, thereby clarifying the construct further. The examples in the following presentation represent analysts who have chosen to travel on the Frommian road. In this regard, there is a commitment to discover experience in the consulting room that can both enable patients to become more aware of that which they cannot account for and also discover new possibilities for self.

Interpersonalists are disposed to focus on the interplay of events during the session—upon the interactions between the participants—rather than upon the content of the patient's productions. What can be observed between patient and therapist is the primary focus. An example that evoked lively discussion when presented at a colloquium follows.

The patient walked into the office, turned off a lamp (the room remained adequately lit), and then said, "Do you mind if I turn this off? It bothers my eyes." His tone was demanding and arrogant and clearly did not suggest a sincere concern with whether his analyst indeed minded the action he had already taken. Not one second passed between the question "Do you mind if I turn this off?" and his lying down on the couch and beginning to talk about another subject. The therapist then asked the patient whether he was aware of what had just happened between them; specifically, that he had asked for permission after he had done what he wanted and that he had neither waited for a response before acting nor displayed any interest in his analyst's reaction. The discussion rather immediately moved on to the various ways he had invariably obtained what he wanted from people. Gradually both of them learned that he was unable to wait for a "yes" or a "no" because of the intolerable anxiety experienced by him in response to the intimacy of hearing another's preference. Listening was too close for comfort for him. Then he became interested in how this anxiety had developed and how early it had begun. Those in the audience of different theoretical views argued that the analyst should have asked for associations to the lamp light or should have raised the issue of the seduction implied by the turning off of the light. To the interpersonalist, however, the behavior of the patient with the analyst was similar to his chaotic interpersonal behavior outside the office. By articulating maladaptive interpersonal behaviors, the analyst helped the patient to see more clearly and objectively the impact of the self on another. Also, this interaction moved the patient to realize other possibilities for the self. This enlightenment can enable the patient to move on to change if he or she so desires.

Another distinction between the interpersonal model and other models, including classical theory, involves the role of rules in psychoanalysis. An interpersonal approach deemphasizes rules of technique; other models provide technical rules about how to analyze resistance, how to listen, how to confront, clarify, and interpret resistance (Greenson 1967). From the interpersonal perspective, analysis is a place to unfold the meaning of communications (verbal and nonverbal) between the patient and the analyst—the two participants—to examine *in vivo* what has happened between them.

An example of this distinction between rule-governed technique and the effort to understand what happens in the session came to my attention when I was discussing supervision with a colleague. He had just begun working with a nine-year-old girl. When a certain therapy session was half over, the child asserted that she needed to go to the bathroom. He showed her where it was; she returned and the session resumed. His supervisor said that he should not have given the child permission to leave because the leaving was resistance that was being acted out in behavior instead of in words. The supervisor determined that, by giving her permission, the analyst had colluded in the patient's resistance.

A supervisor of interpersonal persuasion would be inclined to pursue the following issues and seek answers to the following questions: Was the child aware of her need before the session started; if so, why did she not speak up then? How did she feel about asking for permission? What was it like to return to resume the session? Was her request an assertion of courage when she was uncomfortable about what was happening at the moment or an effort to flee from the discomfort? What did the therapist notice about his own reactions when the child asked? What were his fantasies, thoughts, and reveries while he waited for her to return? Whether he gave the patient permission or not is not the issue to the interpersonalist. Rather, the problem is to try to understand what happened between the two participants.

David Rapaport (1951) has described interpersonal psychoanalysis as a dialogue at its best with each participant free to say anything on his or her mind and with no fear that the relationship may end because of what is said. There is no censorship. It is, in my view, problematic whether analysts should say everything that occurs to them. There has to be some dividing line between spontaneous expressiveness by the analyst, which enhances the process, and grandiose, self-indulgent, wildly intuitive expressions, which can serve to satisfy the analyst's narcissistic needs.

In an original paper by Wilner (1986) in which the author states that participant-observation is a paradox, there may lie a solution to the problem of finding this dividing line. He affirms that one cannot participate and observe at the same time. He makes a qualitative distinction between two kinds of experience: primary experience, which is locked into an isolated, concrete embeddedness; and secondary experience, which has generality and application beyond the self. His paper presents an illustration of these two kinds of experience.

> an upset patient was crying profusely, and used many tissues to dry her eyes. I felt helpless in that nothing that I was able to say could get to the source of her upset or stem the flow of her tears. She commented at some point that she had used up half of my tissues. Her calling my attention to the tissues in this way served to change the "reality" of the situation. For it suddenly occurred to me (and Wilner tells this to the patient) that she was not basically using the tissues because she was crying. Rather, she was crying in order to use my tissues, thereby, perhaps, condensing myself and the tissues in her mind. (11)

Wilner's feelings of helplessness in the session is a primary experience— so too is the patient's endless weeping. When the patient observes what she is doing and tells him—that is, moves from being a participant to being an observer—his reality changes. Wilner sees clearly and objectively the meaning of the interaction and expresses these thoughts spontaneously. (In reaction to her observations, he moves from being a participant to being an observer.)

How to distinguish between the analyst's primary and secondary experience is elusive and mysterious, as are many other tasks in analysis, and could be the subject of another treatise by Wilner. I speculate that primary experience is more powerful, intense, and completing and is more likely to be anchored to concrete images. Secondary experience is more differentiated, objectified, and unlikely to be connected to strong affective experience. It has an abstract quality. Further, I speculate that communication of secondary experience enhances the meaning of the interaction, and this should lead to further associations by both participants. According to Wilner, the participant-observer, when participat ing, is embedded in the context; the observing-participant, when observing, is freed from the context. He believes that the two realities—participating and observing—are qualitatively distinct. Perhaps one way to view the process of analysis is to consider it as an interplay between these two kinds of experience—primary and secondary—whereby the process is facilitated by the flexibilities of the participants to engage in the interplay.

That an analyst be able to see the self clearly and objectively is of particular importance. Hoffman (1983) has written that analysts may be placed on a continuum defined by their use of the patient-therapist relationship as a slice of reality. If one believes, as interpersonalists do, that there is some truth in the patient's perception of the analyst, then a major task of the analyst is to facilitate the patient's ability to distinguish between what is real and what is not real in the interactions between the patient and analyst, as well as to give words to the distinction.

Regardless of the level of activity of analysts, their character styles and personalities are present from the very beginning—in the particular messages on their answering machines; in the furnishings of their offices; their accents; their styles of dress; and, at a more profound level, in their attitudes, ethics, and determinations in the consulting room, and in their rate of intervention, their tone, gesture, and mood. Singer (1977) has argued persuasively that the analyst cannot be anonymous.

The degree to which the analyst encourages or discourages the patient's realistic appraisal of the analyst's character style is a measure of the analyst's commitment to the interpersonal model. What is studied in the analysis is what is observed. In addition, if the patient is becoming more precise in the consulting room, the analyst may conclude that the same precision is developing in the patient's interpersonal world in other significant relationships. Patient appraisal helps the analyst to be more aware of impact of self on other.

There are various ways for the analyst to indicate to the patient the analyst's readiness for this kind of work. (These are recommendations and not rules.) Early on, sometimes during the first consultation, the analyst may ask the patient for any thoughts or feelings, whether positive or negative and no matter how fleeting, about the room, the analyst, comments made by the analyst during the session, and the like. These questions show a willingness on the part of the analyst to hear the answers and to invite the patient to join in as a participant-observer.

Upon hearing annoyance, joy, or any emotion in his or her own voice in response to some remark by the patient, the analyst may ask whether the patient noticed the tone and what reactions occurred. If there were reactive thoughts and feelings, why was the patient silent? Here I do not mean that the analyst self-consciously decides first to express a particular emotion to the patient and then behaves accordingly. Rather, I mean that the analyst has already spontaneously expressed self. Then he or she has observed the expression objectively and communicates his or her observation to the patient. This may be another example of Wilner's primary experience (affective expressiveness) in interplay with secondary experience (objective observation).

In an interpersonal model, the openness on the analyst's part and the willingness to hear the criticism, reactions, praise, and admonitions by the patient demand that the analyst not be the authority figure, the teacher, or the savant but a fellow participant—in other words, more human than otherwise.

To conclude, interpersonal psychoanalysis is a construct, in the sense that it organizes and integrates concepts and theories so that they are available for use, study, refinement, and even replacement, and this construct is both elusive and mysterious.

REFERENCES

Eagle, M. N. 1984. *Recent developments in psychoanalysis.* New York: McGraw-Hill.
Field, T. M., R. Woodson, R. Greenberg, and D. Cohen. 1982. Discrimination and imitation of facial expression by neonates. *Science* 218:179–81.
Freud, S. [1912] 1953. Recommendations to physicians practising psycho-analysis. In *Standard Edition,* vol. 12, 109–20. London: Hogarth Press.
Fromm, E. 1947. *Man for himself.* New York: Ballantine.
Greenson, R. 1967. The technique and practice of psychoanalysis. New York: International Universities Press.
Jung, C. G. 1935. *Collected works.* New York: Bollingen.
Hoffman, I. 1983. The patient as interpreter of the analyst's experience. *Contemporary Psychoanalysis,* 19.
Levenson, E. 1972. *The fallacy of understanding.* New York: Basic Books.
———. 1985. Talk given at New York University Postdoctoral Program, New York City, 6 December.
———. 1985. The interpersonal (Sullivanian) model. In *Models of the mind: Their relationships to clinical work,* edited by A. Rothstein. New York: International Universities Press.

Masson, J. M. C. 1984. *The assault on truth*. New York: Farrar, Straus & Giroux.

Rapaport, D. 1951. The conceptual model of psychoanalysis. In *Psychoanalytic psychiatry and psychology, clinical and theoretical papers,* vol. 1, edited by R. P. Knight and C. R. Friedman. Austen Riggs Center. New York: International Universities Press.

Schachtel, E. 1959. *Metamorphosis: On the development of affect, perception, attention, and memory*. New York: Basic Books.

Singer, E. 1977. The fiction of analytic anonymity. In *The human dimension in psychoanalytic practice,* edited by K. A. Frank. New York: Grune & Stratton.

Stern, D. 1983. Unformulated experience. *Contemporary Psychoanalysis* 19:71–99.

———. 1985. *The interpersonal world of the infant: a view from psychoanalysis and developmental psychology*. New York: Basic Books.

Sullivan, H. S. 1953. *The interpersonal theory of psychiatry*. New York: W. W. Norton.

Tauber, E. 1979. Erich Fromm: Clinician and social philosopher. *Contemporary Psychoanalysis* 15:201–13.

Trungpa, C. 1973. *Cutting through spiritual materialism*. Boston: Shambhala.

Wilner, W. 1986. *Participatory experience: The participant observer paradox*. Paper presented at the Manhattan Institute for Psychoanalysis, New York City, 25 April.

7

THE INFLUENCE OF NEUROTIC CONFLICT ON THE ANALYST'S CHOICE OF THEORY AND PRACTICE

Richard Lasky, Ph.D.

The division of Psychoanalysis of the American Psychological Association sponsored a conference at Clark University on psychoanalytic training for psychologists in 1986. On a panel entitled "On Becoming a Psychoanalyst of One Persuasion or Another," Stephen Appelbaum (1990) postulated that one selects a psychoanalytic theory or perspective primarily as an outgrowth of personality and the nature of one's identity. He stated that personality factors can not only lead an analyst to a particular theory but also can cause an analyst to defend it dogmatically and reject others enthusiastically. A decade earlier, Roy Schafer delivered a paper to the graduating class of the William Alanson White Institute with exactly the same title, "On Becoming a Psychoanalyst of One Persuasion or Another" (1977, published in 1978 with a slightly different title). Schafer thought of belonging to a particular school of psychoanalysis as belonging to an essentially closed system, which, like belonging to any culture, one is locked into unconsciously. He spoke of the tensions that exist between the organization of the analyst's experience and becoming a slave to it, particularly in regard to the problem of the analyst's analytic identifications with good and worthy role models who may have vastly differing points of view. He considered how conflicts will contribute to the analyst's attachment to a particular point of view, identifying the fact that a theoretical viewpoint is not simply an antiseptic intellectual undertaking. However, the main thrust of his paper was on the complementarity of personality and choice of orientation, rather than a particular emphasis on how conflicts can come to actively warp the analyst's views on theory and technique. This question—how neurotic conflict in an analyst can detrimentally influence ideas about theory and technique—seems to be intriguing to a number of analysts at this time. Abend (1986) and Cooper (1986), in articles intended to be directed at each other's related concerns, do take up this question in some considerable detail. Abend points out how some neurotic conflicts are inevitably involved in the formation of both the analyst's analytic ideals and the analyst's analytic idealizations, arguing that our own analyses are imperfect and leave us with residual variabilities in functioning affecting how we theorize and work, which includes "the persistence or reappearance of certain of the less desirable patterns of thought, emotionality, and behavior that are derived from our infantile conflicts" (Abend 1986, 566). He stresses the fact that "specific illustrations of the favorable and unfavorable effects of the analyst's compromise formations on his analyzing capability are not easy to provide" (570). I intend to try and do so at a later point in this paper. I will use four examples: two that are drawn from the analyses of developing analysts, one that is drawn from a supervisory context, and one that arose in a classroom.

Cooper (1986) describes the analyst whose theorizing is overly influenced by conflict as being "deskilled." He states that "it is not always clear, however, whether these kinds of situations should be labeled technical, that is, better training would enable the analyst to overcome them, or whether they are, at least for certain analysts, characterologic and are not alterable by education. Rather, they require a characterologic change in the analyst" (579). He, too, emphasizes that we naturally tend to gravitate most readily toward those theories that are consistent with elements of our own characters and values without suggesting that this attraction is necessarily pathological. Strupp (1986) states the case in the most extreme, and negative, form possible when he asserts that "many mental health professionals start with preconceptions that are relatively immune to scientific evidence, as is true of any issue where strong emotions are involved" (386). Both Abend and Cooper suggest that some neoanalytic developments, such as the Kleinian approach, the British school, the interpersonal, cultural, and sociological approaches, Kernberg's ego-psychological "softening" (Abend) of the Kleinian view, self-psychology, and others may either be used for neurotic purposes by some analysts or may in and of themselves represent a distortion. However, it was not either Abend's nor Cooper's intention to define what actually should be accepted or rejected in psychoanalytic thinking. They share the idea stated by Cooper (1986), that "we require strong belief systems in order to maintain the vigor that our work requires and this, historically, has led to certain intellectual perils" (580).

In this essay I address how a special set of ideas, those having to do with the development of psychoanalytic models based on object-relations theories, can be put to neurotic use. I am concerned here with how an obsessional interest in or an exclusive attachment to mother-child object-relations theories of development, which specifically exclude the developmental processes of later psychosexual stages, can be used to avoid the analysis of oedipal wishes and conflicts. I will examine how the avoidance of an analyst's unresolved oedipal conflicts can lead to a belief that the oedipal conflict is irrelevant and subsequently to a demand on patients to avoid this material so that the analyst's conflicts are not further inflamed. No doubt a similar essay could be written showing how neurotic conflict can distort or influence an analyst's choice of Freudian theory, Jungian theory, Horneyian or Adlerian theory, interpersonal theory, cultural or sociological or existential theory, and so forth. I am neither claiming that every theoretical perspective is neurotically determined nor that analysts with other than a Freudian orientation are merely displaying their neuroses. I will first present some of the conceptual differences between the Freudian psychoanalytic model and the ideas of Fairbairn's British school (and, parenthetically, some of Klein's ideas) and second some of the conceptual differences between the Freudian psychoanalytic model and the ideas of self psychology. Following that I will present some examples in which the reader can see the influence of neurotic conflict on theory and technique.

From a Freudian perspective, there is no such thing as an object-relations theory per se. The classical position suggests object relations cannot be conceived of as belonging to a separate theory of its own. This is assumed because one's object relations are so dependent on the prevailing state of instinctual longings, tied into the development of narcissism, identity, identifications, and the sense of self, deeply critical to the nature of structural development, and are continuously modified by each succeeding psychosexual developmental stage.

Let us consider as an introduction some of the most critical, yet general, differences between the Freudian position and some object-relational theories of analysis. In the British school, founded for the most part by Fairbairn (1952) and augmented by Guntrip (1961, 1968, 1971), a theoretical position is advanced that changes (and, in some instances entirely replaces) many standard propositions in psychoanalysis. The British school essentially abandons the traditional focus on psychosexual developmental stages and disavows the usual emphasis placed on the role of the oedipal complex in the development of character and neurosis. It is also at odds with a number of elements that are basic to the thinking of mainstream psychoanalysis, particularly as it has been influenced by trends in current ego-psychology. For example, analysts of the British school hold very different opinions as to the contents and functions of the psychic structures. Furthermore, they define the mechanisms of sublimation, neutralization, and drive-fusion quite differently and are also in disagreement with an ego-psychological understanding of the dynamics of internalization and the processes of identification (Saretsky et al. 1979).

Kohut's school of "self-psychology" (Kohut 1968, 1971, 1972, 1978) has raised heated debate (Kernberg 1967, 1970, 1972, 1975, 1976; Lasky 1979, 1982) about two related questions that may be inconsistent with mainstream psychoanalytic theory: first, the extent to which the development of narcissism and of object relations can take place outside the influence of object-instinctual strivings; and second, the extent to which narcissism, object relations, and an individual's sense of self can, or should be, elevated to the status of psychic structure.

Theories of development and psychotherapy that are based in their entirety on an exclusively oral-stage object-relations approach can sometimes serve as an intellectualized defense against the emergence into consciousness of unresolved oedipal conflicts. In such cases, they can also reflect an analyst's unconscious insistence on maintaining a fantasy of a successful oedipal union, which develops its disguise from a developmentally downward displacement in the theory. Finally, such theories may also represent the destruction, in symbolic form, of the oedipal competitor. I will later say more about this last point.

A review of some of the more specific points of difference between the British school and standard psychoanalytic conceptions will now be described. Fairbairn chose not to call his new theory "psychoanalysis" and, instead, decided to describe his reworking of psychoanalytic theory as an "object-relations theory of personality" (1952). This review is necessary because in his theory, despite the fact that he does not call it "psychoanalysis," he has retained much of the language of psychoanalysis and that leads to some confusion as to whether his ideas are a variation of, or a departure from, psychoanalysis. This more specific review is intended to particularly highlight the special areas of difference that can, in overdetermined fashion, be used to avoid post–oral-state conflicts and wishes by an analyst who is unconsciously motivated to do so.

Fairbairn (1952) uses a concept of libido that is not a function of the id but of the ego. His concept of aggression is in no way related to drives because for Fairbairn, the only instinct is to be object seeking; thus, aggression is simply an understandable response to frustration or disappointment. In this way, Fairbairn equates aggression with affective anger, rage, hostility, vindictiveness, and so forth. That is a limitation on the meaning and function of aggression not present in traditional psychoanalytic theory. For Fairbairn, both the ego and the id (with a radically altered concept of libido) are fundamentally object seeking. The more usual psychoanalytic formulation is that the ego is adaptational and reality oriented and the id is pleasure seeking and discharge oriented. In addition, psychoanalytic thinking makes an important distinction between being perpetually object-hungry (in the sense that object need is fundamental to the dependency of infancy), as opposed to Fairbairn's concept of being instinctively object seeking (which implies an immediate capacity to distinguish between the self and object world). Much of Fairbairn's description of the ego uses variables that are used to describe aspects of the id and of the superego in conventional psychoanalytic thinking. He uses the concept of internalization not as a regulator of mental functioning but as a defense. Regarding identification processes, Fairbairn assumes a considerably wider distinction between internalization and incorporation than is customary in mainstream psychoanalysis. Standard psychoanalytic theory suggests that (despite the most minimal contents possible) there are precursors to the ego present at birth. It also suggests that one can see functions that will be attributed to the ego's sphere of influence, present at birth (for example, those functions operating with primary autonomy). Neither of these ideas is considered by classical psychoanalysis to be the equivalent of the view that there is a structuralized ego present at birth. Fairbairn axiomatically poses a structuralized ego present at birth that, notwithstanding its need for further development, organizes itself around the primary task of relating to objects.

Melanie Klein (1973) and her followers also posit that the ego, as a structural entity, is present at birth. In her thinking, the primary task of the ego is defense; thus, in common with Fairbairn's thinking, it is incapable of the autonomy suggested in the ego-psychological position. Both theoretical stances suggest that the infant is capable of greater distinctions between inner and outer environments and between self and objects than is usually assumed to be possible in the Freudian point of view.

Fairbairn's concept that excitement arises from the relation of the ego to objects excludes the notion of excitement arising from libidinal and aggressive drives that may, or may not, rest on the involvement of objects. Fairbairn's view leads him to the conclusion that excitation can never exist independently from objects. His concept of the ego-ideal is that it is a fully conscious entity that resides in the ego rather than a partially conscious entity that resides in the superego. He does not view the ego-ideal as serving a bridging function between the ego and the superego; he equates the ego-ideal with an ideal object. His concept of antilibidinal refers to being rejected and being rejecting, and it is not related to the more familiar economic concepts of anticathexis, hypercathexis, and hypocathexis or the more familiar dynamic concept of countercathexis. Finally, Fairbairn's concept of anxiety rests exclusively on the fear of separation.

Fairbairn (1963) himself has provided an excellent summary of the views of his British school. The preceding comparisons by no means represent the totality of Fairbairn's work, just as making an example of his theory does not exhaust the fund of object-relations theories of personality in existence today.

Having made these distinctions, let us return to the original thesis of this essay. An analyst motivated by neurosis to redefine psychoanalysis along exclusively oral dimensions would be able to capitalize on the views of the British school. He or she could readily claim support for an avoidance of oedipal issues by citing the special (that is, nonpsychosexual) conceptual framework of the British school, particularly with its focus on early infancy. That the British school is growing in popularity makes this overdetermined position easy to justify. In further aid of avoiding oedipal conflicts, the theory lends itself easily to distortion; the individual is in a position to claim that psychoanalytic horizons are only being expanded (rather than radically changed) precisely because Fairbairn's nomenclature is indistinguishable from the technical language of traditional psychoanalysis.

The imagery of oral union, which is at the heart of the British school, particularly when expanded by the work of Balint (1968), can be used as a conscious substitute for unconsciously retained infantile assumptions about the nature and the meaning of sexual intercourse in the mind of an analyst (and as such, is not limited to the constellations of boys and their mothers). When such confusions and condensations about what is oral and what is phallic, which are primary process events, come to dictate important elements in the quality of secondary-process thinking, does it not seem likely that the ego has been forced to capitulate to the id and, to a lesser extent, to the superego? In an analyst with a neurotic attachment to early-object-relations theories, the ego serves the id and superego, rather than mediating and regulating their activity. The danger this poses is in developing highly rationalized and intellectualized obsessional attachments to symbolic oedipal unions, in the name, however, of orality, which are then able to be acted out in interpersonal relations (including those with their patients). These apparently nonsexual activities in object relationships are designed to solidify mental representations of consummated mergers between highly instinctualized self and parental representations, thus effecting an oedipal union in one's object relations.

We need to distinguish oedipal relationships in one's interpersonal relations from oedipal relationships in one's object relations.

It is important not to confuse one's object-relations with one's relations with objects. One's relations to objects (and the object-world in its entirety) are one's interpersonal relations. One's interpersonal relations are continuously modifying, and being modified by, one's object-relations. One's object-relations are part of internal sphere of mental representations, which exists as a psychological event. The mental representations of the object-world enter into various levels of merger with self-representations, and these internal psychic phenomena compose the set of one's object-relations. (Lasky 1979, 62)

The confusion, as it spills over into a therapy interaction, will be discussed shortly.

When an oedipal union in object relations is acted out in orally disguised object relationships, the ego's autonomy is highly compromised (and its potential as an adaptive mental regulator is considerably diminished). The neurotic analyst's ego turns its talents to the service of denial, disguise, inhibition, intellectualization, and idiosyncratic modes of reality testing. In the neurotic relation to theory and practice, this unconscious activity, and its "anticonscious" behavioral component, has a conscious representation in an obsessional and intense excitement associated with ideas—that is, the analyst's theory—in the place of conscious recognition of conflictual wishes.

Some of the assumptions of Kohut's self psychology school can be used, as well, to serve similar neurotic purposes. Kohut's primary interest in the mental activity of the oral stage, most particularly, and his attempt to separate crucial mental dynamics from object-instinctual considerations can be used, in some circumstances, to avoid anxiety in someone who strives to circumvent the object-instinctual oedipal conflict. One of the building blocks of psychoanalytic theory, having special relevance to the oedipal complex, suggests that we identify with, and particularly value, those individuals in the object world who gratify instinctual longings: we become attached to and grow to love the mother who feeds us (that is, who provides a libidinally gratifying environment). We do not love the person who simply mechanically and biologically gave birth to us if she is not responsive to our libidinal needs (or anyone else who randomly exists in our infantile environment). Based on this instinctual tie, our attachments undergo a variety of predetermined stage-specific transformations from object attention all the way to object love and, ultimately, in the phallic stage, they become expressed as oedipal wishes and conflicts.

Within this paradigm, which articulates a critical essence of the psychoanalytic model, there are some central notions: (1) the process of identification and the identifications themselves are originated by, continuously supported by, and intimately related to the development and vicissitudes of instinctual strivings, frustrations, and gratifications (excluding some introjective identifications that occur in the structuralization of the superego and that can eventually achieve a considerable amount of autonomy from infantile wishes); (2) since object relations are the result of mergers between self-representations and object representations, and because both object love (as distinguished from object attention) and object representations are intimately related to instinctual strivings, it follows that the sense of one's self that accompanies one's object relations cannot be evolved outside the sphere of object-instinctual considerations; and (3) since the development of object relations occurs throughout all the stages of psychosexual development and since the superego (which is a reservoir of a special variety of identifications and, hence, an important influence on and part of our object relations) is structuralized in response to the oedipal complex, one cannot artifically separate narcissism, object relations, and one's sense of self from oedipal dynamics.

If one disavows instinctual motivations and drive-related mental activities, which is precisely what Kohut does when he posits that narcissism can evolve outside the influence of object-instinctual strivings, one disavows and undercuts the primary foundation of the oedipal complex. In this way, a symbolic destruction of the oedipal complex and an undoing of the oedipal competitor can be made to occur, in the service of conflict, when one encounters a dogmatic insistence on this posture that is empowered by neurosis.

Other aspects of self psychology also lend themselves to a denial of both the phallic stage and the oedipal complex. Kohut's special involvement with the concepts of empathy, self-object transference, and mirroring in positive transference, and his relative disinterest in analyzing negative-transference phenomena (which should not be considered to be the equivalent of a disinterest in the question of narcissistic rage) can easily support a wish to perpetuate an ideal (idealized, idealizing) dyadic relationship without the interference of any triadic competitive and frustrating intrusions. In the oral stage, the model of an ideal (and an idealized) relationship is dyadic and is based on feeding and being taken care of; in the phallic stage, it is transformed into the context of a triadic relationship that now changes the original dyad to the level of a specifically oedipal union. One can also bypass the oedipal conflict and maintain one's ties intact if one refuses to conceptualize dyads except in the context of oral empathy—that is, by relating the behavior of an oral-stage infant to the behavior of an adult as rough equivalents without including the later developing intervening variables that originate in or are transformed by the anal and phallic stages' latency, and adolescence.

Kohut's assertion that the pathological narcissism of an adult is the equivalent of the stage-specific narcissism of an infant, without taking into account the powerful influence of intervening maturational processes, has been challenged repeatedly (Kernberg 1975; Lasky 1979). The crux of these objections argues that the narcissism (including grandiosity, omnipotence, and omniscience) of a child will fluctuate and be formed by successes and failures in reality, thus bringing to narcissism much of the sovereignty of the ego, whereas the pathological narcissism of an adult is relatively impervious to successes and failures in reality, leaving narcissism for the most part under the primary influence of the id and of archaic and primitive aspects of the superego.

As was the case with the British school, this is an incomplete description of the views of self psychology. It has not been the prime intention of this essay, however, to represent and also critique either self psychology or the British school in their entirety (even though some criticism was inevitable), but rather to have selected some specific components of those theories that lend themselves particularly well to the avoidance of what is sometimes a warranted examination of the oedipal complex.

Moving back, once again, to the neurotic use of these theories, we can speculate that turning away from postoral psychological development also serves the purpose of ridding oneself of the oedipal competitor who must inevitably interfere in the dyadic relationship, once he or she enters one's life or one's analysis. Taking the position that phallic and oedipal conflicts are unimportant can be thought of as a way of reducing the presence, impact, and success of an oedipal rival. Hidden in the pretext of an omission, it permits an unchallenged discharge of aggression. It also allows the conflicted individual to reduce libidinal cathexes that ordinarily are extended toward the competing parent to help balance the aggression directed at that parent. The maintenance of libidinal attachments to the competing parent in the oedipal triad forces on the child (and the individual he or she grows up to become) an acknowledgement of the value, importance, and unmistakable presence of that parent (leading to guilt, open conflict, and, one hopes, eventual resolution in the form of the development of affection and the wish to identify). The relegation of the oedipal competitor to unimportance and, in effect, nonexistence behind the facade of a theoretical posture can be a crowning insult in the symbolic language of the theorizer. The idea and the person of the oedipal rival can be diminished without running the "risks" involved in direct contempt, obvious displays of ridicule, and openly acknowledged rivalry. The development of a defensive involvement in oral-level "object-relations-only" theories in the place of confronting oedipal anger, conflict, fears, and wishes reduces anxiety in both consciousness and unconsciousness. It provides a vehicle for hidden assault (libidinal and aggressive) and a shield against danger (from the analyst's wishes as well as from fantasies of retaliation). It organizes an intellectual structure to mask the analyst's fixation and to disguise disruptions in ego and superego functioning.

Obsessional adherence to one's theoretical position is the enemy of scientific curiosity and may represent a defense against love and identification, as well as against the possibility of an oedipal defeat. An obsessional commitment to object-relations theories that are most remarkable for their phallic omissions (or, in other words, to "emasculated" and "castrated" theories) is frequently justified and "legitimized" simply on the basis of consensual validation. Resort to such an argument can be powerful, indeed. Modifications in clinical technique that are outgrowths of this process may act in concert with the particular neurosis of the therapist, who then enacts these conflicts with the patient. For example, implicit and even explicit instructions guiding the patient to focus exclusively, or predominantly, on oral-stage material can be made to look, on the surface, like a thorough examination of the patient's earliest years. Such directedness helps the therapist remain free of the personal conflicts that would arise if the patient was left to express phallic and oedipal material at his or her own discretion. It also serves the purpose of maintaining the oedipally desired parent as the sole libidinal transference object in the patient's neurosis, which complements and supports the neurotic needs of such a therapist (who identifies with the position the patient has in this way been forced into).

I will illustrate some of these notions by presenting some case material. Choosing different contexts for my examples is designed to show how such neurotic influences may be expressed in a variety of circumstances.

During an analysis of one patient, at a time of severe oedipal stress, when competitive rages at his father were emerging into consciousness, this patient, a practicing analyst, commented on what he understood to be my interest in object-relations theory. Commenting further on his own rapidly growing interest in the topic, he suggested that I should take this as a compliment since it was, according to him, strong evidence of positive transference. This was a hypocritical statement that was frequently repeated as negative paternal transferences began to become more pronounced in the treatment, and it was designed to lull, and eventually incapacitate, my defenses against and awareness of his current and future hostile wishes. I was to assume that in the transference I was being loved, instead of feared, hated, and, eventually, attacked.

The patient tried to circumvent his oedipal struggles by acquiring an intense intellectual interest in and theoretical commitment to a theory of object relations that suggested that all important character development and symptom formation occurred in the developmental processes of the oral stage. He began to assert dogmatically that neurosis was defined as a pathological attachment to the nipple and that good therapy involved a "proper weaning." His insistence that psychoanalysis was, at its very highest form, a weaning operation was designed to strengthen and maintain the existence of his mother as the sole transference object, and to refuse his father any emergence into the analysis. Seeing his father as theoretically and realistically unimportant was, for this male analyst, a symbolic act of paternally directed castration. This superficially benign-appearing method of castrating and murdering his father—that is, as part of his intellectualizations—allowed the patient to commit an act of aggression under the guise of an omission. Earlier in the treatment and prior to the emergence of negative paternal transference, the patient's associations were rich with material about his father; now, however, this patient's spontaneous comments about his father were virtually non-existent. Father became a focus of attention only when the patient was pointing out to me how unimportant his father was in comparison to his mother in his psychic development. Thus, his interest in object relations had three motives. Initially it began with a healthy sublimated intellectual interest more or less unrelated to the content of his analysis. Then, it became a vehicle for a circumvention of his anxiety-laden oedipal struggles. Finally, it expressed the wish to be victorious in the struggle. His obsessive interest in the oral character of relationships then led him to insist that I change my style and use the analysis as if it were a "weaning process." During this time my patient quoted to me Guntrip and Balint, chapter and verse. He used those authors to serve his own very special purposes: his fantasy that he was attached to the nipple of his mother was the conscious representative, in a developmentally downward displacement, of his unconscious wish for an oedipal union. His claim that he was orally fixated and united with his mother was, in reality, the expression of his wish to be genitally, or perhaps one should say phallically, united with her. The request for "weaning" was eventually understood by us to be a derivative of superego prohibitions regarding incest and as an even more transformed prohibition regarding patricide. He was caught in a frightening conflict between his need to do away with his father in order to have his mother and the terror of achieving this aim. Throughout it all, his wishes toward his parents were expressed almost exclusively in these rationalized and highly intellectualized theoretical beliefs. Thus, one can say that his interest in object-relations theory may have started out as an attempt at sublimation, but his obsessively organized study of the topic became a castration and murder with ritual aspects. Ultimately, given its multiple functions, even his wish to be weaned (as the terror of oedipal success caused prohibitions to emerge) was, on another level, a symbolic insistence on an oedipal victory over his father. Incidentally, these conclusions were borne out by him by the time we reached the end of his analysis. We examined with considerable profit his insistence that I shared and agreed with this theory that stood, in the middle and late phases of his analysis, for his struggles with his father over his mother.

Taking the stance that psychoanalysis is, in its best condition, a "weaning" process, as some therapists do, suggests the wish for an unbreakable instinctual relationship. For the analyst to pretend that psychoanalysis is a weaning operation means that the therapeutic undertaking of the patient to develop the ego's capacities to resolve conflict and to enhance in general the adaptive structuralization of the entire mental apparatus is undermined. The patient's struggle to be free of archaic object choices and conflicts is transformed into a struggle to be free of the analyst's fantasy life. This includes the analyst's rationalized insistence that it is the patient's conflicts rather than the analyst's that are being introduced into the treatment.

The following supervisory vignette reflects the problem under discussion in analytic trainees rather than in working analysts. It is possible that this example represents the kind of case that Cooper (1986) might have viewed as only requiring more and better education. The training process itself involves strong identifications and strong enthusiasms that tend to temper slowly over time as one gains experience. Some markedly extreme involvements may often occur that have, nonetheless, a relatively transient quality in the long run. The supervisee in this example seemed to me, however, to go beyond the simple problem of being someone who was new to the field and who simply needed to learn more about what he was doing. He did not give the impression that his therapeutic posture would change as he gained more experience. If anything, he seemed to show an active hostility to new and different points of view and gave an impression of adamancy rather than enthusiasm in his thinking. Most importantly, he appeared to take an unquestioning position that he was justified in refusing to study points of view different from his own. There is no way of knowing what the final outcome of his analytic development might have been after his training was over and his analysis complete; but the questions that are raised in the following example, about the degree to which neurotic conflict had affected his thinking and influenced his work in this intermediate stage of his training, are, nevertheless, pertinent.

In our first supervisory hour, the supervisee said he wanted to work with me because he had heard that I was interested in object relations. Although he had not had personal contact with me previously nor read anything I had written, he thought that I would be helpful to him based on what he had casually heard about me. He hoped that I would complement his own strong interest in object-relations theory. That settled, he presented to me the following case material: He had seen a young woman, only a few times, who had come to treatment because she was about to engage in a relationship that was causing her considerable anxiety. All of her previous love and sexual experiences were with older married men, and she was about to begin a love affair with a single man of her own age. On the way to his apartment for what was planned to be their first sexual encounter, she fell off her bicycle and fractured her arm. She began treatment immediately afterward and had a reasonably accurate if intellectual understanding of the relationship between her injury and her anxiety. Her second, less immediate reason for seeking treatment (almost as if it was an after-thought) was to change a predominantly passive, dependent, and infantile posture she characteristically assumed with her older, married lovers. Concerning her mother she reported only that they did not get along very well and had little to do with each other. She had an older sister who did get on well with the mother, and the patient reported that she herself was the father's favorite. Each child appeared to be the favorite of one of the two parents. Her father was, in her words: "a sailor, or a seaman, or a merchant—something like that." She then stated that each time he returned from a cruise she would sleep in the same bed with him (the mother slept in a different bed with her older sister). Her father abandoned the family when the patient was twelve-and-a-half years old, which was when she began to menstruate, and had never been heard from since. When she was eighteen, she left the city of her childhood and came to New York City. She quickly fell into a deep depression and eventually made a suicidal gesture that led to a brief hospitalization. Since that time she had made no other suicidal attempts but remained chronically depressed. In describing his work with the patient, the supervisee mentioned that she had forgotten her wallet during her second session and so had no carfare with her to get home. He loaned her a dollar, and his question was "Two sessions have gone by since I loaned her the dollar. She hasn't offered yet to repay me. Should I bring it up, or should I wait for her to bring it up?" I pointed out to him that carfare was, at that time, only thirty-five cents and asked what his rationale was for loaning her any money at all. He replied that he thought that she was a very oral and needy person and that it was consistent with his interest in object-relations theory to be a better object for his patient than were the significant figures in the patient's past. He went on to tell me that his view of analysis was that it served as a corrective emotional experience, by which he meant that it was a better repetition of the mother-child interaction. He thought his patient wanted to see if he would be as absent as was her "grossly inadequate" mother (these were his words, not hers). He was determined to be a better nurturer. He felt that her depression was due to the fact that she had lost her mother to her sister, and that her sexual difficulties reflected her difficulty in establishing an adequate relationship with her mother. He gave her the dollar because anyone could have given her just the right carfare. He would do better, so that she could use him to form good introjects and enter into a corrective self-object transference (clearly not the use of his concept that I think Kohut intended).

I thought his views were somewhat too speculative and not directly related to the data. I suggested that she was overstimulated by her father or by her fantasies about her father. I reminded him of the special sequential connection between her thinking of him as a seaman (pun on the male ejaculate: *semen*) and her memory of being in bed with him. It occurred to me, since he was her bed partner, that her father, leaving as he did just as she began to reach sexual maturity, might have severely wounded her and that she experienced his leaving as a personal rejection rather than as a rejection of her mother or of family life. It seemed to me possible to wonder whether her moving to New York City, one of the most active port cities in the United States, may have been a search for her lost father, which she had only been waiting to be old enough to conduct. To support this, as a not unreasonable question, I also pointed out her consistent interest in older, married men. I suggested the possibility that it wasn't until she made the attempt to give up her repetitively incestuous object choice, as represented by her involvement with older married men, that she began to experience the new anxiety—different from her chronic depression—which led her to break her arm. (It was almost as if her superego and her id were in league to punish her for abandoning the father who had abandoned her.) While it is possible that her mother may have been uninvolved with her, there is no clear evidence that she had an incapacity to provide a nurturing environment. Further, from the information he gave me—which is the information I have presented here—there is no real evidence that the mother was "grossly inadequate" to any of the tasks of mothering; she was, after all, able to provide good mothering to her sister.

My summation of the patient's dynamics, based on the information up to that point, was that she was exhibiting problems that were primarily related to oedipal difficulties. I saw her suicidal gesture as possibly being connected to her disappointment at having failed in her search for her father. Her almost exclusive involvement with married men may have been a refusal to accept her failure and may have been her way of insisting on a symbolic reunion with her father in addition to reflecting an incestuous object choice. She seemed to have a hard time mastering the depressive struggles that attended this object loss. I thought that her interest in this new man was possibly a good sign but did not know how yet to explain this shift in object choice (if, indeed, it was a shift).

I emphasized that analysis might be possible with her, all other conditions being satisfied, only if the supervisee could avoid being drawn into precisely the transference gratifications that would diminish her capacity to strive for a new, nonincestuous object. What disturbed the supervisee most was my suggestion that he gave the dollar in countertransference, playing into her pattern of passive, dependent, infantile sexual relations with men, and that he acted out with her, instead of analyzing, a basically taboo and incestuous event. He indignantly stated that I was mistaken when I suggested he was, in effect, being symbolically seduced by her. At that point, he reiterated that he had chosen me for a supervisor because I had had the reputation of being interested in object-relations theory and that if he had known that I was going to turn out to be "just another Freudian" he would never have made this choice. He was adamant about the fact that he wanted to do what he called "object-relations analysis" and told me that it was the generally accepted opinion in sophisticated circles that the oedipal complex was passé. His impression was that the oedipal complex was like an animal that had become extinct. He suggested that I read Fairbairn and then "advance" to Kohut. I suggested that he take a look at Jacobson and Loewald, and both our first supervisory session and the agreement to work together came to an end.

It was from his insistence on adhering to a theory, rather than adherence to the data, that I assumed he was engaged in an active avoidance of his own oedipal conflicts, as their impact was heightened in response to the oedipal issues presented by his patient. He was my supervisee and not my patient and so I can only present this as a speculation. His attempt to fit the patient into a preconceived notion of an object-relations theory of development that excluded the father did not seem to me to attend to the limited, but revealing, information that we had about her. When in the course of our supervisory session I had suggested to him that everyone's object relations bear examination and that we could look more closely at hers when we had more material to go on, he accused me of trying to force him to my "outdated" point of view and used the metaphor of my trying to force something down his throat. He then made a complaint to the director of training of his institute, suggesting that I be removed from the supervisory faculty. Never before, nor since, have I had such a conflict-laden relationship with a supervisee. Needless to say, such an extreme reaction to an intellectual difference of opinion suggests that the supervisory setting is also not without its oedipal overtones.

When a therapist attempts in an active way to be a "better" object and means by this to make up for the deficits in the original parenting process, there is established an instinctualized and regressive relationship in the place of treatment. In addition, one may also see this as an attempt on the part of the therapist to transform the patient into an idealized parent. If the patient makes transference demands that are met by the therapist in the guise of being "available" and "nurturing," the patient gives in return an unconditional love and admiration, which is what every child is prepared to give (in a reasonably normal family environment) and what every child wants and needs intensely from its parents. Unconditional love, admiration, and commitment from the patient may be, in the primary-process reasoning of the therapist, a surrender to childhood oedipal love from and toward the desired partner. Clearly in this circumstance, as well as in a number of other possible circumstances, the interests and the avoidances of patient and therapist can be highly complementary.

To give another, very brief, example: I was present when a class received the information that a prominent female group therapist was going to combine a group of her own patients with a group of her son's patients (he was also a therapist). Then, the two of them, together, would run a doubly long session with a doubly large group. Many intellectual comments were passed by members of the class on the highly experimental and unorthodox nature of such an undertaking, and then the comments (in a rather light-hearted way) began to center on what they thought the patients' sexual fantasies would be concerning this mother-son dyad. Ultimately, a number of comments became rather playfully descriptive. These comments were interrupted by the remarks of an irate fellow student, who was known for her interest in object-relations theory. She said, "The hell with the oedipal fantasies! What about the oral ones?" She then began with obvious anger to lecture the rest of the students on what she described as their "archaic" views of personality and psychotherapy. The language involved—"the hell with the oedipal"—and what seemed to be real vehemence in her tone of voice suggested that her lecture on object-relations theory was strongly linked to conflict.

Her description of her classmates' views as "archaic'" was an attack and suggested the wish to shame them rather than the wish to educate them. She seemed to be unable tolerate the sexualized fantasies about the mother and son (or, in reversal, about the father and daughter) and may have been relieving her own growing anxiety when she insisted, absolutely, on replacing all oedipal images only with oral images. She seemed bent on influencing the other students in a way designed to produce shame and guilt, which led me to think that she was attempting to inhibit the production of oedipal imagery and fantasies. Her efforts were designed to set up prohibitions and not truly designed to educate; her goals seemed tied to prohibitions against sexual fantasies, against oedipal conceptual formulations, and against any openly aggressive aims that might emerge if those prohibitive restraints were absent.

I will conclude this discussion with an example of how neurotic conflict can be expressed in the traditional psychoanalytic model, since, as stated from the outset, every theory has the potential for neurotic misuse. I have been thus far illustrating how the hidden expression of oedipal conflicts can be couched in a defensive obsession with "oral-stage-only" object-relations theories. The following is an example of how unconscious preoedipal conflicts were enacted through an exaggerated Freudian posture by a different analyst-patient in my practice.

My patient had a generally schizoid character style that was not so severe that she was soothed by emptiness, but which did contribute to some serious problems in achieving appropriate trial identifications and meaningful empathy with her patients. This character style formed in response to having been raised by a very narcissistic mother who used the patient as a means of acquiring gratifications for herself and who often attempted to reverse the roles of parent and child. Part of the patient's schizoid posture accurately reflected the psychic emptiness of her early childhood environment and the shallowness of her mother in reality. Another part of her "flatness" was a direct defense against a rather overwhelming rage at her mother for her depriving deficiencies. The patient's father died when she was two years old. Part of her lack of feeling and the impairment of her inner spontaneity was also associated with this loss. This loss was in reality also a loss of part of her childhood sense of self and, in fantasy, of her sense of integrity (as his loss prevented normally and ordinarily expressed concrete mergers between self and parental representations appropriate to that age). Her feelings of detachment in this regard repeated the actual absence of her father and also served, as with the mother, as a defense against powerful recriminations.

When entering into the toilet-training process, the patient's mother seemed to be oblivious to those aspects of the process that would aid in her child's development and seemed to be focused only on how successful toilet training would free her from the noxious burdens of infant care. Her mother's ultimate aim of successful toilet training was not to enhance her child's capacity for internal impulse control and to foster fuller abilities in the direction of social adaptability but rather to qualify the child for day-care services so that her mother would be free to pursue more desirable activities. Rather than a narcissistically enhancing act of self-mastery, toilet training became just another activity in which the patient was to make an adaptation to her mother's needs. The patient had many legitimate grievances against both her parents, but since the age of two she had no father, and the mother she had—no matter how unsatisfactory—was the only mother she had. As a young child, barely out of infancy, she did not have the luxury of being able to express her anger and disappointment, since her mother's commitment to her seemed tenuous at best. Her compromise formation, which was also in part an identification with each of her parents as well as a means of not losing them, was to defend against her rage and resentment through inhibition, repression, and suppression. She, too, became a person who was there but "not there."

In her analytic work, the patient took the most extreme positions possible regarding the concepts of "the blank screen," abstinence, neutrality, and the deprivation of transference demands. At one point, before these issues were sufficiently examined in her own analysis, she even insisted that an analysis could be conducted without a word passing from the analyst to the patient (except for "come in, please" and "we have to stop now"). At times she sadistically withheld interpretations from patients, justifying her behavior on the basis of what she described as "technical requirements of the analytic process," but which when finally subjected to analysis turned out to be a symbolic and satisfying withholding of her bowel contents from her unreasonably demanding mother, in which role she then had unconsciously cast her patients. She repeatedly reenacted the lack of depth in the relationship with her mother and the absence of her father by withholding the rich panoply of emotions one feels in the conduct of an analysis, and she attempted to master the trauma of her own disappointing childhood by "being the child" in the analytic relationship. She supported her conduct in this regard by emphasizing a caricature of the legitimate Freudian stance in which the analyst is not supposed to gratify, but rather to analyze, the infantile longings of their patients—not recognizing that she was neither gratifying nor analyzing but only being depriving in precisely the way she was deprived as a child. Her use of certain aspects of Freudian theory and technique that easily lend themselves to abuse—for example what, when, how, and how much to deprive patients of in the course of analysis—fit directly into the very intense and problematic conflicts with which she had not yet come to terms. Thus, before resolving this in her own analysis, she was able to capitalize upon certain aspects of the Freudian approach with regard to her specifically preoedipal problems.

This patient's transference to me was also in character with her distortion of what constituted legitimate Freudian theory and technique. For example, if some preconscious material made its appearance and I commented on it, she would chide me for being "directive." Or, when I remark on how disappointing and painful it was to have had such a self-centered mother or on how sad it made her not to have had a father who could have made up for some of the deficiencies of her mother, she told me to start practicing analysis and stop fooling around with "touchy-feely psychotherapy." She required an austerity in our relationship that was, in actuality, very much like the layman's worst stereotype of the cold, unrelated, uninvolved, and ungiving analyst. She demanded that I be like a piece of ice, lacking any human qualities as "the analyst" (and she behaved similarily with her patients). She justified this by frequent references to "neutrality" and "abstinence," misunderstanding these concepts to mean the equivalent of the deprivations she suffered in early childhood.

Before leaving this case material I want to indicate that this patient had conflicts other than only the preoedipal ones briefly described here, just as it is important to note that the first patient had preoedipal as well as specifically oedipal problems. This patient's other problems did not play into a misuse of Freudian theory in the way her preoedipal problems did; in the case of the other patient, preoedipal problems did not play into the misuse of object-relations theories the way his oedipal problems did. Although I think that some conflict and theories may have an implicit affinity for one another, I do not believe that they must always necessarily be linked to one another.

In closing, it seems useful to remember that during the shift from anality to the phallic stage both boys and girls, by way of entering the oedipal conflict, will need to renounce their more primitive attachments to their mothers and make numerous shifts, some temporary and some permanent, in both aim and object. Aside from the obviously important issue of biological stage-specificity, the task for children involves the renunciation of many infantile aims that were lodged in orality, and also in anality, and beginning the phallic transformation of others, so that they may continue the process of growth and development. Regressive pulls will exist, of course, throughout life. In a healthy outcome, most oral and specifically anal wishes undergo reshaping via numerous psychic channels into displaced and sometimes even biologically predetermined genital formats, which then undergo even more drastic and complex transformations. When an analyst has not successfully integrated some of these childhood aims but has achieved highly organized and structuralized ego functioning (one is not completely dependent on the other), the capacity to disguise the continued existence of these aims is greatly enhanced. Therapists who fall into this category (with their easy access to compliant theoretical frameworks) can defend against knowledge of these infantile genital aims via massive displacement to orality. The orally disguised but actually phallic attachment to the desired parent is not exhibited as infantile and conspicuous symptoms per se, as one might ordinarily expect in nontherapists, but, rather, the oedipal attachment is demonstrated by an intellectual return to orality where the symptom itself occurs in the context of a higher-order ego process—that is, the contents of one's thinking.

Many approaches to personality and to treatment seem accurate and valid. It is the use to which these approaches are put that concerns us here and not the truth of these approaches. Where there is a high level of consensual validation regarding valid observations in a legitimate context, it can be very difficult to recognize the difference between a genuine difference of opinion and a disguised oedipal maneuver. Subjecting such material to analysis can be extremely difficult because therapists, just like other patients, are inventive in finding (or, if necessary, creating) realities in conformity with their inner needs; such patients are in a position to rebut most oedipal interpretations with attachments to, and the free use of, highly popular theories that exclude (or can be understood to exclude) the father (who is the archetypical oedipal competitor) and thus exclude the oedipal conflict itself.

A nontherapist male patient once said he felt he had no way of becoming a man outside of performing fellatio on his father or killing him. In either case, this represents a wish to rob and murder the competition. One's analytic objective should include the intention to influence the infantile wish to kill by facilitating the development of a well-structuralized ego and superego, and to change the act of fellatio from an act of robbery through sadistic oral incorporation to one that uses the less aggressive and more benign mechanisms of the identification process (a process that leads to the development of a noninstinctualized love relationship with one's parents while making their desired characteristics one's own). For the sophisticated patient who is also a psychotherapist the task is no different.

This essay's primary concern has been focused on the way exclusively oral object-relations theories can be used within the constraints of a neurosis and to speculate about how the contents of any theory can be colored by the influence of a neurosis.

The study of object relations in general is susceptible to being used as a defense against the conscious recognition of oedipal conflicts because of its capacity to be viewed, I believe incorrectly, as a set of developmental phenomena exclusive to the oral stage. When the full range of object-relational development is studied as it progresses through all the psychosexual stages, the theory, while perhaps lending itself to other kinds of abuse, will not lend itself so readily to a posture that abandons or ignores oedipal and phallic dynamics.

REFERENCES

Abend, S. 1986. Countertransference, empathy, and the analytic ideal: The impact of life stresses on analytic capability. *Psychoanalytic Quarterly* 55:563–75.

Appelbaum, S. 1990. Reflections on the role of theory in psychoanalysis. In *Tradition and innovation in psychoanalytic education*, edited by M. Meisels and E. R. Shapiro. Hillsdale, N.J.: Lawrence Erlbaum Associates.

Balint, M. 1968. *The basic fault*. London: Tavistock.

Blos, P. 1962. *On adolescence*. New York: International Universities Press.

Cooper, A. 1986. Some limitations on therapeutic effectiveness: The "burn-out" syndrome in psychoanalysis. *Psychoanalytic Quarterly* 55:576–98.

Fairbairn, W. R. D. 1941. A revised psychopathology of the psychoses and psychoneuroses. *International Journal of Psycho-Analysis* 22:21–33.

———. 1952. *An object-relations theory of personality*. New York: Basic Books.

———. 1963. Synopsis of an object-relations theory of the personality. *International Journal of Psycho-Analysis* 44:224–25.

Freud, S. [1914] 1953. *On narcissim: An introduction* In *Standard edition*, vol. 14. London: Hogarth.

Guntrip, H. 1961. *Personality structure and human interaction*. New York: International Universities Press.

———. 1968. *Schizoid phenomena, object-relations and the self*. New York: International Universities Press.

———. 1971. *Psychoanalytic theory, therapy, and the self*. New York: Basic Books.

Jacobson, E. 1961. Adolescent moods and the remodeling of psychic structures in adolescence. *Psychoanalytic Study of the Child* 16:164–83.

———. 1964. *The self and the object world*. New York: International Universities Press.

——— 1971. *Depression*. New York: International Universities Press.

Kernberg, O. 1967. Borderline personality organization. *Journal of the American Psychoanalytic Association* 15:33–52.

———. 1970. A psychoanalytic classification of character pathology. *Journal of the American Psychoanalytic Association* 18:800–802.

———. 1972. Early ego integration and object-relations. *Annual of the New York Academy of Science* 193:233–47.

———. 1975. *Borderline conditions and pathological narcissism*. New York: Jason Aronson.

———. 1976. *Objection relations theory and clinical psycho-analysis*. New York: Jason Aronson.

Klein, M. 1930. The importance of symbol formation in the development of the ego. *International Journal of Psycho-Analysis* 11:236–50.

———. 1932. *Psychoanalysis of children*. London: Hogarth.

————. 1948. *Contributions to psychoanalysis: Collected papers, 1921–1945,* edited by E. Jones. London: Hogarth.

————. 1957. *Envy and gratitude.* London: Tavistock.

————. 1961. *Narrative of child analysis.* London: Hogarth.

————. 1973. *Contributions to psychoanalysis.* London: Hogarth.

Klein, M., P. Heimann, and R. Money-Kyrle. 1955. *New directions in psychoanalysis.* London: Tavistock.

Klein, M., and J. Riviere. 1964. *Love, hate, and reparation.* New York: W. W. Norton.

Kohut, H. 1968. The psychoanalytic treatment of narcissistic personality disorders. *Psychoanalytic Study of the Child* 23:86–113.

————. 1971. *The analysis of self.* New York: International Universities Press.

————. 1972. Thoughts on narcissism and narcissistic rage. *Psychoanalytic Study of the Child* 27:360–400.

————. 1978. *A casebook.* New York: International Universities Press.

Lasky, R. 1978a. The impact of object-relations theory on psychoanalysis: Theory and treatment techniques. In *Changing approaches to the psychotherapies,* edited by H. H. Grayson and C. Loew. New York: Spectrum.

————. 1978b Neurotic investment and object-relations theory. *Colloquium* 1:23–25.

————. 1978c. Comments on treating the narcissistic character disorder, *Colloquium,* 1:35–38.

————. 1979. Archaic, immature, and infantile personality characteristics. In *Integrating ego psychology and object-relations theory: Psychoanalytic perspectives on psychopathology,* edited by L. Saretsky, G. D. Goldman, and D. S. Milman. Dubuque, Iowa: Kendall/Hunt.

————. 1982. *Evaluating criminal responsibility in multiple personality and the related dissociative disorders: A psychoanalytic consideration.* Springfield, Ill.: Charles C Thomas.

————. 1984. Dynamics, and some problems in treatment, of the "oedipal winner." *Psychoanalytic Review* 73:351–74.

————. 1986. Primitive object relations and impaired structuralization in the abusive patient. *Psychotherapy Patient* 1:95–109.

————. 1989. Some determinants of the male analyst's capacity to identify with patients. *International Journal of Psycho-Analysis* 70:405–18.

————. In press. *Key concepts in psychoanalytic theory and the basic treatment model.* New York: Jason Aronson.

Lasky, R., and D. Brandt. 1977. Object loss and mourning in adolescence. Paper presented at New York Center for Psychoanalytic Training Symposium, New York Academy of Medicine.

Mahler, M. S., and M. Furer. 1967. *On human symbiosis and the vicissitudes of individuation.* New York: International Universities Press.

Mahler, M. S., F. Pine, and A. Bergmann. 1975. *The psychological birth of the human infant.* New York: Basic Books.

Reich, A. 1954. Early identifications as archaic elements in the superego. *Journal of the American Psychoanalytic Association* 2:15–31.

Reich, A. 1960. Pathologic forms of self-esteem regulation. *Psychoanalytic Study of the Child* 15:215–32.

Rosenfeld. H. 1969. On the treatment of psychotic states by psychoanalysis. *International Journal of Psycho-Analysis* 50:101–16.

Sandler, J. 1960. On the concept of the supergo. *Psychoanalytic Study of the Child* 15:128–62.

Saretsky, L., D. Goldman, and D. S. Milman, eds. 1979. *Integrating ego psychology and object-relations theory: Psychoanalytic perspectives on psychopathology.* Dubuque, Iowa: Kendall/Hunt.

Schafer, R. 1960. On the loving and beloved superego in Freud's structural theory. *Psychoanalytic Study of the Child* 15:163–88.

———. 1978. On becoming an analyst in one persuasion or another. *Contemporary Psychoanalysis* 31:7–20.

Segal, H. 1964. *An introduction to the work of Melanie Klein.* London: Heinemann.

Spitz, R. A. 1957. *No and yes: On the genesis of human communication.* New York: International Universities Press.

———. 1959. *A genetic field theory of ego formation.* New York: International Universities Press.

———. 1965. *The first year of life.* New York: International Universities Press.

Strupp, H. 1986. Book review of *Psychotherapy of schizophrenia* by B. P. Karon, and G. P. Vandenbos. *Psychoanalytic Psychology* 3:385–88.

Winnicott, D. R. W. 1958. *Collected papers.* New York: Basic Books.

———. 1965. *The maturational process and the facilitating environment.* New York: International Universities Press.

8

ANNIHILATION ANXIETY: AN INTRODUCTION

Marvin Hurvich, Ph.D.

In his writings on anxiety, Freud (1894, 1926, 1933) delineated two forms: automatic-traumatic and signal. In the former, the ego becomes overwhelmed by excessive internal or external stimulation that it cannot master. In the latter, the person evolves an anticipation of danger related in part to memories of earlier states of overwhelmed helplessness. This expectation of potential danger, accompanied by an attenuated anxiety response, triggers the mobilization of defenses and other ego functions to deal with the subjectively perceived threat before it reaches traumatic proportions.

Compton (1972), in his comprehensive review of Freud's anxiety formulations, contrasted the two varieties of anxiety from each of the metapsychyological points of view (Freud 1915; Rapaport and Gill 1959). There is a signal of approaching helplessness *or* an experience of current helplessness (dynamic point of view); signal (nonenergic) anxiety *or* economic (generated) anxiety (economic point of view). Anxiety is a function of the ego organization *or* a reflection of the disruption of ego organization (structural point of view). Anxiety can be a reaction of the differentiated mental apparatus *or* a response of the undifferentiated apparatus (genetic point of view). And lastly, the anxiety response may be expedient *or* inexpedient (adaptive point of view).

Compton further states that Freud does not consider anxiety in the psychoses as a kind of reaction that may be different from either neurotic or realistic anxiety. But in "The Neuro-psychoses of Defense" (1894), Freud did distinguish between incompatible ideas pertinent to neurotic defenses and intolerable ideas as germane to psychoses. In "Neurosis and Psychosis" (1923b), Freud again made the distinction, here in regard to the intolerable frustration by reality of important childhood wishes in the genesis of some acute psychoses.

In this essay, I will discuss and illustrate aspects of the "intolerable" anxiety that Freud understood in 1926 as a response to a traumatic state of helplessness that overwhelms the ego. My aim is to provide a variety of clinical descriptions of annihilation anxieties together with a consideration of some theoretical underpinnings. Other papers have focused primarily on theoretical issues (Hurvich 1987, 1989, 1990), and on empirical measurement (Hurvich 1987; Hurvich et al. 1988).

In addition to Freud's basic distinction between traumatic and signal anxieties (1894, 1926), he delineated a number of basic danger situations: fears of loss of the object, loss of the object's love, of castration, and of superego disapproval. I have elsewhere argued in detail (Hurvich 1989) that the danger of being psychically overwhelmed and related fears of annihilation be included as a basic danger, indeed as the first basic danger. Freud also described overwhelmed helplessness as the first psychic danger and pegged its occurrence at the stage of the ego's early immaturity (1933, 88). It is primitive anxiety that Freud believed was without mental content. To quote him from an earlier source: "What it is that the ego fears from the external world and the libidinal danger cannot be specified. We know that the fear is of being overwhelmed or annihilated, but it cannot be grasped analytically" (1923a, 57.) This has been called the danger of overstimulation (Gedo and Goldberg 1973) and is related to what Mahler meant by organismic distress (1968). Many psychoanalytic authors have described versions of this anxiety (Hurvich 1989; Hurvich et al. 1988).

Jones (1911) described a fear wider than castration, a fear that the personality itself be lost, which he called "aphanisis." He assumed it to be based on a preideational primal anxiety *(Urangst)* and understood it to be a defensive response to the helplessness from the growing tension due to need, about which Freud wrote in 1926.

Anna Freud (1936) included ego disintegration as a basic danger. She later underscored (1951) how threats to ego intactness can result from psychic merger with the love object, leading to loss of personal characteristics.

Fenichel (1937) wrote that what is feared in excessive excitation is a collapse of the ego and loss of voluntary control. Bak (1943) surmised that anxiety seen in the early stages of schizophrenia is based on a threat to the well-defined ego sinking into impersonality, with loss of personal identity and the sense of a unique and separate self. He also held that schizophrenic anxiety is a reaction to the danger of damage to ego functions or to the dissolution of the self.

Melanie Klein stated that the fear of annihilation is the origin of anxiety (1946) and that its ultimate source is the destructive instincts (1932). She described persecutory anxiety as universally typical of the paranoid-schizoid position. It involves a fear of engulfment and annihilation from an uncontrollable, overpowering object that may be experienced as internal or external. The pain resulting from insufficient gratification is presumably experienced by the infant as an annihilation-threatening persecutory assault (1958).

Winnicott (1962) held that annihilation anxiety develops in the early postnatal period, but only in response to environmental failure and as a result of excessive reaction to impingement. An excess of such reacting produces not *frustration* but a threat of *annihilation*. "This in my view is a very primitive anxiety, long antedating any anxiety that includes the word death in its description." He portrays "unthinkable anxiety" in terms of going to pieces, falling forever, having no relationship to the body and/or having no orientation (58). While these are described in the framework of child development, Winnicott states that he is talking about psychotic anxieties and that clinically they belong to schizophrenia or to a schizoid factor in a nonpsychotic personality.

Little (1981) characterized annihilation anxiety as the most primitive anxiety of all, not anxiety about death. It involves "losing one's identity, of being merged in some undefined homogeneous mass, or lost forever in a bottomless pit."

Frosch (1970) has described a fear of dissolution or disintegration of self and of reality. He believes that much psychotic symptomatology is understandable as a fear of psychic death through dissolution of self and object, or as an attempt to preserve contact with reality and object in the interest of psychic survival (1967). Eissler (1953) pointed out that schizophrenic defenses operate to prevent ego dissolution. Indeed, a major function of all defensive activity is the maintenance of ego integrity; but in the severely disturbed, protection against ego disintegration is central.

For Kohut (1971, 1977), fragmentation of the self and disintegration anxiety are important concepts in his self psychology. He differentiates anxieties of the person with a cohesive self, involving fears of specific danger situations, and disintegration anxiety, which is an anticipation that a break up of the self is approaching. And he sees the pathology of the fragmented self as encompassing the range from schizophrenia to the narcissistic personality disorders. Kohut characterizes annihilation anxiety as dread of loss of the self, fragmentation of and estrangement from the body and mind in space, and the break up of one's sense of continuity in time (1977, 305).

Predictably, the different authors cited do not share precisely the same vision of annihilation anxiety. Little (1981), for example, claims that her annihilation anxiety (the loss of boundaries and the merging with another) is developmentally earlier than Klein's persecutory anxiety, which involves fears of destruction by something outside the self that is already (presumably) recognized as distinguished from the self. There is the issue of an annihilation dread more primitive than a concern with death. And Kohut's definition covers a range of experiences from either threatened to actual fragmentation and disintegration.

My interest in this topic was stimulated initially by attempts to understand the difficult and sometimes refractory resistances in more disturbed patients. Clinical work revealed that fears of change, of growing up, of relinquishing maladaptive patterns, of accepting substitutes and revising negative self evaluations—these and other ingrained patterns—were sometimes underlain by anxiety that was experienced as catastrophic and annihilatory. Symptoms, thought patterns, affect states, and behaviors are especially resistant to change when they are defending against annihilation anxieties.

Some fears conveyed by patients that often are expressions of or derivatives of underlying annihilation anxieties are fears of overstimulation, of loss of control, of going insane, of dissolving, of intolerable feeling states, of being absorbed or shattered, of exploding, melting, fading away, and being destroyed. As one patient said during a regressive interval: "I feel someone could easily violate me, mentally, physically and emotionally. And I would be shattered to pieces. Everything inside me would become like shattered glass, and couldn't come back together."

Another patient put it this way: "It means coming into the world was like an airplane crash; it's total annihilation, like getting burned and broken, limbs scattered for miles. This is how I experienced my childhood. The experience was so violent that I was emotionally destroyed: it was an emotional death."

Annihilation fears *can* underlie a number of specific behavior sequences, character patterns, and symptoms. Some examples are vengeance, fears of growing up and of change, the need to be right or to have one's way, the inability to be committed to a partner, maintaining and defending a low self-esteem, fear of any strong emotional experience, and schizoid and paranoid states.

But a psychoanalytic observer would not conclude that signs of vengeance or the need to be right necessarily reflect underlying annihilation anxieties. Nor should statements about feeling destroyed by the summer heat or blown away by the local baseball team's unexpected defeat be taken at face value. Indeed, neither the implications nor the meaning to the patient are immediately clear from a stated fear of being annihilated; these must be explored, like any other content. But clinical experience as well as this writer's empirical research findings indicate that conscious concerns that manifestly suggest overwhelming worries about ego integrity repeatedly turn out to reflect underlying annihilation anxieties. This finding in no way contradicts the fact that unconscious fears of annihilation will be represented in a way that reflect the unique quality and organization of each person's unconscious fantasies.

Clinical criteria have been put forth for differentiating between regressive expressions of castration anxiety and annihilation-type anxieties. These criteria include whether or not the fears become more specific over time, whether associations suggest competition with a superior rival, and whether there is evidence for fears of guilt-related retribution (Kohut 1971).

There are thus a number of considerations relevant to defining annihilation anxieties and a range of experiences from various developmental periods and with different levels of organization. On the lower end of the scale, patients have described a virtually intolerable anxiety experience, felt and believed to be over psychic survival and accompanied by fears of imminent death or psychological destruction. There is a sense of helplessness in the face of an utterly frightening danger experienced as having no forseeable end. It is a danger against which the person feels he or she can take no constructive action and that threatens to overwhelm and disorganize him or her. It may lead to panic, paralysis, and other maladaptive responses rather than to effective or adaptive behavior; in some cases, primitive fight-or-flight reactions occur, such as blind assaultiveness, running headlong into oncoming traffic, or jumping out of windows.

Elsewhere the author and collaborators (Hurvich et al. 1988) have delineated experiential correlates of annihilation anxieties. These are fears of being overwhelmed, of merger, impingement, loss of needed support, inability to cope, loss of self cohesion, concern over survival, and the presence of a catastrophic mentality. Each of these headings is further elaborated, and the entire schema provides the basis for the construction of scales to assess annihilation anxieties from Rorschach and TAT responses.

Persons who repeatedly show this kind of annihilation anxiety are prone to demonstrate a number of the following: significant weaknesses in mental boundaries; marked oral and anal fixations; and an easily activated tendency toward regression of ego and superego functions, resulting from a weak defense organization. There tends to be a prominence of primitive defenses and a tendency to loss or erosion of effectiveness of the anxiety signal function in mobilizing adequate defenses. Internalizations are unstable and overly negative, the self organization is markedly defective, object constancy is relatively lacking, symbolization capacity is poor or readily subject to regressive interference, and there is a low overall integrative capacity. These weaknesses, whatever their origin, often contribute centrally to the predisposition and vulnerability to annihilation anxieties.

Meanings tend to be attributed to annihilation anxieties consistent with the person's past experiences, particularly of traumatic events and the elaboration of these in unconscious fantasies. Some patients who repeatedly experience annihilation anxieties are not able to specify what is frightening them. The threat of an annihilation-anxiety experience or the experience itself can also be used for secondary gain or can lead to additional psychic consequences, especially the fear of reexperiencing the fear.

Stimuli that typically trigger these anxieties in susceptible persons are the basic danger situations described by Freud (1926), especially threats of or actual object loss and loss of love but also threats of bodily harm and fears of intrusion from others. Direct challenges to self-esteem, such as humiliation and degradation, are important activators, as are any events (such as the basic danger situations) that may be experienced as affronts to self-esteem by the susceptible person.

The basic dangers, such as loss of love, do not remain at that level for the annihilation anxiety—prone individual; rather, like the small anxiety that triggers greater anxiety, the specific fear begets the fear of catastrophe (Fenichel 1945). While there are individual differences in responses, the appearance of this basic level of annihilation anxiety is associated with a decrease in the degree of mental organization (regression), which then triggers more annihilation anxiety in a downward spiral. Such manifestations as panic attacks, night terrors of children, nightmares in adults, and acute psychotic episodes that include turmoil states reflect this basic level most clearly.

In addition, high affect arousal, high sensory stimulation, and environmental threats and demands are also potential mobilizers. The person's current state, his or her mood, the relative intactness of his or her defenses and sense of well-being influence the arousal of annihilation anxieties in the susceptible person at any particular time.

A connection between the ego weaknesses detailed above and annihilation anxieties can be seen in psychotic children. Psychoanalytic observers who have extensive experience with psychotic youngsters report that these unfortunate children—whom we know to have the ego weaknesses already mentioned—show an unrelenting fear for their lives, a constant fear of destruction (Bettelheim 1967), and an anxiety "similar to that which imminent death gives rise" (Rodrigue 1955).

Others have found that latency-age children who may be characterized as borderline show both a host of ego weaknesses (marked defect in repression, difficulty in maintaing body ego and self boundaries, difficulty in maintaining object cathexes, concrete thinking, and so on) and a quality of anxiety different from that of neurotic children. The anxiety of the borderline children was more intense, diffuse, and paniclike and "seemed to involve an experience of disintegration and annihilation" (Kut-Rosenfeld and Sprince 1963, 628).

BASIC ANNIHILATION ANXIETY

The following description a patient gave of a panic attack she experienced the previous evening is an illustration of basic annihilation anxiety in an adult (aged twenty-seven).

At the beginning of the attack [the patient had felt ignored by someone important to her], I felt inundated from my head and body, bombarded, then my body felt bigger, my wrists throbbed and felt cut, I was extremely aware of my heart and other parts of my body, my hands began to tingle, different parts of my body got tense, my stomach knotted up and I felt cramps in my muscles. Everything was going very fast, and when she [the person by whom the patient had earlier felt ignored] began to talk, the words were cut up into little pieces and scattered around. The sound of her words made me feel more shaky; they hurt because they added to the inside noise. At that point I felt threatened, like someone was going to assault me, and that I had to get away from the words because if I didn't I would get hurt. Then I felt I was really losing control, and it snowballed and I got panicky and started to shake and pant. There was nothing clear on my mind, just pure panic, like adrenalin rushing, like a sound getting louder and louder. It's not anything like a thought. But it's like the feeling you'd have if you were about to get raped or mugged, and you can't get away. At some point it got into such a salad that I wanted to scream or throw things. There were a million things going on at once.

It was like if someone would hook you up to a machine and jumble up your thoughts, like print that's not clear, parts of words taken out, or like a newspaper that's been underwater and you can't read it. It's big and chaotic. Like words are on an assembly line and it's going so fast I couldn't select any in time. And if I could select some, this would stimulate the whole crazy process again and activate it even more.

I felt like a victim watching it all and being helpless to straighten it out. It was beyond me, and the more it went on, the more helpless I felt and stupid. At that point, any kind of mental exertion would make it worse, any noise, movement, or activity, by me or others.

It reached some kind of peak and then I got exhausted. It started to decrease, like a car slowing down that's been going very fast. I felt depressed. The jumble began to sink away, like something going underwater, receding into the background, and few sentences came out like generalizations: "I can't do it." The emotions went up to a peak then broke, and there was some relief. When I start to feel any fear, even a little, I start to feel I'm going to have an anxiety attack. I have to push it away, get away from it. I'm so afraid of fear.

This panic attack was triggered by disappointments with a significant person, which likely meant for her some combination of loss of love, loss of the object, and a slight to her self-esteem. As with other panics she has reported or I have witnessed, anger played an important role. Feeling bombarded and inundated reflect a turning round on the self of the activated anger. Regressive sensations of a large body put her in a better position to defend herself. The throbbing wrists that felt cut recalled in a concrete feeling the actual wrist cutting during previous anxiety attacks. It was "to let the poison out" as she had previously told me, referring to the ego alien anger and hateful fantasies associated with negatively toned internalized object representations.

The racing thoughts suggest a loss of cognitive control and the weakening of various inner boundaries as the defenses are unable to keep order in consciousness. The words that she experienced as cut up and scattered around reflect her anger toward the frustrator and a regression in synthetic-integrative functioning. The inability to tolerate any additional stimulation, the feeling of threat, and the fear of being ineffective indicate that she feels a threat of being overwhelmed by stimuli.

The friend's attempt to talk to the patient when she can bear no further input and the anger generated by both are followed by a sense of more loss of control, accompanied by panic, shaking, and panting. Now the annihilation experience is central, with a sense of helplessness, and the experience that there is no way to escape the danger. The awareness of cognitive functioning is like a television screen showing static, and there is a sense of thoughts being jumbled and fragmented, while the racing sensation continues and feelings of chaos and helplessness pervade.

Typically for this patient, the regression is time limited, and she describes the jumble receding into the background. The build up and release also suggest sexual arousal, orgasm, and relaxation. The patient is nonorgasmic. The final comment about her fear of fear points to how the anxiety signal can lead to panic and underscores the vulnerable defense organization. An anxiety signal, rather than aiding in the protection against a traumatic state, here tends to usher it in.

When I later inquired about her self experience during the panic attack, she answered as follows:

My sense of self was hollow, like I didn't have a self, like it was outside myself. Like a ghost—I'm watching, like I have absolutely no impact on what's going on. I felt like I was being literally ripped apart. There are all these characters which feel separate, not part of me, and they start fighting, I can't stop them or integrate them.

The ingredients of overstimulation, threat of disorganization, and fragmentation of the self are all there. The panic attacks only began after a suicide attempt while she was in treatment. There were traumatic occurrences in her past: her father had a volatile temper and sometimes broke things when he was upset. The patient was very frightened of him and believed on several occasions that he would kill her in the course of a beating for misbehavior. She was the oldest of four closely spaced children, and it appeared that her attachment to her mother was repeatedly interfered with by the arrival of each successive sibling. She has had panic attacks a number of times in the office, which decreased in frequency and intensity during psychotherapy. She has intense separation anxiety, weak ego boundaries, vulnerable integration of self and of object representations, and a tendency to regress deeply although reversibly. She has regressed to a psychotic state on a number of occasions but less frequently over the last year. There are indications of failures throughout the separation-individuation subphases, beginning with unsatisfactory symbiotic attachment.

A Kohutian formulation here would stress that a less than optimal self-object merger has resulted in a weakness in affect-taming capacity and in defective structures. This would suggest a primary disorder of the self with protracted break-up, enfeeblement, and serious distortion of the self, with some defensive covering that is easily incapacitated.

Such reactions as a blocking of emotional awareness, temporary motor paralysis, a loss of will, a constriction of cognition, and a decrease in the capacity for pleasure have been found in concentration camp survivors and other victims of adult psychic trauma (Krystal 1978). These are characteristics of this patient during regressive periods.

A different manifestation of annihilation anxiety without panic is in the patient who has a catastrophic mentality. An example is the patient who is unsure he put a stamp on the rent-check envelope. As a result, he begins to fantasy that he will be evicted from his apartment and will then be forced to move back to his parent's home, which is seen as a calamity. This example illustrates how even a fantasied mistake (together with a fear-wish over getting close to the parents) triggers images of disaster. Such reactions are characteristic for this patient and approximate the pan-anxiety Hoch and Polatin (1949) found to be typical of pseudoneurotic schizophrenia.

What can be considered another level of annihilation anxiety is where protection against these anxieties is a central feature of the character defenses. As with the basic level, there is also a range. And among patients who experience annihilation anxiety together with disruptive affect, the defensive functions also operate in the service of protecting the person against these dread experiences, but less successfully than on this second level.

Defenses against fears of annihilation as a result of separation can be seen in agoraphobia (Weiss 1964), both in the clinging and in restrictive anxious attempts to control the other. Another variation involves attempts to protect the object against the patient's own anger, envy, and revenge (Deutsch 1929), which would threaten to destroy the object. This then would leave the patient feeling abandoned and trigger annihilation fears.

Some defenses against merger fears can be withdrawal, assaultive behavior, negativism, sexual inhibitions, contamination fears, claustrophobia and agoraphobia, intractable obsessive worrying, and desperate compulsive orderliness. Many paranoid mechanisms, in addition to defending the patient against awareness of his or her own aggressive impulses, also protect the patient against closeness, which threatens merger because of weak boundaries. Together with underlying merger wishes this threatens loss of the sense of self (Blatt and Wild 1976). A patient with rigid though weak and permeable ego boundaries expressed fears her husband was trying to kill her following times when they have been close. In the therapeutic situation, she used argumentativeness for the same distancing purpose. In these cases, attempts to analyze the narrowness and suspiciousness may threaten the patients' sense of survival.

One male patient who showed aspects of funtioning on higher levels than other patients so far presented expressed his annihilation fears over getting involved in a relationship as follows:

When I get involved, I feel I have no rights, no prerogatives. The other person can make decisions, I can't. They can do what they want, I can't. I feel like I can't maintain my separate existence, I can't be a person when I'm involved in a relationship. It makes me feel panicky.

Since childhood, this patient experienced a sense of overwhelming dread:

I can't stand the fear; I need comfort. Once fear steps in, I can't see anything or do anything. There are so many things I do out of fear. I'm afraid I'll fall apart, lose control, be taken over, be shot down with a machine gun. . . . The fear was always of something extreme happening. I won't get smacked; I'll get bombed. Some people fight or run away. When I'm cornered, I crumble.

A related variation in a more disturbed patient is a traumatic response to imposition. In the therapy situation, the patient would speak more rapidly or loudly if he anticipated that I was about to speak, and he would experience any reaction from me as an intolerable interference. These experienced intrusions triggered fears of annihilation. He could not bear to have any activity interrupted, felt what he was doing would be completely ruined, and that interrupting and spoiling were related to driving him crazy. Reading an article or a chapter in a book without interruption calmed him and decreased his fear of going insane.

In some persons, close derivatives of annihilation anxiety are an ongoing concern and reflect a compulsion to repeat (Wilson and Malatesta 1989). One patient showed a continual preoccupation with fears of being destroyed. This meant he felt unable to grow psychologically, to be creative, and to approach his potential. His fears of being destroyed were also reflected in a repeated concern with the condition of his teeth. He would poke his tongue into one of his teeth until he believed he had loosened it. He would then begin to ruminate on whether or not he had destroyed the tooth. An anxious visit to the dentist (he had consulted dozens) resulted in his being reassured that his tooth was intact and in being advised not to poke at it further—which he proceeded to do anyway, and the cycle would start over. This is an example of annihilation anxieties that suggest castration imagery in an oral context.

The patient displayed a primitive repetitive undoing mechanism in the attempt to deal with annihilation fears. If he accidentally dropped his camera or bumped his arm, he would then intentionally drop the camera again or willfully bang his arm once more. This was an attempt to make it come out better the second time. This time, he hoped, the camera would not be damaged, or his arm would not be hurt. By repeating an act of damage, he would (magically) undo the damage. His associations around such issues make it clear that he was attempting to undo the feeling that he had been permanently destroyed by his parents.

He also showed a number of maladaptive and dangerous action patterns that were manifestations of vengefulness. These acts of revenge threatened his marriage, friendships, and health. In spite of a clear awareness of the consequences and an uncovering and working through of the bases for the revenge patterns, the patient clung to these for dear life and twice quit treatment when he anticipated that remaining in therapy might result in his giving up these behaviors.

As a child he felt his parents never acknowledged his existence. His mother talked about him to her friends in his presence as though he was not there. His father downgraded his interests and efforts because he did not follow the father's religious ideas and practices. He felt humiliated, rejected, and destroyed—the latter because he believed his parents had crushed his ability to grow mentally and to express himself creatively. The protection against annihilation served by the revenge was pieced together as follows: When he was a child and his parents mistreated him, the patient did not speak out. He felt he thus contributed to his own sense of destruction. Now, the only way he can feel strong, good, worthwhile, and that he is a person is to destroy other people. As he stated it:

> The act of hate is a way of ridding myself of what they've done to me. It's a way of defending myself against my parents. If I could kill them, then I could prove to myself that they did not destroy me. It would show that I am strong enough to defend myself, and it disproves the feeling of being destroyed. It means I'm strong, not an incompetent, worthless freak. Hate is for me a way of self-enhancement.

So to give up his revenge, hostility, and hatred would make him feel vulnerable to being destroyed once more.

The discharge of hatred, over and beyond an attempted compensation for the narcissistic injury, was a way of expressing uninhibited anger and provided the patient with a feeling of instinctual pleasure. He described it as being so much more gratifying and invigorating than the tame and colorless way adults express emotions. Analysis of the defensive aspects of these trends was experienced by the patient as an attempt to take away from him what he most needed to protect himself from being destroyed. Even so, the defensive aspects can often be analyzed over time.

This patient, who was preoccupied daily with close derivatives of annihilation anxiety, did not have panic attacks and showed no loss of the signal function. His annihilation anxiety was consistent with the attempt to avoid the mortification of being reexposed to the narcissistic injuries of childhood, but a number of other issues and factors were integral to the persistent concern with being destroyed, as this vignette indicates.

The hypothesis has been stated earlier in this essay that symptoms, behavior, thought patterns, and attitudes are especially resistant to change when they are defending against annihilation anxiety. Stern (1968) has offered a somewhat similar idea: "This paper suggests that the patient's clinging to neurosis might also be due to his use of infantile gratification for warding off the fear of death" (460). The man just described emphasized fears of psychic, not physical, death. But there is much overlap between the two. This same patient maintained a fantasy that pointed to a fear of death. The fantasy is that as long as he avoids being like an adult, time stands still, the possibility remains for him to get the love and recognition from his parents previously denied him, and that he is subject neither to aging, illness, nor death.

In what is here labeled basic annihilation anxiety, there is evidence that the patient experiences stark terror associated with a fear of imminent death or destruction. I also identified a higher level where defenses against annihilation anxieties are prominent. Stated along the way was the point that verbal statements of being destroyed, blown away, or annihilated would only be considered examples of annihilation anxiety with confirmatory evidence, but also that when such fears are repeatedly verbalized, confirmatory evidence is often found.

A third level of annihilation anxiety can be found in relatively well-functioning patients who demonstrate no evidence of borderline trends. In these cases, the annihilation fears are associated with childhood traumas around surgery, accidents, deaths, adoption, and the like. A distinction is being made between the content of annihilation fears and the degree of uncontrolled anxiety (Schur 1953) associated with it. The extent of anxiety—terror and ego disruption depends on the relative ego-function intactness versus ego weakness, on the one hand, and on the timing, context, and intrapsychic meanings of significant traumatic experiences past and current, on the other.

During the early phases of ego development, some frightening and overwhelming situations will be traumatic. It is here assumed that these experiences will increase the likelihood of later vulnerability to annihilation anxiety, with major individual differences. This does not rule out the possibility that such anxieties can arise from later periods. The kinds of noxious overstimulation at the beginning of and during the phallic phase described by Shengold (1967, 1971), such as severe and repeated beatings, sexual seduction and primal-scene stimulation, overintrusion in the form of body violation, force feeding, enemas, and interference with the child's self-initiated activity, all tend to be associated with massive defensive efforts that often cover annihilation fears.

Generally speaking, too much sexual, aggressive, or even sensory stimulation during the early years can lead to the kinds of developmental arrests and ego weaknesses that increase the likelihood of annihilation anxieties. Events that are especially frightening and ego disruptive and are perceived as life threatening become the basis for unconscious fantasies, sometimes massive defensive efforts, a tendency to repeat, and symptom formation. The panic-attack patient had some panic episodes that we were subsequently able to understand as a later version, in action and fantasy, of her father's beatings when she was a child.

With regard to structural considerations, we can assess the patient's capacity to use the signal function and the conditions under which it breaks down. The patient who described her panic tended to have less signal anxiety when faced with separation and when she was confronting possible bodily harm. For some years she would deny any concern about my annual approaching summer vacation and would be subjected to panic attacks after I left. She was especially prone to annihilation anxiety when her capacity for synthesis and integration were regressively decreased. The seriousness of the suicidal risk with this patient varied in relation to the degree of her capacity to anticipate the consequences of her actions. When synthesis was at a more regressed level, her capacity for anticipation was near zero, and she experienced time as "a blank wall right in front of me," with every moment like an eternity, together with a feeling that she dare not think past the immediate present and an overwhelming urge to end the pain.

The level of defensive functioning also varies, as well as the adequacy of the repression barrier. The patient who worried about his teeth relied heavily on projection, splitting, and denial, while another patient who avoided close relationships because he feared losing his separate existence used higher level defenses of isolation, undoing, and reaction formation.

The patient who used paranoid projection to fend off closeness (and argumentativeness in the therapy situation to accomplish the same purpose) demonstrated the vulnerable repression barrier and the triggering of annihilation anxieties when paranoid defenses were compromised. He explained:

My mind is being deluged with all sorts of frightening thoughts and images. My body is all nerves. I can't sit down for any period of time; I'm constantly up and down. I feel like I'm going to crack up. At my job I can't do a thing; I just feel I can't go on.

The defense organization, when weak, leaves the person prone to regressions that are often deep, precipitous, and disorganizing. Since disorganization is a major trigger for annihilation anxiety, the integrity of the defense organization is an important factor. For the schizophrenic, say Burnham, Gladstone, and Gibson (1969), disorganization is equivalent to destruction. The patient who regained his equilibrium by reading a chapter in a book without interruption was experiencing intrusions as disorganizing, leading to the feeling he was about to go crazy. The later preoccupation with survival can also be understood in terms of the baby having been forced to recognize the separateness of the object before he was able to form stable introjects and identify with them (Winnicott 1965). This could result from a low stimulus barrier, the others' failure to serve as an adequate protective shield, too strong an increase in baby's instinctual drives, other inner stimulation such as pain—or some combination of these.

From the economic point of view, we can raise questions about the fears of being overwhelmed by sexual and aggressive urges and about the amounts of stimulation involved. Some workers (Bak 1954; Hartmann 1953; Spitz 1965) have emphasized the pathogenic effects of unneutralized aggression on structural development, such as interfering with perceptual organization (in hindering the integration of contact and distance perception) that obstructs the formation of a stable body image and of stable self and object representations.

In his later formulations on trauma, Freud (1920) emphasized the intensity of the stimulus and psychic unpreparedness due to surprise, leading to overstiumulation, paralysis of ego functions and psychic helplessness. In his earlier writings, primarily focused on sexual trauma (1895), Freud said that the original response to the trauma was usually not obvious and that its effects would only manifest themselves later as memories, often after puberty.

My data suggest a wide range in the degree of flooding, especially from activated primitive affects and traumatic memories. This is consistent with a range of arrests and conflicts at various levels in different patients. With ego development, as Schur (1958) has pointed out, reality testing and other ego functions, together with desomatization become more dominant in the anxiety response, and the largely somatic discharge moves toward a more thoughtlike awareness of anxiety. Developmental arrest, leading to ego deficits, inner conflict between impulses and defenses, and regressions influence the degree of the feeling and fantasy of being flooded or overwhelmed.

With regard to adult psychic trauma, the question can be raised whether strong affects and/or the strength of external stimuli are crucial. The formulation has been put forth (Krystal 1988) that the key issue may rather be that the person is faced with a situation of danger that he or she cannot escape and that this triggers the psychic numbing, depersonalization, and other reactions seen in concentration camp victims and others. The case of panic presented earlier clearly demonstrates experiences of massive flooding of the psychic apparatus, but other examples of annihilation anxieties do not.

Kohut has written a good deal about threat to the self organization as triggering fears of disintegration, as already stated. Such fears are related to what is here being referred to as annihilation anxiety. While annihilation anxiety often involves a fear of loss of the self, I feel this formulation is too narrow and that rather than reducing all annihilation fears to the threatened break-up of the cohesive self, we can assume that what Kohut describes is one basis for annihilation anxieties.

There are a variety of specific deficits that increase proneness to annihilation anxieties and that can be variously implicated in different cases: boundary weakness, inadequate internalizations, interference with sensory processes due to early denial mechanisms triggered to avoid psychic pain, laying down of defective memory traces, serious interference with the development of symbolic functioning, weakness of the defense organization, and various features in integration of structures, including both self and object representations.

The internalization of self-soothing and with it the capacity for recall or evocative memory that allows intrapsychic contact with the protective and loving aspects of previous experience with the mother have in recent years been designated as essential to the development of signal anxiety. The failure of self-soothing can be based on a failure of internalization (a deficit) or on psychic blocking (a defense).

A detailed consideration of these ego deficits as well as of traumatic experience and unconscious fantasy elaborations will further our understanding of the manifestations and implications of annihilation anxieties.

SUMMARY

Aspects of automatic-traumatic anxiety described by Freud are further discussed and elaborated. Annihilation anxieties are illustrated on different levels of mental organization and with different degrees of directness. Clinical examples highlight a complex interaction among congenital predispositions, ego weaknesses, traumatogenic experiences, degree of self cohesion, unconscious fantasies, and intrapsychic conflicts. The hypothesis is offered that symptoms, thoughts, affects, and behaviors are particularly refractory to change when they are defending against annihilation anxieties.

152   MARVIN HURVICH

REFERENCES

Bak, R. 1943. Dissolution of the ego: Mannerism and delusion of grandeur. *Journal of Nervous and Mental Diseases* 98:457–64.

———. 1954. The schizophrenic defense against aggression. *International Journal of Psycho-Analysis* 35:129–33.

Bettelheim, B. 1967. *The empty fortress.* New York: Free Press.

Blatt, S., and C. Wild. 1976. *Schizophrenia: A developmental analysis.* New York: Academic Press.

Burnhan, D., Gladstone, A., and Gibson, R. 1969. *Schizophrenia and the need-fear dilemma.* New York: International Universities Press.

Compton, A. 1972. A study of the psychoanalytic theory of anxiety. part 1: The development of Freud's theory of anxiety. *Journal of the American Psychoanalytic Association* 20:341–94.

Deutsch, H. 1929. The genesis of agoraphobia. *International Journal of Psychoanalysis* 10:51.

Eissler, K. 1953. The effect of the structure of the ego on psychoanalytic technique. *Journal of the American Psychoanalytic Association* 1:104–43.

Fenichel, O. [1937] 1954. Early stages of ego development. In *The collected papers of Otto Fenichel* edited by H. Fenichel and D. Rapaport, Second series. New York: Norton.

———. 1945. *The psychoanalytic theory of neuroses.* New York: Norton.

Freud, A. 1936. *The ego and the mechanisms of defense.* New York: International Universities Press.

———. 1951. Notes on a connection between the states of negativism and of emotional surrender. In *The writings of Anna Freud, vol. 4.* New York: International Universities Press, 1968.

Freud, S. 1894. The neuro-psychoses of defense. In *Standard edition,* vol. 3, 45–61. London: Hogarth.

———. 1895. Project for a scientific psychology. In *Standard edition,* vol. 1, 295–391.

———. 1915. The unconscious. In *Standard edition,* vol. 15, 166–204.

———. 1918. From the history of an infantile neurosis. In *Standard edition,* vol. 17, 3–122.

———. 1920. Beyond the pleasure principle. In *Standard edition,* vol. 18, 7–64.

———. 1923a. The ego and the id. In *Standard edition,* vol. 19, 3–63.

———. 1923b. Neurosis and psychosis. In *Standard edition,* vol. 19, 149–53.

———. 1926. Inhibitions, symptoms, and anxiety. In *Standard edition,* vol. 20, 75–125.

———. 1933. New introductory lectures on psychoanalysis. In *Standard edition,* vol. 22, 1–183.

———. 1937. Analysis terminable and interminable. In *Standard edition,* 23, 216–53.

Frosch, J. 1967. Severe regressive states during analysis: Introduction and summary. *Journal of the American Psychoanalytic Association* 15:491–507, 606–25.

———. 1970. Psychoanalytic considerations of the psychotic character. *Journal American Psychoanalytic Association,* 18:24–50.

Furer, E. 1964. The development of a preschool symbiotic psychotic boy. *Psychoanalytic Study of the Child* 19:448–69.

Gedo, J., and A. Goldberg. 1973. *Models of the mind.* Chicago: University of Chicago Press.

Hartmann, H. 1953. Contribution to the metapsychology of schizophrenia. *Psychoanalytic Study of the Child* 8:177–97.

Hoch, P., and P. Polatin. 1949. Pseudoneurotic forms of schizophrenia. *Psychiatric Quarterly,* 23:248–76.

Hurvich, M. 1987. The assessment of annihilation anxiety. Paper presented at the Memorial Meeting in Honor of the Work and Memory of Lloyd Silverman, APA Division of Psychoanalysis, New York.

———. 1989. Traumatic moment, basic dangers, and annihilation anxiety. *Psychoanalytic Psychology* 6:309–23.

———. 1990. Fears of being overwhelmed, threats to ego integrity, and the psychoanalytic theory of anxiety. Weil Memorial Lecture, Institute for Psychoanalytic Training and Research.

Hurvich, M., P. Beneviste, J. Howard, and S. Connerty. 1988. The assessment of annihilation anxiety from projective tests. Paper presented at the Conference for Psychological Testing and the Psychotherapuetic Process, Austen Riggs Center, Stockbridge, Mass.

Jones, E. [1911] 1938. The pathology of morbid anxiety. In *Papers in psychoanalysis.* 4th Edition. London: Bailliere, Tindall and Cox.

Klein, M. 1932. *The psychoanalysis of children.* London: Hogarth.

———. 1946. Notes on some schizoid mechanisms. In *Envy and gratitude and other works (1946–1963).* New York: Delacorte.

———. 1958. On the development of mental functioning. In *Envy and gratitude and other works. (1946–1963).* New York: Delacorte.

Kohut, H. 1971. *The psychology of the self.* New York: International Universities Press.

———. 1977. *The restoration of the self.* New York: International Universities Press.

Krystal, H. 1978. Trauma and affect. *Psychoanalytic Study of the Child* 33:81–116.

———. 1988. *Integration and self-healing.* Hillsdale, N.J.: Analytic Press.

Kut-Rosenfeld, S., and M. Sprince. 1963. An attempt to formulate the meaning of the concept "borderline." In *Psychoanalytic study of the child,* vol. 18. New York: International Universities Press.

Little, M. 1981. *Transference neurosis and transference psychosis.* New York: Jason Aronson.

Mahler, M. 1968. *On human symbiosis and the vicissitudes of individuation.* New York: International Universities press.

Rapaport, D., and M. Gill, 1959. The points of view and assumptions of metapsychology. *International Journal of Psycho-Analysis* 40:153–62.

Rodrigue, E. 1955. The analysis of a three-year-old mute schizophrenic. *New directions in psychoanalysis* edited by M. Klein, P. Heiman, and R. Money-Kyrle, 140–79. New York: Basic Books.

Schur, M. 1953. The ego in anxiety. In *Drives, affects, and behavior,* edited by R. Loewenstein. New York: International Universities Press.

———. 1958. The ego and the id in anxiety. *Psychanalytic study of the child,* vol. 13, 190–220. New York: International Universities Press.

Shengold, L. 1967. The effects of overstimulation: Rat people. *International Journal of Psycho-Analysis* 48:277–88.

———. 1971. More about rats and rat people. *International Journal of Psycho-Analysis* 52:277–88.

Spitz, R. 1965. *The first year of life.* New York: International Universities Press.

Stern, M. 1968. Death and trauma. *International of Journal of Psycho-Analysis* 49:457–61.

Weiss, E. 1964. *Agoraphobia in the light of ego psychology.* New York and London: Grune & Stratton.

Wilson A., and C. Malatesta. 1989. Affect and the compulsion to repeat: Freud's repetition compulsion revisited. *Psychoanalytic and Contemporary Thought* 12: 265–312.

Winnicott, D. 1962, Ego integration in child development. In *The maturational processes and the facilitating environment.* 56–63.

———. 1965. *The maturational processes and the facilitating environment.* New York: International Universities Press.

9

WHERE THERE IS RELATEDNESS, CAN THERE BE AUTONOMY?

Helen L. Wintrob, Ph.D.

T he purpose of this essay is to explore one aspect of the primary parent-child relationship, which traditionally Western society has considered to be the mother-child relationship, as the prototype for later significant relationships—namely, the child's submission to the parent in order to be cared for and loved and the consequent power that this bestows on the parent in the context of the development of intense emotional bonds. The long-term consequences of this form of early attachment will be considered by examining current relationships between man and women. It is suggested that these relationships have retained their hierarchical and dependent qualities despite changing social mores. It appears that intense emotional connections more frequently seem to occur in the context of hierarchical and dependent relationships, and one wonders whether profound involvement is possible where both partners are "independent," or if, in fact, autonomy is an illusory goal.

INDIVIDUATION VERSUS SYMBIOSIS?

A substantial body of psychoanalytic literature addresses the struggle between the wish to individuate or be autonomous and the desire for symbiosis or merger. Fromm (1975) sees the striving for autonomy and the yearning for symbiotic unity with some person, group, or power "outside" of oneself as the essential dilemma that all humans encounter throughout their lives. In this context, symbiosis is defined as the union of one individual with another self in such a way as to make each lose the integrity of the self and to make each completely dependent on the other. This kind of merger is thought to define the relationship between mother and child. Alice Balint (1933) describes the relationship between mother and child as one of mutuality from the beginning, with the child considered as much an object of the mother's gratification as the mother is of the child's. In the same way that the child does not recognize the separate identity of the mother, the mother looks upon the child as part of herself and one whose interests are identical with her own. Although Mahler (1968) writes primarily about the child's experience, rather than the mother's needs, her view of childhood as a struggle from original oneness to a loss of a symbiotic partner clearly reaffirms the dilemma. Subsequent intense attachments often thrive in similar hierarchical relationships that mimic the mother-child bond. In such relationships, the capacity for merger is omnipresent, and people feel that abandonment will lead to disintegration. A person then experiences a conflict of two equally untenable alternatives: either being engulfed or being abandoned. Theorists such as Fromm (1975) have asserted that symbiosis in adulthood is only possible in a relationship that denies one's uniqueness and potential for creativity. From this perspective, those plagued by a "fear" of separateness, aloneness, powerlessness, and inferiority will become involved in symbiotic relationships as a consequence of a failure to achieve adequate differentiation of the self from the other. In keeping with the theory of preoedipal and oedipal attachments, Fromm distinguishes between primary ties, which are seen as "organic" in the sense that they are part of normal development and existed before the process of individuation, and secondary bonds, which are a substitute for the primary bonds that have been lost. He describes these secondary bonds as mechanisms of escape from freedom or bondage. Under such circumstances, one is unaware of the freedom to attach oneself, and only experiences anxiety when the freedom from certain attachments is considered (Basescu 1974). Basescu asserts that when one only experiences freedom from attachments without the concomitant freedom to attach oneself and commit oneself to something new, one is left feeling empty and powerless.

Humanist psychologists such as Maslow (1962) tried to understand what interfered with what they considered predictable developmental urges, such as "actualizing one's potential." They argue that the sense of separateness associated with using all of one's powers and creativity engenders such intense anxiety that it is likened to a sense of "going wild" or "being totally out of control." Maslow called it the "Jonah

Syndrome," which he saw as a fear of being torn apart, losing control, being shattered and disintegrated, even of being killed by the experience.

Given this dilemma, how then do we understand "adult love"? Isn't one of its more enjoyable components the capacity for merger with another human being so that usual boundaries are permeated? Perhaps it is not the quality of the relationship that is so different but the belief that one can exercise choice about beginning and ending it. Basescu (1974) attempts to deal with this paradox when he states that humans are terrified of separateness when they are unaware of the freedom they have to attach themselves and are terrified of closeness when unaware of the freedom they have to detach themselves; thus, they only experience the anxiety engendered when attachment and freedom from certain attachments are considered. While it appears that people fear merging as well as being separate, it is more likely that what they actually fear is a loss of choice and control over these experiences.

POWER AND POWERLESSNESS

The type of intense emotional bond being discussed is predicated on the basis that one person is seemingly powerful and controlling, and the other is seemingly powerless and controlled. In traditional Western societies, men are typically seen as powerful and aggressive, and the usual role for women is to be submissive and compliant. These roles persist despite recent herculean efforts to redefine them. One cannot help but wonder why people cling so tenaciously to role definitions characterized by power inequities. Perhaps it is the complementarity of these roles that leads to the profound and seemingly inextricable belief that one person cannot live without the other. A man cannot be powerful and aggressive unless he has someone to control, and a woman cannot be compliant and submissive without someone to dominate her. By necessity, any view of power requires a dyadic relationship like that of the mother and child. The various theories of psychoanalysis address the issue of the development of personality within the context of a significant emotional connection between two people of seemingly unequal status. Although each school ascribes a different rationale for this bond, all agree on its intensity. Freud's definition of sadomasochism is drive determined; the interpersonal position looks at issues of power and powerlessness from an environmental perspective; and attachment theory considers these dynamics as directly related to object loss, both real and fantasied. If this is what we know as love and relatedness, can we feel love when we sense that our survival is not dependent on the other's existence?

Men and women have always had complementary roles that have evoked feelings in each that survival without the other is impossible. Men have occupied the position of breadwinner and women that of caretaker/nurturer. For many reasons, both men and women seem to have agreed that the work of men is strong and powerful and that "women's work," primarily that of childbearing and caretaking, is less valued and less powerful. To counteract these notions, one goal of the women's movement was to eliminate status distinctions based on traditional views of power. Early feminists had hoped that heading a corporation and being responsible for childcare would be given equal status and that these roles might be interchangeable between men and women. However, even with the best intentions, the same hierarchical distinctions have remained. Being a corporate executive is still regarded as more prestigious and consequently more powerful than taking care of children. This is true irrespective of gender. Sociologists studying role theory assert that these distinctions are related to class and that in a society where one's social status is unequivocally connected to how much one earns, people who earn more are valued more highly. However, this explanation seems to be inadequate when one looks at Socialist societies where one's worth is purportedly not equivalent to one's earning power, and it appears that the same biases persist.

Chodorow (1978) offers another explanation to account for these distinctions. She states that issues of power and control are, at least in part, related to the fact that women are the primary caretakers in our society. Because women have been the nurturers, she suggests that what we describe as feminine may well be related to current child-care arrangements. Since women are brought up by their mothers, feelings of softness, tenderness, compassion, empathy, and emotion are developed through a process of identification with the mother. For women, these feelings are not particularly threatening. However, these capacities are viewed by both women and men as belonging to women and, therefore, as feminine. If men were to express these same sentiments, their masculinity would be jeopardized. In addition, since men were reared by women, feeling helpless and vulnerable reminds them of a time in their past when their mothers (women) had the power to calm those anxious feelings. Remembering themselves as so powerless—and their mothers as so powerful—is perhaps threatening for men. Chodorow speculates that since men unconsciously view all women as quite powerful, they have to devalue women in order to come to terms with this fear. Not only are women diminished, but the work that women do is devalued. The work of being caretakers, homemakers, or any career that requires nurturing skills and the ability to bond emotionally is denigrated and seen as women's work. Thus, traditional "women's work" still carries a low status, whether it is done by a man or a woman. To complicate the issue further, in middle-class families where both the husband and wife work outside the home, it is a woman that is hired to handle child-care duties. If we look at relationships between men and women in the 1980s, we find that the same conception of power and powerlessness experienced before the feminist era has remained. Women are now free to be "powerful" like men—for example, to head corporations—and men are free to be "powerless" like women—to take care of children. Interestingly, many women in "powerful" positions seem to have a hard time finding mates. Why this should be so raises some interesting questions. Traditionally, women marry "up," meaning that they marry an older individual with more formal schooling and greater earning power. If the traditional arrangement was for women to marry "up," the correlate was that men married "down," which meant marrying a younger individual with less formal schooling, lower social status, and less money. This, the usual mode for intimate connections, involves a hierarchical arrangement. If this is true, it may help to explain why women in high-status positions are frequently unattached. The most intensely connected relationships are those in which one person seemingly has power, whether it be economic, political, social, psychological or sexual, and the other seemingly does not. In the parent-child relationship, the traditional husband-wife paradigm, the boss-worker dyad, the teacher-student relationship, and so on, one is a conventionally powerful position and the other is not. Each is dependent on the other, and one needs the other, irrespective of how need or dependence are defined. These relationships are referred to as "fierce attachments" by Vivian Gornick (1987) in her book that described the relationship between mothers and daughters.

If one examines the traditional male and female roles in greater depth, it becomes clear that this mode of interchange maintains an apparent hierarchy. Rather than viewing the woman's position as reflecting a passive sexual attitude, Caplan (1985) suggests another explanation: it is the ability to delay gratification, wait for rewards and pleasure, and the capacity to put other people's needs ahead of her own. Implicit in this formulation is that based on past experience, most women feel that what they have is about all that they can expect to get. An effort is directed at avoiding punishment, rejection, or guilt. A woman's position has traditionally been that of nurturer and caretaker, the one who has enabled others to function. She functioned as a behind-the-scenes mother, wife, and secretary. Do women take on this role because they have an unconscious, psychosexually determined need to suffer, or do they do it because it is a culturally determined mode of relating that they have learned? It is the writer's opinion that through a set of social arrangements, women have learned to subordinate themselves to men in order to maintain the quality of relating and "intimacy" that for both people parallels the dynamics of the earlier mother-child relationship.

If in order to continue this hierarchical mode of relating women are obliged to maintain a seemingly subordinate position, what happens to men who must counter the female's submissive stance with one that is powerful, strong, independent, decisive, and in charge? Being human means that at times a person will feel anxious, vulnerable, insecure, inadequate, "dependent," and so forth. However, if expressing these feelings or even acknowledging them to oneself implies a feminine stance, what is the impact on men when they experience these feelings? It is probable that experiencing a range of emotion, including a sense of vulnerability, is frightening for men who are taught to relate to the world through competition and aggression. From a very early age boys are instructed to "take it like a man"—to hide their feelings of weakness and fear. One result of hiding emotions is that feelings become hard to regulate and in time become so intense that they can no longer be suppressed. At such moments men may feel out of control but attempt as soon as possible to revert to a constricted position that allows them to feel powerful and dominant. As stated previously, however, a person cannot feel powerful and dominant in isolation. One must have power and dominance over someone. If men have achieved a sense of power in the world by being nonemotional, dominant, and in charge, what happens to men when they feel normal human feelings of inadequacy and dependence? One option is to become involved with a partner who will express these taboo emotions and thus behaves in a complementary mode. Bowen (1961) states that people will often seek out a mate who will express what they deem as unacceptable thoughts and feelings. Men who find it particularly difficult to express and/or experience intense emotion will become involved with women who are "emotional." In such relationships women express the thoughts and feelings that men are loathe to reveal. One could consider this form of relatedness to be symbiotic.

IS CHANGE POSSIBLE?

The goal of psychoanalysis has always been to help a person to become separate, individuated, and capable of an intimate relationship that is mutually validating. Interestingly, however, this process of separation and individuation takes place in the context of an intensely connected relationship to a psychoanalyst whom the individual sees several times a week for many years. In this relationship, one person ostensively has more power than the other. Despite the efforts of many modern psychoanalysts to define the analytic relationship as nonhierarchical and between two peers, it is rarely seen or experienced in that way by either member of the dyad. Psychoanalytic theory maintains that the patient's experience with a powerful other who is experienced differently from significant others of the past is what constitutes a major part of "the cure." However, it is generally thought that a hierarchical relationship implies oppression. If one person has more power than the other, the assumption is that the more powerful person will use his or her position to hurt the other. In a society that espouses egalitarian values, the notion that relationships between two unequal partners must, by their very nature, be abusive are values with which most of us have grown up. Paradoxically, when one speaks with people who have a positive sense of their analyses, what they describe is the feeling of being understood, listened to, given permission to live their lives fruitfully and successfully, and so on.

Although the outer constraints of a psychoanalysis imply something very different, the aforementioned aspects of being validated and confirmed by a powerful person are generally shared phenomena. If being in that kind of relationship over a prolonged period of time facilitates change, what factors serve to inhibit or limit change? Matter has a basic tendency to return to previous states of organization, and humans exhibit this tendency to return to past states in both physical and behavioral terms. Freud's concept of the repetition compulsion suggests that there is a tendency for humans to repeat previous acts over and over again. Sullivan (1953) offered another explanation. He thought that anxiety engendered by disapproval was the most unbearable of human experiences and suggested that methods for avoiding anxiety-provoking situations and interactions were developed from the earliest days of life. Consequently, in later life when a person is in a situation that reactivates old anxieties, the individual will employ patterns of anxiety avoidance that proved useful at some previous time. While these two explanations are seemingly different, there is an underlying similarity between them. Each underscores the fact that people will revert to earlier ways of behaving to avoid anxiety: one theory states this explicitly; the other implies it. Behaviors that were developed during an early period of a person's life were formed in the context of hierarchical relationships where one person is dependent on the other for satisfaction of his or her needs. It is likely that acting as one did during that time evokes feelings of security that are related to the intense connectedness that was felt in the mother-child relationship. The suggestion is that it is not the behaviors themselves that lessen anxiety but rather the relationship that is recalled with all of its intensity that is so reassuring. Anxiety-producing behaviors threaten one's sense of connection.

Change is difficult in psychoanalysis because it implies the loss of a relationship in which the person felt an intense bond, hierarchical in nature, that reminds him or her of an earlier period of dependence. While acknowledging that one is no longer dependent in that way should be liberating, the fear of loss becomes overwhelming and serves to inhibit change. On a social level, this premise has its additional implications in that we continue to define the world hierarchically, in terms of high status and low status—being powerful and powerless.

ARE RELATIONSHIPS BETWEEN TWO "POWERFUL" PEOPLE POSSIBLE?

It seems that the most intensely connected relationships are those in which one person has power and the other does not and where these power inequities are seemingly synonymous with the relationship itself. Is it possible to have intense involvements when one is on an equal basis, or must there be a hierarchy to experience a connection? We have always thought of people in powerful positions as males and women in the less-powerful positions as nurturers and caretakers. Carol Gilligan (1982) and others have asked for a redefinition of power so that there is not one specific type of power but one in which the differences between the sexes is acknowledged rather than ordered. It would appear, however, that we have not yet incorporated the concept of being different but equal and that we still do consider one mode of relating as being more powerful than the other, whether the person in power is a man or a woman. One question that we may ask ourselves is to what extent does our sophisticated and enlightened jargon reflect a true shift of feelings and to what degree is it just jargon? We say chairperson, spokesperson, doctor (he or she), child-care person, and so on. But what do we think and what is our mental representation? When we say chairperson, do we visualize either solely? When we say corporate lawyer, do we visualize either a man or a woman or solely a man? When we say child-care person, do we visualize either a man or woman or just a woman? I am suggesting that our definitions of power and powerlessness have not changed and that we cling to these definitions mainly because they perpetuate a hierarchy with which we are familiar and at ease. Since profound attachments are developed with members of a dyad in unequal positions of power, we adhere to this scheme, for with equality there is a freedom that terrifies us and makes us experience our own separateness in the universe—a terror we strive to avoid.

IS RELATEDNESS CONSISTENT WITH AUTONOMY?

When someone whom we have loved dies, we say: "I have lost a part of myself. A part of me has died." Such feelings have been romanticized in movies and novels that never seem to lose their appeal. Yet, those of us who take pride in our psychological maturity feel compelled to see these as theatrical depictions belonging to a world of fantasy, not a world of mature reality. The mature person feels sadness in the presence of loss, mourns, and moves on. Perhaps we are juxtaposing two alternatives that cannot really be compared by adhering to a definition of autonomy that denies what it means to be human. The American ideal reveres individualism and the person who pulls him or herself up by his or her own bootstraps. This is also true of psychoanalysis in its maintenance of the belief that we can connect with others but not really need them.

When psychoanalysis was dominated by Freudian conceptions of preoedipal and oedipal stages of development, the theme of autonomy as synonymous with health flourished. As time has moved on and new ideas have emerged, the work of Kohut has influenced much of our current thinking. Kohut (1969) talks about the self-object connection that individuals find in each other and the regulatory nature of that function. Even though Kohut acknowledges the "need" that one individual has for another, he understands these connections in terms of the functions that each performs. He makes the assumption that one person can fulfill these functions just as easily as another. Kohut has been criticized because he fails to consider the significance that one person has for the other that is special and cannot easily be replaced. One might speculate that this thinking is consistent with the idea that the autonomous person acknowledges that he or she has certain needs and is then free to have these needs met by a variety of people.

Theorists such as Miller (1976) assert that a model of autonomy is impossible and that we must acknowledge the needs we have that are related to a specific person. Numerous studies have shown the increased incidence of illness and death following the death of an intimate other. Independent men seem to fare less well than women after death or divorce. Perhaps this is an indication that to be human means that we "need" other people and that the quest for total autonomy is a spurious ideal. While intense connections are most often hierarchical, this may also disguise the need that we have for others. If we were to be fully conscious of our feelings of dependence and interdependence, and such needs were not stigmatized, the quality of our connections might change. Even though autonomy and relatedness may be incongruous, relatedness and hierarchy do not necessarily have to be synonymous.

REFERENCES

Balint, A. 1933. Love for the mother and mother-love. *International Journal of Psycho-Analysis* 14:251–57.
Basescu, S. 1974. The concept of freedom. *Contemporary Psychoanalysis* 10:231–38.
Bowen, M. 1961. Family psychotherapy. *American Journal of Orthopsychiatry* 30:40–60.
Caplan, P. J. 1985. *The myth of women's masochism.* New York: New American Library.
Chodorow, N. 1978. *The reproduction of mothering.* Berkeley: University of California Press.
Ehrenreich, B. 1983. *The hearts of men.* New York: Anchor Press.
Ehrenreich, B., and D. English. 1979. *For her own good.* New York: Anchor Press.
Eichenbaum, L., and S. Orbach. 1983. *Understanding women: A feminist psychoanalytic approach.* New York: Basic Books.

Freud, S. 1942. *Beyond the pleasure principle.* London: Hogarth.

———. 1962. *Three essays on the theory of sexuality.* New York: Basic Books.

Friedan, B. 1981. *The second stage.* New York: Summit Books.

Fromm, E. 1941. *Escape from freedom.* New York: Avon Books.

———. 1975. Of human bonds and bondage. *Contemporary Psychoanalysis* 11:435–52.

Gilligan, C. 1982. *In a different voice.* Cambridge: Harvard University Press.

Gornick, V. 1987. *Fierce attachments.* New York: Farrar, Straus & Giroux.

Horney, K. 1942. *Self analysis.* New York: W. W. Norton.

Kohut, H. 1969. *The search for self.* New York: Pantheon.

Mahler, M. 1968. *On human symbiosis and the vicissitudes of individuation.* New York: International Universities Press.

Maslow, A. 1962. *Toward a new psychology of women.* Princeton, N.J.: Van Nostrand Insight Book.

Miller, J. 1976. *Toward a new psychology of women.* Boston: Beacon.

Orbach, S. 1979. *Fat is a feminist issue.* New York: Berkeley Books.

Stone, C. 1975. Three mother daughter poems: The struggle for separation. *Contemporary psychoanalysis* 11:227–39.

Sullivan, H. S. 1953. *The interpersonal theory of psychiatry.* New York: W. W. Norton.

Winnicott, D. W. 1960. Ego distortions in terms of true and false self. In *Maturational processes and the facilitating environment.* New York: International Universities Press.

Wolstein, B. 1982. The cornerstone of psychoanalysis. *Contemporary Psychoanalysis* 18:291–301.

10

NARRATIVE IN PSYCHOANALYSIS
AND EVERYDAY LIFE

Leanne Domash, Ph.D.

This essay is a discussion of our need for narrative in everyday life as well as its relevance to the development of narrative in the psychoanalytic situation. Positing a basic human need—the need to put experience into meaningful narrative form—I shall first discuss some normal cultural expressions of this need and the restorative functions they serve. After describing the role of narrative in the psychoanalytic situation from a more traditional perspective, I shall then present some clinical material that demonstrates how the analyst might borrow from the cultural expressions of everyday life to facilitate the analytic process.

In everyday life, the need for narrative is reflected in our fascination with such things as reading novels, attending the theater and movies, listening to popular music. In contrast to the notion of the psychopathology of everyday life, this essay emphasizes the creativity and health of everyday life, in that we have fashioned any number of cultural expressions that are healing. We are gripped, for instance, by the song that tells a narrative of a feeling state to which we resonate. As these various narrative are told, they provide both cathartic relief to our scattered, half-formed feelings and help us in our struggle to complete the basic life tasks of separation from the original caretaker and the ensuing, complicated oedipal struggles.

As we gain understanding, narrative also answers our need for meaning. It helps us integrate, at times, seemingly random happenings and, in a sense, create our soul. Our need to reconstruct and then understand our life stories assists us in mastering past trauma. Without a meaningful narrative, we are left feeling unconnected and futile. In a recent novel by Schaeffer (1983), the heroine, although markedly emotionally disturbed, expresses this essence as she begins to write a narrative of her life: "What I want now is what I suppose I've always wanted. If I've had to stay alive so long, I want to know what my life has meant" (17).

In another example from everyday life, Bettelheim (1977) speaks of the importance of fairy tales for children in helping impart a sense of meaning to their lives. These are narratives that encompass the difficulties in life without being overwhelming. While transmitting our cultural heritage, the fairy tale helps the child make sense of the turmoil of his or her feelings. The young child needs ideas about how to bring his or her inner house in order and on that basis create order in his or her life. Fairy tales offer sufficient distance from the conflict to allow perspective and mastery. Fairy tales also speak about the child's severe inner pressures in a way the child unconsciously understands. And without belittling the most serious inner struggles that growing up entails, they offer temporary and permanent solutions to difficulties, thereby offering hope.

The act of giving words or visual representation to our conflicts and struggles is in many ways healing and is probably the "silent stuff of everyday life" that helps us synthesize our experience into a meaningful system. At times we may be blocked, overwhelmed by trauma, or in a particular conflict, and we may not be able to use narrative in this healing sense. In addition, we may be unable to organize our experiences into meaningful narrative but instead develop what I call pseudonarratives, which reflect repetitious patterns from which there is no obvious means of escape.

An extreme example of this is a Holocaust victim exposed to overwhelming horror, unable to construct a meaningful narrative and therefore finding that life becomes futile. There then develops a perseverative need to construct a narrative, while at the same time this is impossible to do. This also speaks to the powerful grip of the numerous current accounts of the Holocaust. Auerham and Prelinger (1983) discuss a concentration camp survivor and her child and the mother's inability to construct a true narrative for herself. She instead repeated, in a perseverative way, the horrors of the camp to the child. The mother was attempting to carve her experience into a coherent whole and confer meaning upon it. Instead, however, she overwhelmed her child by recounting experiences the child could not possibly understand. A central trauma for the mother in the camps was of seeing truckloads of children dumped into a bonfire and consumed alive, leaving the mother horrified, feeling an endless despair that life had no meaning. In repeating these experiences to the child, the mother prematurely imposed a sense of meaninglessness, contributing to the death of hope in her child and the absence of a view toward the future. This mother was so overwhelmed that she was unable to find a coherent narrative for herself or her child.

While this is an extreme example, it is an analogy to many patients who come for treatment overwhelmed by past circumstances and unable to find narratives for their lives. The bald repetition of horrifying events is not a narrative. Some sense of aesthetic shaping, some sense of distance, some thread of meaning must be found to release the person from the event, to place it in perspective, to create a sense of a past that is settled so the person can live in the present. In this respect, the use of a true narrative helps to shape and reshape the ego as it maneuvers through the vicissitudes of life.

Psychoanalysis can be seen as specifically addressing our repetition compulsions or false narratives and eventually helping us to construct more accurate and ultimately truer narratives. The use of reconstruction in psychoanalysis is a crucial part of this process. In a review of the use of reconstruction, a JAPA Panel (1982) refers to Freud's original discussion of working with the patients' resistances to undo repressions and to lead to a coherent complete history or reconstruction. Freud also spoke of the analyst filling in gaps of memories from other data where this reconstruction becomes as valid as the patients' memories. An additional aspect of this reconstruction is the progressive work in the analysis to reconstruct or restructure the patients' inner world. For example, Schwaber (JAPA Panel 1982) presented vignettes from a case in which the patient remembered very little of the first thirteen years of his life and through numerous reconstructions by the therapist reunited his first thirteen years with the rest of his life, thus reconnecting his inner experience on a continuum. There may be a current movement away from planful reconstruction to an almost exclusive preoccupation with transference.

However, in varying degrees with various patients, there may be points in the analysis where the usual psychoanalytic narrative is not enough—that is, when the associations of the patient (or frequently the lack of associations) and the interpretations of the analyst are not producing the desired therapeutic result. At these times, the analyst may consider borrowing from the therapeutic, cultural experiences of everyday life—those expressions that represent our need to put our experiences in narrative form, such as dramatic writing or the use of wit—and using them in some way in the analysis. For example, the patient may need strengthening or mobilizing of his or her observing ego and/or a channel for expressing overwhelming feelings of anger. Elsewhere I have discussed an example of children and adolescents' use of writing in this regard, both in the session with the analyst and in the form of journal and letter writing (Domash 1976). An interactive example is a child patient's use of wit, as an ego-strengthening device, including the ability to express aggression in a more neutralized form, with the analyst being the straight man (Domash 1975). Another example when the psychoanalytic narrative is not sufficient may be an extremely masochistic patient or a patient who needs help in being able to give symbolic meaning to events and to construct a narrative at all. Aspects of these latter two problems will be given later in this essay in describing the analyst's use of fairy tales.

Regarding the therapist, there may be times with an extremely difficult patient when the therapist needs to regain perspective—that is, mobilize his or her own observing ego—or times when he or she feels at an impasse. To take this one step further, there may be instances in some analyses when the analyst himself or herself has to work certain issues through before he or she can help the patient. It is with extremely difficult patients that the inner processes and struggles of the analyst become clear. I have discussed elsewhere the case of a severely masochistic woman and my attempt to resolve feelings within myself about working with her rage, hopelessness, and addiction to pain by my writing about her in dramatic form (Domash 1985)—that is, constructing a narrative about her. I depicted an imaginary case presentation where she and several analysts are speaking together about her in a round-table discussion. It was felt that by my taking her point of view as well as that of the analysts and attempting to express it in dramatic form, I was able to resolve sufficiently my feelings about her addiction to suffering and then work with her more effectively. Writing my own narrative gave me a sense of meaning about her suffering (and mine, in working with this type of patient), which then enabled me to get sufficient distance to be of more help. This narrative was not shared with the patient.

Another form of narrative the analyst might consider is the use of a fairy tale constructed for the patient, either for the analyst's own use or to be shared with the patient at a certain stage of the analysis. By fairy tale, I mean the construction of an imaginary story set in a distant time and place with the patient as the main character. The fairy tale should capture the essence of the patient's inner struggle and conflict and give an imaginary or unusual solution, but one that provides opportunity for discussion of meaning. It should approximate, as much as possible, aspects of the true narrative of the patient.

This technique can help the patient gain distance and perspective, in a manner similar to watching a play in which the central character has conflicts to which we resonate. And by saying it metaphorically and pictorially, the patient is urged to stop and think—in short, to do more work.

The use of creativity—for instance, imagery—as discussed by Hammer (1968), or in this case the construction of a fairy tale, takes the analyst and patient into transitional space by attempting a creative act. Transitional space is the area of healing and renewal. The area of "magic" and temporary "illusion" may allow the patient to lower the boundaries between self and other and to listen more openly and flexibly and, therefore, admit more possibilities. Similarly, the analyst can look at the patient from a new perspective and gain additional insights into both transference and countertransference phenomena.

For the narcissistic patient, the use of a fairy tale may also provide a strengthening of the self representation. It can help rebuild both the inner and outer world, contributing to greater cohesiveness and stability. Writers have frequently commented that narcissistic patients attempt to "self-heal" in a manner that eventually results in difficulty for the patient. Stolorow (1975) writes of the use of masochism and sadism in this regard; Domash and Balter (1978) refer to antisocial trends. The analyst, of course, by working with the narcissistic transference attempts to strengthen the self representation in positive ways. The fairy tale is a dramatic form of this that, in a concrete way, knits together the patient's past in a way that respects the defenses but also points out the current cost. Because the solution is a fantastic rather than a real one, the therapist is not saying what to do, only that there is a way out.

The fairy tale also speaks to the narcissistic patient in a language more appropriate to his or her concerns. There is frequently a need for specialness, a belief in magic, a wish for omnipotence—all of which are natural ingredients of the fairy tale. The more intense the feelings of vulnerability in the narcissistic patient, the more the need for illusion and omniscience. The analyst of such a patient must tread lightly. The path resembles that of the creator of the fairy tale, which reflects the dilemma back to the patient and respects the turmoil but also offers hope for structure and a solution.

CLINICAL USE OF FAIRY TALES

The following is a brief clinical description of a patient, Diane, followed by a fairy tale about the same phenomena.

Clinical Description

When under stress, thirty-year-old Diane, a professional singer, identifies with her cold, rejecting, narcissistic mother. She experiences alternating ego states as she relates to her husband. At times she relates to him as a whole person and at other times as a part object—one who does not have a beautiful face. At these times she becomes imperious and rejecting. He is not good enough for her (who is seen as highly desirable, very beautiful, and so on). This occurs as a result of her feeling challenged and vulnerable elsewhere. For example, her voice student challenges her; Diane then becomes like her cold, disdainful mother, attacking or rejecting her husband in some way. Afterward she feels alienated from her husband and upset with herself.

Fairy Tale

There once was a pretty little girl who suffered at the hands of a vain but beautiful mother. She longed for the touch, the kiss of this beautiful creature whose skin was so white, hair so black, and lips a crimson red. Only occasionally would the mother kiss her. The girl would sit on the steps outside the cottage and wait and wait for her mother. She would listen to the birds sing, as their voices filled the still forest. She too had a melodious voice and sang to accompany the birds. She felt so bad because she thought she was to blame. She was always dreaming, waiting for her mother to return. The little girl did not feel loveable. Finally this girl grew to be a beautiful woman who still felt bad inside. But when she sang she got rid of this bad feeling and for the moment was healed. A handsome traveling musician heard her singing. He liked the sounds he heard. They sang together and were married. Funny things started to happen. They would be happy for a while, singing, holding hands, and kissing. Then, if something bad happened to the girl, like if somebody said a mean word to her, she would suddenly not remember her husband as she knew him; but he would only be a face, an unfamiliar face, and she would notice every flaw. This way she did not have to think about her own hurt. She became so convinced of this that she did not want to sing with him anymore. She wanted to get away from his (and her) flaws. Finally an old fairy came and made her feel better. She gave her a magic wand that allowed her to heal her own flaws, so she could kiss her husband again. They sang together in the forest for many years to come.

While acknowledging the pain the patient suffered, this story attempts to analyze the patient's narcissistic defense. It fosters structural repair by (1) knitting together parts of the patient's past into a coherent story, therefore serving an organizing function; (2) allowing further discussion of the mother's coldness and the patient's anger, promoting cohesion as the anger becomes more integrated; and (3) fostering differentiation of the self and object by extended discussion of the mother's defense that currently "overwhelms" her. With continued discussion, the patient felt less at the mercy of her mother's defensive structure.

This approach is a relatively unthreatening attempt to foster separation. It therefore reduces the necessity for negative therapeutic reaction, which I view as, in part, a fearful, spiteful rejection of the analyst's offerings to ward off separation from the bad object.

I read this fairy tale to the patient only after she had discussed this dynamic with me many times. I was mindful of the timing, not wanting to overwhelm her or to have her feel the insight was mine and not hers. Her reaction to the fairy tale was that it served as a "crystallization" of her thoughts and that it offered hope. She cried after she heard it and requested a copy. It helped generate more discussion about her mother's aloofness and her feelings of anger and emptiness.

The patient is now at a point in treatment where she feels only partly identified with her mother, instead of being overtaken by her. This can be viewed as movement in the internalization process. Initially, as described by the fairy tale, the mother was experienced as a transitional presence that "hits" her from without. More currently she is a selective identification that has been integrated into the self representation (Schafer 1968). In parallel fashion, in the past she would get very upset with her husband whenever he had a problem because, as she would state it, there was "no separation." She can now listen to his difficulties, realize they are *his,* and not get overwhelmed. She feels an increasing sense of her separateness with him. Just as her mother no longer "overtakes" her, neither does her husband.

Clinical Description

The following is a second clinical example of a patient with prominent narcissistic difficulties. Twenty-seven-year-old Mary is anxious about her abilities and afraid of exposure. Mary has to be "right" and all-knowing so she will not look foolish. As a child, she was repeatedly told by her father, who was prone to psychotic rages, that she was stupid. Each time she is given a new assignment at work, she becomes frightened. This is, in part, because she does not know how to do it immediately, precisely because it *is* a problem to be solved. Her sense of humiliation during the problem-solving period compels her to attempt to complete the task quickly, without sufficient thought. Regarding the transference, she also cannot fully trust the analyst, from whom she fears criticality and intrusiveness.

Excerpt from a Session

Mary had been talking about her difficulties at work, part of which involve attempts at creative problem solving, and how anxious this makes her. She cannot take the time to deliberate for fear she will look foolish.

ANALYST: A girl, in the middle of the woods, got caught on the wrong path. It was a long windy route, but it did lead to home. She was unsure of the way, unsure if she had the ability to try, although she had been told there were many treasures and many adventures to be had. The other route to the left—she wasn't sure how to get over there—was short and quick. She thought she would be better off there.

PATIENT: This brings up a lot of things—I always think there's a right way, and I always compare myself to others to see if I'm doing it right! For instance, I have an ideal of how relationships should be and mine never turn out like the ideal. Or in here I can't say what's on my mind. I keep wondering what I *should* be saying.

ANALYST: She met someone who promised to help her along the path to discover its riches and mine the gold. But she wasn't sure. She hesitated and the day grew late. The sun was setting through the trees. The cool October day was growing to an end.

Could you try out some less "right possibilities" with me. Just say things that come to mind.

PATIENT: I still have a problem with trust. I still have to plan the "right" thing to say before coming into the session.

This vignette attempts to discuss her problem with feeling humiliated if she takes the time to ponder or consider a problem, a dysfunctional thinking pattern typical of some narcissistic patients (Domash and Shapiro 1978). It also alludes to her difficulty in forming an alliance and in trusting the analyst. Since this is a pervasive problem with Mary, one that is slow to be solved, I presented her with a fragment of a tale to mirror where she was and to help her consider alternatives. By "surprising" her with this fragment, I hoped to encourage her to take a chance to say something from deeper within herself.

This is a patient who has great difficulty revealing anything of substance to the analyst. She finds it nearly impossible to reveal fantasies or dreams. Shortly after this vignette, she recounted the following dream:

I was living in a very drab place—dark, dreary, broken furniture—which suddenly turned beautiful. It had an open veranda, lush vegetation. A handsome man came by and spent the day. We sat on lounge chairs.

In the dream, there are some possible relationships to my story. Her life becomes brighter, and a person comes who makes things more pleasant. The lounge chairs made me think of my office. However, the patient gave very few associations to the dream. This patient and I continue to struggle through periods of intense resistance to any deepening of analysis alternating with periods of some greater willingness to attempt it. Unlike the previous patient, she tends not to give confirming evidence, further associations, and so forth, directly to my interventions. Instead, she seems to respond inwardly so that the work does move forward, at least intermittently.

CONCLUSION

This essay has been a discussion of the creation and use of narrative in everyday life and in psychoanalysis and, further, of times when the standard psychoanalytic narrative is not enough. In these instances, the analyst may borrow from the cultural narrative of everyday life for use in the analysis. This may help strengthen certain aspects of the patient, provide a model for the use of narration, or help the analyst work through countertransference issues within himself or herself. The use of a fairy tale, particularly with the narcissistic patient, may help restore the patient's sense of hope and may help her or him feel less alone while at the same time gain greater perspective. I am reminded of an anecdote reported by Issroff (1983) about Winnicott. She remarked that his most effective comments were the most poetic and illusive. For example, instead of making a father interpretation directly, Winnicott might have first talked about a walk he had taken that day and about the young women he had seen on the street. He would wonder what these pubescent women might expect from a father. She quotes him as saying, " 'Loving. One could almost eat them, perhaps loving is eating, I suppose.' " And then he might shift his gaze from the past to his present listener and say, " 'By the way, over these past years I've noticed you changing. . . . I think you should know that I have the capacity to dream about you.' " He was a master in creating an area in which people could discover themselves. It is in this spirit that the fairy tale is ideally offered.

Countertransference pitfalls with this type of technique are several. There is the risk of the therapist wanting to demonstrate his or her creativity, with the patient serving as an admiring self object. In addition to self analysis of this dynamic, timing can help counteract this—that is, if the patient already feels the insight is his or hers, the fairy tale will be confirming rather than imposed from without. Another problem is that the story may draw too heavily on similar conflicts in the therapist. By this I mean that we all resonate to certain similar difficulties in ourselves as we listen to our patients. If we choose a conflict to elucidate because that is what is central to us at that moment rather than the patient, we will of course be in error as therapists.

Another problem is that of overgratifying the patient, of fulfilling a transference wish that they be given "special" treatment. I think, however, that the nature of this gratification is that of ego instincts rather than id instincts, a distinction articulated by Modell (1975). Ego instincts include the maternal holding environment and the need for reaffirmation of the constancy and reliability of the analyst. This results in an identification with a "good" object. This identification does require that something be provided by the human environment and should lead to a growing individuation on the part of the patient. By giving the patient reconstructions, including a fairy tale form, we seek to understand the unique, individualized self of the patient and provide a holding environment where the patient is affirmed as a coherent whole whose life has had, does have, and will have meaning. We are reaching out to enlarge meaning and to encourage patients to step into that comfortable space that allows them to find meaning for themselves.

REFERENCES

Auerham, N. C., and E. Prelinger. 1983. Repetition in the concentration camp survivor and her child. *International Review of Psycho-Analysis* 10:31–46.

Bettelheim, B. 1977. *The uses of enchantment.* New York: Vintage Books.

Domash, L. 1975. The use of wit and the comic by a borderline psychotic child in psychotherapy. *Journal of Psychotherapy* 29:261–70.

———. 1976. The therapeutic use of writing in the service of the ego. *Journal of the American Academy of Psychoanalysis* 4:261–69.

———. 1985. *Tragedy, masochism, and the heroic confrontation.* Unpublished paper.

Domash, L., and Balter, L. 1978. Restitution and revenge: Antisocial trends in narcissism. *Journal of American Academic Psychoanalysis* 7:375–84.

Domash, L., and R. Shapiro. 1978. Dysfunctional patterns of thinking in the borderline personality. *Journal of the American Academy of Psychoanalysis* 7:543–52.

Hammer, E. F. 1968. *Use of interpretation in treatment: Techniques and art.* New York: Grune & Stratton.

Issroff, J. 1983. A reaction to "Boundary and space: An introduction to the work of D. W. Winnicott" by M. Davis and D. Wallbridge. *International Review of Psycho-Analysis* 10:231–36.

JAPA Panel. 1982. Construction and reconstruction: Clinical aspects. Arthur Malin, reporter. *Journal of the American Psychoanalytical Association* 30:169–84.

Modell, A. 1975. The ego and the id—fifty years later. *International Journal of Psycho-Analysis* 56:57–68.

Schaeffer, S. F. 1983. *The madness of a seduced woman.* New York: Bantam Books.

Schafer, R. 1968. *Aspects of internalization.* New York: International Universities Press.

Stolorow, R. D. 1975. The narcissistic function of masochism and sadism. *International Journal of Psycho-Analysis* 56:441–48.

11

ON THE TRANSITION FROM PSYCHOTHERAPY TO PSYCHOANALYSIS WITH THE SAME ANALYST

Helen Gediman, Ph.D.

Not so long ago there was a widespread conviction among psychoanalytic practitioners that any patient seen in psychotherapy by one analyst should, if and when psychoanalysis proper is indicated, be referred to another analyst. There appeared to be a caveat prohibiting transition under any circumstances from psychoanalytic therapy to psychoanalysis with the same analyst.

We have come a long way since Freud (1919), in his metaphor of alloying the pure gold of psychoanalysis with the copper of suggestion, implied that there were only two fundamental types of psychotherapy: psychoanalysis proper, involving interpretations of the transference, and nonanalytic therapies, involving manipulation of the transference, or suggestion. Yet, only one major article (Bernstein 1983) and two major panels (Panel 1983a, 1983b) have been devoted to the topic of conversion or transition. In the panel entitled "Converting from Psychotherapy to Psychoanalysis," (at the December 1983 meeting of the American Psychoanalytic Association) I would characterize panel members such as Otto Kernberg and Ernst Ticho as conservative on conversion, while I would see Merton Gill as standing alone with a radical position.

The conservatives upheld a need to differentiate sharply between psychoanalysis and psychotherapy. But since the psychotherapies they addressed were fundamentally nonpsychoanalytic, their conclusion that the two processes are fundamentally discontinuous seem to me tautological in that it derives from their predefining the processes as essentially different to begin with. Such predefinitions also are made to conform to their conviction that patients can be strictly differentiated diagnostically in advance, with the treatment plan, psychoanalysis or psychotherapy, then tailored to that diagnosis. From the conservative position, psychotherapy underplays interpretation and deliberately omits free association, evenly hovering attention, fostering of the regressive transference neurosis, and most transference and resistance analyses. These psychotherapeutic processes are defined in a way that obviously rules out the possibility of analyzability emerging as a function of the psychotherapeutic work. It is, therefore, a foregone conclusion—a self-fulfilling prophecy—that few, if any, conversions can be made to psychoanalysis with the same analyst.

Gill, on the other hand, addressed himself to both psychoanalysis and psychoanalytic psychotherapy. He saw the two processes as identical, with neither—and this is where I regard him as radical—fostering a regressive transference neurosis. Only certain manifest behaviors can be seen as different, and these Gill regards as not intrinsic to the treatment process. Like the discontinuities of the conservative group, however, this identity is based on predefinition, so that many of Gill's conclusions can also be regarded as tautological: since there are no fundamental differences, conversion is a nonproblem.

I believe that we can understand psychoanalysis and psychoanalytic psychotherapy as occupying positions on a continuum, varying in most important respects only in matters of degree. However, past a certain point, depending on context, these quantitative differences do become functionally qualitative. We should be able to state the conditions of psychoanalysis; to state some variations that are a matter of degree tending toward psychoanalytic psychotherapy; and then also state the conditions that are functionally discontinuous, characterizing a fundamentally different process that can no longer be called psychoanalytic psychotherapy but something else—another process, another modality, another kind of psychotherapy. I propose that the greater the difference between a psychoanalytic psychotherapy and a psychoanalysis and the longer the period of time that elapses before the conversion is attempted, the more difficult will be the work required in the transition. When the quantitative differences have crossed the hypothetical delimiting point into the qualitative, the nonanalytic psychotherapy we are doing with a patient, if recommended and feasible, might well need to be taken on by someone other than the original therapist.

There are various reasons for a psychotherapy to be converted eventually into a psychoanalysis. These reasons derive from two nodal situations: In the first, the analyst has felt psychoanalysis to be the treatment of choice and has recommended it but the patient chose not to enter it. The second nodal situation, in contrast, has the analyst judging initially that psychoanalytic psychotherapy, not psychoanalysis proper, is the treatment of choice but that the patient eventually may benefit from psychoanalysis. In the second situation are to be found the "more difficult" patients: those described in connection with Stone's (1954) indications for the "widening scope" or those considered to have ego defects requiring preparatory work employing variations, modifications, and parameters of psychoanalytic technique. In the first situation, one which has received very little attention in psychoanalytic literature, with the exception of the excellent paper by Bernstein (1983), a stated goal to analyze the patients' reasons for refusing analysis, whether those reasons are based on feasibility concerns, resistances, or combinations of both. That is, the option of switching to psychoanalysis is kept in mind and reviewed continuously, for as Bernstein has pointed out, some of the problems for which such patients seek treatment are the very problems related to their doubts and concerns about analysis. These problems, broadly conceived, include fears of dependency, regression, and commitment, as well as anxieties connected with diminished interactional manifest behavior.

The clearest and least controversial case one could make for transition is the first type, and I shall present some brief clinical material illustrating how such a conversion comes about, offering some suggestions for analyzing the meaning that the transition process itself has for the patient. For the more difficult patients where psychoanalytic psychotherapy is recommended initially, the literature abounds in good clinical examples. I shall therefore restrict my discussion to some relevant clinical-theoretical matters centering on issues of conversion itself. These have to do mainly with my conviction that practically speaking analyzability is often, if not always, an emergent phenomenon, dependent on conducting a psychoanalytic psychotherapy within the bounds of the basic treatment model. I shall also offer some reflections on certain specific problems of the more difficult patient, relevant to conversion: those involving patients' difficulties in comprehending the realm of psychoanalytic discourse or in being able to utilize interpretations in the service of insight and therapeutic benefit; and those involving severe early trauma and subsequent ego weaknesses. Finally, I shall comment on the development of an analyzable transference neurosis as a condition for transition and shall conclude with some remarks on the very meaning, in terms of the transference neurosis, of making the transition.

It is axiomatic that theoretical orientation, which does in fact influence our definition and subsequent conduct of an analysis or a psychotherapy (as it did for the panel of the American Psychoanalytic Association), will also influence the criteria of analyzability we employ. It is erroneous to believe that there now exists some sort of universally accepted objective and theory-free assessment of analyzability. I also believe that analyzability, although sometimes discernible in advance, is often emergent from the analytic process itself, independent of the analyst's initial conviction as to the patient's potential for analyzability. Further, the way that the process itself evolves must be influenced by the analyst's view of human beings, personality development, and personality change. Thus, the analyst's theoretical orientation necessarily affects not only which patients are selected for analysis but also those selected for transition from psychotherapy to psychoanalysis. Hopefully, further developments in comparative psychoanalysis will clarify the ways in which diverse theoretical orientations control our questions and answers about analyzability.

A MODEL FOR PSYCHOANALYTIC TREATMENT

The basic treatment model should subsume both the analytic point of view, or stance, and the requisite arrangements for conducting an analytic treatment according to a specifiable process. When viewed as a continuum, it should apply to psychotherapy but not to other psychotherapeutic modalities.

Consider the following vignette: A patient anxiously and angrily revealed to me her belief that she was in psychotherapy and not in psychoanalysis because I had been greeting her warmly and saying "Good morning" each day as I went to meet her in my waiting room. Her conviction was buttressed by her accurately perceived variations in my facial expressions at the sessions' end as she got up off the couch and glanced at me on the way out. She had at certain times detected me smiling restrainedly, regarding her with a pleasant expression, while at other times, she noticed me pondering thoughtfully, perhaps puzzling over something that had transpired in the session that had remained ambiguous as to its meanings. While her perceptions were accurate, her interpretations of them were idiosyncratic. She concluded that my end-of-session enigmatic smiles conveyed my appreciation of her hard work toward resolution of her difficulties and that my looks of perplexity were intended by me, consciously and deliberately, to signal her that she was not doing good work as a patient. I was letting her know, she thought, that I myself was struggling vainly for the kind of closure that would permit me to offer analytically valuable interpretations. She imagined that both of these signs of my personal expressiveness, along with my cordial morning greeting, were clear and calculated departures from analytic neutrality on my part; that I, either in ignorance of the correct analytic approach or in a reasoned departure from it, such as a decision to employ behavior-modification techniques by rewarding and punishing her, was not doing analysis but "only" psychotherapy.

This vignette raises some important questions, for any consideration of the transition from being in psychotherapy to being in analysis and must deal with the issues of arrangements and of free association as a tool in the analysis of transference and resistance, but also with the centrality of the analyst's maintaining the analytic stance and the ways in which the patient consciously and unconsciously perceives that stance. Only then can we identify the limiting conditions of psychoanalysis that more or less differentiate it from psychoanalytic psychotherapy and also from those other psychotherapies that cannot be called psychoanalytic.

THE ANALYTIC POINT OF VIEW

What constitutes the analytic stance in the basic model for either a psychoanalytic psychotherapy or a psychoanalysis proper? For the sake of clarity, I shall present in my exposition some polar opposite or functionally discontinuous qualities that eventuate in a fundamentally nonpsychoanalytic treatment process, generally counterindicating a transition to psychoanalysis with the same therapist. These discontinuous qualities set limits on, or at least influence, what can be worked out later in analysis, particularly in the analysis of the transference. This argument assumes the basic treatment model of free association as a tool toward the analysis of unconscious intrapsychic conflicts originating in childhood.

The first cardinal aspect of the analytic approach is neutrality. Returning to my vignette, I do not wish to belabor the obvious—that psychoanalytic neutrality refers not to whether the analyst's face is expressive or deadpan but to the analyst not taking sides in the patient's conflicts, thereby remaining equidistant from id, superego, defensive, and reality considerations. Related to neutrality are issues of anonymity and abstinence. Examples of extreme departures from analytic neutrality might be siding with instinctual gratifications at the expense of superego analysis or overly judgmental attitudes at the expense of id analysis. Other departures involve working toward a specific goal, such as encouraging the patient one-sidedly in a conflictually based paralysis about a job decision; encouraging a homosexual to become a heterosexual; or evangelically promoting a "norm" of mental health. Guidance, advice, and life management are all significant departures from neutrality. However, at certain moments and in context any of these potential deviations conceivably may be employed as means to an analytic end. For example, if accepting a particular job is the only course of action that makes analysis feasible, then in that context supportive accents on interpretive interventions may be compatible analytic goals.

A second characteristic of the analytic stance is the avoidance of either/or thinking, in favor of a consideration of multiple meanings, of overdetermination of all psychic phenomena, and unflagging appreciation of the role of ambivalence and conflict. At the extreme end of this continuum are simplistic interpretations focusing on one or a few lines of dynamics or of genetic reconstruction. This extreme is exemplified by certain brief psychotherapies that employ repeated confrontations in the form of simple dynamic interpretations and do so in the absence of the patient's associations and in the absence of transference and resistance analysis. Another case in point is the singular goal of desensitization or other behavior-modification work in eliminating a specific phobia or symptom. Single-mindedness of understanding and of purpose might be manifest in the therapist's insistence on exploring only one overriding defensive style or only one life-historical theme—which often turns out to be a screen memory—such as "very early maternal deprivation," to the exclusion of all others. From the patient's point of view, narrowness of purpose is frequently manifest in demands upon the therapist for idiosyncratic versions of the corrective emotional experience. Therapists lacking the analytic point of view might acquiesce.

A third constituent of the analytic approach is listening to the patient's associations with evenly hovering attention in order to offer judiciously timed interpretations of psychic reality following preparatory confrontation and clarification. In contrast, the nonanalytic approach addresses external reality, but only in its manifest terms. The analytic approach focuses on external reality as manifest content and as historical truth, but it is regulated by the aim of eventually seeing such content as means to an end of associating further into the realms of inner psychic reality. At the symposium (Panel 1983b) presented at the American Psychoanalytic Association, all four participants included clarification and confrontation as proper techniques for psychotherapy; it was only Merton Gill, however, who focused on the centrality of the interpretation of psychic reality in psychotherapy. All of the others took a position that, according to the criteria that I am proposing and not theirs, eliminated any possibility of conversion or transition with the same analyst because they did not see the cardinal feature of analyzing—the interpretation of psychic reality—as relevant for psychotherapy but only for psychoanalysis. Either they did not consider psychotherapy to be psychoanalytic or what they seemed to mean by psychotherapy was nonanalytic therapy conducted by an analyst. Nonetheless, they believed conversions were occasionally possible even under these limiting circumstances.

A fourth hallmark of the analytic approach is analyzing with an appreciation of the constraints involved in that process. Deviations in the direction of omnisciently purveying wisdom or deliberately responding countermanipulatively or counteractively to emotional overtures or to acting out depart from an analytic stance. Employing parameters, to be subject to analysis eventually, comes within the realm of analysis but deciding which deviations are definitely and totally analyzable in the future tends toward the omniscient and the nonanalytic.

Offering cures and remedies may be appropriate in the care of certain individuals, but it tends to foreclose the possibility for adequate transference and resistance analysis and could interfere with maintaining an analytic attitude. These tactics are prototypical of many nonpsychoanalytic therapies. They may be required for a given patient at a given time, but they are techniques that, along with the other departures from an analytic stance just reviewed, impede a reasonably smooth transition to psychoanalysis with the same therapist, although they might still allow for transition to another therapist. The new therapist might be more able to work psychoanalytically in a way that is worthwhile and effective, even if, at times, burdened by the contrast with the previous therapist. Yet, it is conceivable that the patient, even when treated with the grossest departures from the analytic attitude and arrangements, might be more burdened by switching to a new therapist than by continuing with one who would gradually modulate the ways in which he or she works.

ARRANGEMENTS

It is particularly important to focus on the arrangements required for conducting a psychoanalysis. Although these widely accepted arrangements have a solidly psychoanalytic rationale, they have been the subject of much attack in recent years. They have been called arbitrary, mindless, and rigidly focused on numbers, with no rationale other than blind adherence to an outmoded legacy. Let me briefly review those arrangements that characterize psychoanalytic psychotherapy. I believe these conditions are not arbitrary or anachronistic. They are intrinsically related to the methods, aims, and processes evolving from the basic treatment model of Freudian psychoanalysis, although they are not necessarily related importantly to psychotherapies based on other models.

First, a psychoanalysis is best conducted at a frequency of four to five times a week, in contrast to a psychoanalytic therapy, which may be conducted appropriately three or fewer times a week. Second, a psychoanalysis is best carried out with the use of the couch, while psychoanalytic psychotherapy is generally conducted face to face. (I realize the idea of a continuum may be a bit difficult to justify for this particular difference.) Third, psychoanalysis involves formally establishing the rule of free association and the requirements of paying close analytic attention to its observation and any departure from it. In psychoanalytic psychotherapy, the same conditions are maintained, but not as rigorously and with a greater emphasis on active exploration and clarification relative to interpreting the meaning of unconscious conflicts, unconscious resistances, and the resistances to resolving transferences. Finally, in psychoanalysis proper, there is a strong, though not absolutely exclusive, emphasis on psychic reality: fantasy, dream, and ego analysis. While the focus is similar in psychoanalytic psychotherapy there may be relatively more emphasis on "outer" reality. The conditions for psychoanalysis proper are aimed at promoting more regressive transferences than are those for psychoanalytic psychotherapy.

To recapitulate: The eventual and gradual switch from psychoanalytic therapy to psychoanalysis proper will be facilitated when the following four conditions intrinsic to an analytic stance are met, even though there may be some limited variations with respect to arrangements. (1) The therapist remains neutral, paying consistent attention to anxiety and resistance, leading to the analysis and resolution of transference. (2) The therapist remains relatively anonymous or opaque. (3) The therapist remains abstinent, not gratifying the patient by offering life decisions, reassurance, or guidance. (4) The therapist does not overinterpret dynamics alone at the expense of attention to anxiety and resistances within the transference. When there have been major departures from the above conditions it is usually better to refer the patient elsewhere if and when analysis is indicated. The principle underlying this recommendation is that the longer you work with a patient using significant departures from the analytic mode and from optimal arrangements, the more transference there will be that may be unanalyzable by you and ultimately unresolved for the patient.

Other variations in arrangements of the basic model, which blur our customary distinctions between psychoanalysis and psychoanalytic psychotherapy, can be effected flexibly and temporarily without ruling out eventual conversion to psychoanalysis proper with the same analyst. In addition to trusting an initial or emerging conviction that the patient is potentially analyzable, the analyst must also be able to wait patiently for the patient's readiness for transition. There are times when a psychoanalysis may be conducted on a three- or even a two-times-a-week basis; for example, if it is not the first analysis or if it is all that can be feasibly arranged at the time. The patient may be seen off the couch at times when anxiety seems temporarily to produce regression too severe to analyze and when this parameter is understood to be a transitional arrangement and its meaning to the patient is stated, eventually to be analyzed. There may also be a need to tolerate temporarily gross violations of the fundamental rule, as with the narcissistically vulnerable patients who might require certain preparatory work.

In psychoanalytic psychotherapy, a patient may be seen on the couch, if this facilitates associative flow in self-exploration, even though the lesser frequency of appointments does not usually facilitate a regressive transference development. A period of exploratory psychotherapy may need to be conducted on an extended basis, when analysis proper is not feasible, for example, when there is an acute crisis, when analyzability is still being assessed, or when a patient's potential as an analysand requires and is permitted substantial time and preparation to emerge. Ultimately, the conscious and unconscious meanings of all these improvisations should be subjected to analysis.

ANALYZABILITY

Since a discussion of the transition from being in psychotherapy to being an analysand depends first and foremost on one's view of analyzability, I am going to raise some questions about analyzability itself before continuing with the problems of transition. Analyzability is not an entity but a process emerging over time as a function of the analytic situation. This position would hold for both nodal situations of potential transition referred to earlier.

Although I do believe that criteria for analyzability are often not discernible during an initial consultation and often emerge only as outcomes of the analytic process itself, I also believe that there are some fairly reliable, consensually agreed upon criteria for analytic potential that can sometimes be discerned independently of the analytic situation. That is, patients meeting certain criteria may be identifiable as analyzable rather quickly. Among these criteria are conscious agreement to the basic rule and paying attention to its violations. Others are psychological-mindedness; conscious motivation to ease psychic pain; adaptive resilience or the capacity to shift back and forth in timely ways between primary and secondary process thinking, between expression and reflection, or between participating and observing. We look also for the capacity to use insight for change, to distinguish fantasy from reality and inner from outer—or at least to do so over the long run despite transient regression—and the capacity to question the previously self-evident. These cases would fall in the first nodal situation of potential transition: the patients meet criteria of analyzability; analysis is recommended, at the outset, but for one reason or another, the patients choose not to accept the recommendation.

Other cases, falling in the second nodal situation, appear doubtful in the beginning based on diagnostic assessments traditionally viewed as counterindicative for analysis proper. Among them are those whose history suggests early environmental, interpersonal, biochemical, neurological, or other developmental deficiencies or trauma.

THE FIRST NODAL SITUATION: A CASE EXAMPLE
OF A FAILED CONVERSION ATTEMPT

A thirty-year-old woman without significant ego impairment chose not to accept the recommendation for psychoanalysis and, in essence, determined unilaterally that once-a-week psychotherapy was the best for her. "I'm not one of those people whose whole life centers around their analysis. My job and my personal life are in crisis, and I frankly don't see the point of coming here and working on my feelings toward you when a critical career decision, my life, hangs in the balance for the next few months. I do not want to be distracted from the task at hand." She also did not want to demean herself by asking her powerful and wealthy father to help make analysis feasible by asking for his financial assistance. She had an unshakable conviction that analysis was not feasible because of external reality: lack of money or being embroiled in real-life crises requiring rapid decisions involving possible change of career and of geographical location. She believed that analysis made no realistic sense for her because so much effort and concentration had to go, within a limited time span, toward making real-life critical decisions; and any focus on feelings about therapy, particularly about the analyst, seemed absurd, postponing as they would inevitably do, decisions that were urgent, thereby working against her own long-term interests. It was also clear to me that for this patient, objective reality was used in the service of powerful resistances and served to foster rationalizations about delving deeper into the inner psychically real world. Her resistances against analysis conformed to the type described by Bernstein (1983). She was afraid of commitment, of getting overly embroiled in personal battles, as she had with a former therapist, or of having treatment become disproportionately important in her life. It was clear that objective reality was used in the service of these powerful resistances and served to foster rationalizations about delving deeper into the inner psychically real world.

Analytic neutrality required appreciating that the patient did feel to be in crisis, that the crisis about reasonably unequivocal commitment to only one career path paralleled fear of commitment to an intensive analytic treatment, and that the crisis was exploited to buttress potentially analyzable defenses. Sometimes real crises never abate, as with certain individuals who appear to possess limitless resourcefulness in creating and exploiting them. Then, the psychotherapy, when it appears to reach a point ready for conversion, never quite takes off because the patient, who in many other respects appears to have the potential to work analytically, will be hard on the trail of resolving a real-life crisis once again.

But with the patient under discussion, a time did come to attempt conversion. She appeared to have exhausted her repertoire of crises. The career path chosen provided deep gratification; the man whom she worked so hard to get to marry her before her "biological time clock" ran out had proposed to her. He wanted children immediately, as she did, and the last real-life crisis disappeared. Everything she had ever wanted was about to materialize. At this juncture, she developed severe anxiety. She was fearful that the impending marriage, which had just seemed a dream come true, albeit one involving certain compromises that she apparently had accepted, would not be a success. She, who rarely reported dreams, reported having two on the night following the marriage proposal. In the first, she had been in prison on Central Park South in New York City for three years, in a cramped cell. The only hope of avoiding total incarceration was the wonderful view over Central Park that her cell window afforded her. The second dream was brief: "I dreamed I had a penis." She associated that the third year of psychotherapy was drawing to a close. The window in my office, which was large and on a high floor, commanded a panoramic view of Central Park from the east. She feared incarceration in marriage and believed it might be worth risking incarceration in analysis to avoid the worse trap. To the second dream she associated much of the thematic material of our work together. She was afraid that her preference for clitoral over vaginal orgasm would be discovered and that her fiancé would reject her as too masculine. She confessed to him that she faked vaginal orgasm. He was not deterred. It made no difference to him. She felt the masculine side of her personality tended, to her chagrin, to overpower the feminine. Here, she referred to her keen and penetrating intelligence and to her aggressively crafty skill at strategic social and professional maneuvers. She also believed she had a more aristocratic breeding and bearing, similar to her father's and brother's, than her fiancé possessed. In her own particular variant of penis envy, or, more likely, awe, she expressed yearning for completion by a man whose masculine attributes could mirror what she designated as her own masculinity. She believed that was the only way she could happily integrate the masculine and feminine sides of her nature. It must be said at this point that the patient was unusually competent, outstanding in a highly competitive field dominated by men, and was exceptionally gifted in the art of argumentation. All along, she feared that I would have difficulty keeping pace with her resourceful wit and that since I was, to her way of seeing it, a "demure" woman, I would not be able to empathize with what she insisted on calling her masculinity. It is of interest that she described her fiancé as boyish, not a man like her father. Whenever I attempted to analyze the unconscious transferential nature of these conscious fears, she felt I was unempathically distracting her from the tasks that beset her in real life and averred that I was interested only in proving my own psychoanalytic theories of transference.

But a turning point occurred as her desires verged on successful materialization. She could hardly function and feared she might be psychotic in her wish for a "clone" to consolidate the masculine and feminine sides of her nature. She asked me if I thought she should come in more often. Perhaps I would tell her, as she heard Freud had done for some of his patients, to postpone the marriage until she embarked upon analysis and completed it. Although I did no such thing, I did interpret her longstanding anxieties that characterized all of her relationships as well as her full commitment to treatment.

In the preparatory psychotherapy, some paranoid anxieties abated. While she took the active role most of the time with me, there were moments of stark contrast where she craved total submission to and authoritarian direction, wanting to submit passively to my directives. During this period, there were no inroads for interpretation, for she was inaccessible to any interpretation of transference feelings toward me. Now, however, to make a long story short, she was no longer content with her previous explanations to herself and an analysis was agreed upon and begun. But it had hardly begun when yet another crisis led the patient eventually to flee.

A demystification of her reluctance to commit herself to an exploration of transference feelings occurred as the transference neurosis finally could develop into analyzable form. She became aware, gradually, that her fear of commitment was but one side of a conflict. The other side was embedded in fears about not feeling enough connectedness with me, paralleling her fear of not enough connectedness with her fiancé. It emerged on attempting deeper analysis that connectedness, to her, meant quite specifically a passionate, sadomasochistically overstimulating attachment, such as she had in childhood to her father, to the previous therapist, and to some ill-fated previous relationships that deteriorated when she found herself feeling defeated in abject submission. Further, she fantasized that such sadistically exciting subjugation of herself to awesome male powers was a precondition for absorbing into herself the male phallus, which would, in turn, tame the cruelty of her abuser and transform him into a respectful egalitarian (previously called a "clone") who would finally recognize her as a powerful woman on equal footing with him.

In retrospect, it seems as though conflicts about a commitment to analysis proper constituted the transference neurosis itself. Access to analyzing that transference neurosis was made possible during a long but aborted conversion process with many shifts back and forth between traditionally conceived psychoanalysis.

THE SECOND NODAL SITUATION: SOME DOUBTFUL CASES

We have just seen how, with a patient for whom analysis was initially recommended, the potential for analyzability emerged from a psychotherapy that departed in arrangements from the basic treatment model, but which did not depart from a fundamentally analytic stance. There are, in addition, some doubtful cases, conforming to our second nodal situation of patients who are not initially recommended for psychoanalysis proper. With these patients, particularly, any final assessment of analyzability will arise only in the context of the analytic situation, for what we are assessing initially is a potential for or the probability of the emergence of "analyzability" through the process itself. A corollary of this position is that settling the question of analyzability always hinges on a trial run, which may vary in length from one consultation, to exploratory psychotherapy preparatory to psychoanalysis, to a trial analysis whose length may be in fact indeterminate at the time of its embarkation. In a trial run, early confrontation or otherwise addressing the meaning of repetitive patterns, especially those that look as though they would disrupt continuous analytic work, is called for in some treatments. This active analysis of negative transference is necessary whenever intensely experienced feelings that appear to be revivals of early pathogenic interactions are repeated and directed toward the analyst in ways that threaten to disrupt treatment. The analyzability of patients of this sort cannot always be determined solely by any a priori nosological assumptions or theoretical account of psychodynamics. The analyzability of such patients may be discernible only after the analyst makes consistent efforts at analyzing each eruption of the disruptive repetitions and, when possible, even begins to predict more of the same before it occurs.

Activity level is, then, very important in the context of considering transition from psychotherapy to psychoanalysis. The kind of active efforts I am describing here would be criticized by some as precluding analytic work. I believe the matter is more subtle and more complex, involving in this instance an apparent paradox: more is sometimes better than less if less is eventually to be better than more. Including negative transference in the analytic dialogue from the beginning, before it escalates to disrupt the analytic process, or even an exploratory therapy, is useful not only therapeutically but as a diagnostic tool for assessing eventual analyzability. It can also serve to rule out those with limited potential for analyzability. It permits the analyst to develop a judgment about the extent to which the patient can also hear an interpretation on its own terms: as a communication offering understanding that expands meaning and insight. Sometimes, after numerous opportunities, a patient cannot hear interpretations in this way but only, for example, as oral, soothing gratification; as simply shameful exposure; as symbolizing an invasive procedure such as anal rape; as proof of phallic defeat; or as a defensive victory for the analyst. The patient who cannot achieve optimal secondary process distance reflectively is unlikely to become an analysand, even though the therapist is, on his or her part, being the quintessential analyst. Nor would a patient be a likely prospect for analysis if he or she seems unable to grasp multiple and ambiguous meanings. The patient's limits in comprehension to a single track of meaning (such as early maternal deprivation) leave the process in a rut, sometimes interminably; then, the possibility of transition to analysis, a process requiring multiple transformations of meaning, seems highly unlikely.

We know there are occasions when it is more analytically neutral to discourage the patient from embarking on analytic therapy and analysis than to hold on to him or her. Such attempts to hold on may stem from misguided efforts to counteract or correct for past traumatic rejections. The principle of analytic neutrality would require more analysis and less determined counteraction of past environmental failures. Psychotherapeutic procedures employing these determined efforts to counteract the past, as with "corrective emotional experiences," set significant limits on the possibilities for further conversion to psychoanalysis with the same analyst.

Certain cases are particularly relevant to issues of eventual and emergent analyzability and ultimate conversion because they illustrate how even severely traumatized patients struggling to deal with a lifetime of stimulus overload and "flooding" excitement do present with analyzable content. However, I believe that what is critical for determining analyzability is the potential for endowing even extreme disorganizing, chaotic early states with representational content and symbolic meaning. Then, when idiosyncratic fantasy content gets to be linked associatively with the great universal themes of separation, otherness, incest, castration, mortality, and so on, analysis may be possible. The patient who initially requires a holding environment to manage painful tensions and traumatic excitability may be analyzable eventually, when meaning and structure can be provided by classical methods of interpretation. I should mention, though, that I think there are hazards in a one-sided emphasis on environmental- or biological-limiting factors, which is conducive to the view that the severely traumatized are discontinuous with the so-called normal neurotics, those who may have been spared some of the real trauma and lifelong suffering. It is true that for the traumatized, aspects of their universal incestuous fantasies, for instance, have been actualized idiosyncratically. When we are faced with real cumulative trauma of chronic early interpersonal and other developmental-environmental failures, such as parental psychosis or seriously defective maternal empathy, then we are dealing with extreme versions of universals. In these cases, the type and degree of insight and change that are achieved may not be exactly as they are in other cases, but conversion to a procedure where the analytic stance and arrangements will be optimal cannot be ruled out a priori as a viable possibility.

In recent years, I have had occasion to work with several patients who as children were presumed to be "learning disabled" or dyslexic from neurological causes. These patients' own accounts of their lives emphasized "deficit," and, indeed, they displayed many of the stigmata of the early traumatized. They seemed overwhelmed at times of chaos, but their temporary susceptibility to traumatic states did not seem specific to any particular precipitant or conflictual constellation. At such times, there also seemed to be signs of dedifferentiation as, for example, in affect and in a failure to identify a source of psychic pain as coming from within or from some external situation. While this transitory boundary-confusion in these patients had some quality of projection and projective identifications—that is, it was not clear to the patient who was doing what to whom—it turned out on analysis to be an intermittent "state" that responded to "holding" and other noninterpretive interventions. However, I have found occasions when such patients are able to move into a psychoanalysis proper, with timely and gradually fewer shifts in technique, back and forth from the less to the more interpretive. The deficit here, especially, is a matter of degree, where the quantitative may sporadically pass over into the qualitative, even resembling, at those temporary revivals of traumatic moments, a formal thought disorder. However, at a later time, following the gaining of composure and the reduction of confusion to therapeutically manageable levels, the psychically traumatic "states" and their symbolic elaborations, secondary or otherwise, may be articulated interpretively in terms of their defensive functions in the context of the compromises of intrapsychic conflict. For example, it may be shown that excited, confused states gratify a wish to seek out dangerous thrills at the same time that they defend against acknowledging the reality of the danger and the subsequent renunciation of a familiar source of gratification. Analysis may then take place.

Victims of early neurologically based confusions, unempathic mothering, or incestuous abuse do repeat these traumas idiosyncratically, but they also create via their fantastic elaborations, just as we all do. For example, for a woman who has been incestuously abused or raped to begin to understand that even women who have not had actual incestuous experiences wish and fantasize them guiltily can be therapeutically valuable. To deal with acting out only as the repetition of real and specific traumatic occurrences and not also of the universal, shared human experiences embedded in the fantasies accompanying it and that gives it meaning can exacerbate the patient's narcissistic anxieties about being damaged.

Most important to the question at issue, a sense of despair when feeling one's experience and psyche as discontinuous with those of others works against the possibility of emergent analyzability. Such an outlook is especially pessimistic if both potential analysand and the analyst collude by deciding in advance that structural "deficit," such as presumably irreversible damage, rules out analyzability. Further exploration of the particular symbolic representation of "deficit," whether dyslexia or sequelae of early maternal deprivation, or anything else, together with their elaborated associated fantasies, must enter into the joint work of analyst and potential analysand; and when they do, we often see a prime example of how analyzability itself emerges and develops.

In sum, for all of these doubtful cases, if we remain open to the possibility of either analysis *or* some other therapeutically valuable modality of treatment, we do not limit the patients' options prematurely. We give it a try. We empathize with the patient's pain without transferentially based zeal to do analysis and without being provoked into countertransferentially based emotional reactions to the patient's attempts to "sabotage" our thoughtful efforts. That is, we respond with the analytic neutrality that is a necessary but not sufficient condition of all psychoanalytic psychotherapeutic work.

TRANSFERENCE NEUROSIS

Our views of nosology and of the transference neurosis are intimately related to issues of converting a psychotherapy to a psychoanalysis. These views have advanced in many quarters from the older contention that only those with the diagnosis of psychoneuroses, particularly the "transference neuroses," could develop an analyzable "transference neurosis."

My understanding of the transference neurosis, recently further elaborated by Brenner (1982), is close to Freud's initial formulations; it allows for the widening scope of its applicability in practice much more than the all-too-common misusage of the term as denoting an instantly discernible nosological entity rather than a process emerging in the analytic situation. It is this unfortunate misusage, misapplied as a so-called objective device for determining analyzability, that I think is rightly open to criticism.

While we accept that "the" transference neurosis can no longer be regarded as an entity differentiating one category of patient, nosologically, from others, we still must await its development in the treatment situation before considering transition. The term is acceptable as a convenient shorthand way of referring to those aspects of unconscious conflictual aims, fantasies, and compromise formations originating in childhood that are enacted repetitively and concentrated cohesively on the analyst as well as on significant others outside of the analytic situation. We saw how the conflicting fear of commitment and wish for a passionate attachment to a powerful phallic figure formed the core of the transference neurosis, which signaled the timing of conversion for the patient discussed earlier. The transference "neurosis"—that is, unconscious and displaced *oedipal and preoedipal* conflicts—is ubiquitous, whether or not the "primary" diagnosis is neurotic. Borderline patients, too, struggle with oedipal conflicts along with hallmark prestructural, preoedipal conflicts. "Prestructural" issues of distance regulation are of paramount importance for neurotic and normal people as well. What makes a person analyzable, then, is not some advance determination of whether or not he or she *has* a discernible transference neurosis, because everybody "has" one. The relevant prognostic issue for psychoanalysis, when we are considering a transition from psychoanalytic psychotherapy, is whether or not "it" appears especially and with increasing transparency with respect to the analyst, and whether or not the patient can tolerate working on it analytically in the analytic setting, despite the regression that the psychoanalytic method encourages. It is important to note that while psychoanalysis proper would promote formal regression or the primitivization of function in the transference neurosis, this is not generally a stated aim of a psychoanalytic psychotherapy. So, its appearance is a good harbinger for transition, as it was in the dream and subsequent developments of the patient described earlier.

The transition, with the same analyst, should present no insuperable difficulty if the psychotherapy has been conducted all along in a way that is close to an analysis proper and has remained in accordance with the variations in arrangements and in the analytic stance reviewed here. Once analyzability has been determined, or adjudged as probable, facilitating the switch should involve little more than conveying whatever changes in goals and procedures are necessary or highly desirable and interpreting whatever resistances are then generated. Even with the most variable early arrangements, such as three or fewer sessions per week, a face-to-face set-up, and relatively more active exploration than interpretation—an eventual though gradual switch to psychoanalysis may be made as the analyst adheres more and more to the basic treatment model as each occasion for its application emerges in the context of the work. This includes analyzing the conscious and unconscious meanings of the transition itself as Bernstein did in his 1983 paper and as I did with the woman who feared overwhelming me phallically and thereby expunging the possibility of therapeutic affirmation. Another patient believed I recommended the couch in order to gratify my own voyeuristic impulses. Yet another believed my wish to intensify and deepen the experience reflected my wish to violently get "inside her head"—a symbolic rape. These meanings to the patient of the transition process itself were interpreted and linked to other life situations where the same anxieties prevailed, and analysis could proceed.

Conversions are easiest when the following conditions, now restated, are met: there has been consistent attention to anxiety and resistance leading to some analysis of the transference; the therapist has remained relatively opaque with regard to personal matters not relevant to the patient's analytic goals; no life decisions, reassurance, or guidance unrelated to the treatment arrangements have been offered; and the therapist has refrained from interpreting too much along one favored line of psychodynamics to the exclusion of the multiple and various perspectives required for psychoanalytic understanding and insight.

When there have been major departures from this approach and analysis is indicated, the patient, in principle, should be transferred elsewhere. The longer the patient is seen with significant departures from the optimal analytic attitude and arrangements, the more the transference with be unanalyzable and unresolvable by the same therapist. However, even with extreme departures, the cost-gain ratio may tilt toward switching to analysis with the original therapist. This may be indicated when a critically valuable working relationship has been established and where transferring would involve starting anew that essential part of the process, which may have been a hard and long-gained accomplishment. It is here a matter of individual judgment.

The possibility for transferring the patient who has benefited from psychoanalytic psychotherapy to analysis with the same therapist is maximized when the departures are within what is generally agreed upon as the broadened limits and widening scope of psychoanalysis.

REFERENCES

Bernstein, S. G. 1983. Treatment preparatory to psychoanalysis. *Journal of the American Psychoanalytic Association*, 31:363–90.
Brenner, C. 1982. *The mind in conflict*. New York: International Universities Press.
Freud, S. 1919. Lines of advance in psycho-analytic therapy. In *Standard edition*, vol. 7. London: Hogarth.
Panel. 1983a. Transition from a psychotherapy to an analytic patient. Arlene K. Richards, reporter. Paper presented at the Midwinter Meeting of Division 39, The American Psychological Association, Palmas del Mar, Puerto Rico.
Panel. 1983b. Converting psychotherapy to psychoanalysis. Charles P. Fisher, reporter. Paper presented at the Fall Meeting of The American Psychoanalytic Association, New York City, 16 December.
Stone, L. 1954. The widening scope of indications for psychoanalysis. *Journal of the American Psychoanalytic Association*, 2:567–94.

12

RELATIVISM REVISITED: THE IMPACT OF LIFE ON PSYCHOANALYTIC THEORY

Barbara Schlachet, Ph.D.

There is an unfortunate, albeit largely unconscious, tendency among us as members of the mental health professions to view professional activities that tend to change the status quo as political, while viewing those that tend to support it as scientific or neutral. The central thrust of this essay will be to question whether psychoanalysis, or, for that matter, any science is, should be, or can be apolitical; whether science is, as it is generally conceived to be, a body of "pure truths," replicable under all properly controlled circumstances, until those truths are found inadequate to explain new phenomena, at which time they are supplanted by other truths, based on new techniques and knowledge. Such a view of science assumes its linear development; an accumulation of knowledge that is continuous builds upon previous knowledge, in which old hypotheses are revised and augmented as more and more new "truths" come to light. Those hypotheses that cannot be so revised and augmented are seen as errors, as unscientific formulations owing their tenure in the scientific community to the lack of available technique and knowledge at that time.

This view of science and scientific progress has raised questions among philosophers and historians of science, and they are questions that have great relevance for psychoanalytic theory. In his important book, *The Structure of Scientific Revolutions* (1962), Thomas Kuhn posits that historians of science must attempt to display the historical integrity of a science in its own time. Edgar Levenson, in *The Fallacy of Understanding* (1972), makes reference to Foucault's position that there is an underlying paradigm that pervades every aspect of a culture, not just its science but its aesthetics, politics, social structure, literature, even its form of aberrancy. Levenson posits that no aspect of the culture can be comprehended without reference to the underlying paradigm.

According to Kuhn, paradigms provide models from which spring particularly coherent traditions of scientific research. In the absence of a paradigm, the scientist cannot focus; all of the facts that could possibly pertain to the development of a science would appear to be equally relevant. Scientists work to solve the puzzles presented by the paradigm, and normal science consists of the effort to fit nature, or data, into the boxes that the paradigm supplies. Those that will not fit are often not seen at all. Kuhn reminds us of the Bruner and Postman (1949) experiment with playing cards, in which subjects were asked to identify on short and controlled exposure a series of playing cards, most of which were normally marked but some of which were anomalous, for example, a red six of spades and a black four of hearts. In short exposure times and without any awareness of difficulty, the anomalous cards were almost always fitted into one of the conceptual categories prepared by previous experience. However, with greater exposure, subjects began to hesitate and became confused, until finally, and sometimes quite suddenly, they did begin to display some awareness of the anomaly.

My point here is that our paradigm prepares us for what we are going to see, what areas are to be investigated, and how we will interpret what we find upon investigation. This is not simply a position of cultural relativism but, rather, a position that views science, in general, and psychoanalysis, in particular, as an interactional part of a whole. What one chooses to examine from a scientific vantage point and the explanation that one offers for phenomena are those that give the closest possible fit to nature as it is understood and observed. This is not to say that scientific theory is corrupt or the handmaiden of politics, economics, and so forth. Rather, it is part of an interactional whole; it is both a description of and an attempt to understand phenomena within the cultural framework. This view obscures the distinction between so-called hard science and soft science, with the value judgments that inhere in each, for it posits that no science is independent of the paradigm. Relativism has been equated with the soft sciences, usually understood as the social sciences; and our aim has been to emulate the hard sciences, the physical sciences, with their "real," that is, quantifiable data. It is interesting to note, as Stephen Jay Gould does in *The Mismeasure of Man* (1981), that one of the first biological theories of intelligence supported by extensive quantitative data was early nineteenth-century craniometry. The problem here was certainly not the accuracy of measurements for they were, in fact, objective. However, their interpretation by well-reputed scientists of the time was inextricable from prevailing models based on a theory of superiority and inferiority of races and sexes. Paul Broca (1824–1880), who at that time was professor of clinical surgery in the faculty of medicine in Paris and founder of the Paris Anthropological Society, singled out the few egalitarian scientists of his century for debasing their calling by allowing an ethical hope or political dream to cloud their judgment and distort objective truth.

As social scientists, we have had a tendency to reify numbers and to underplay the fact that science, whether physical or social, is rooted in creative interpretation; that numbers suggest, constrain, and refute but do not by themselves specify the content of scientific theories, which are built upon the interpretation of numbers, and it is this interpretation that is determined by the paradigm.

However, if what is paradigmatic appears to be truth during the time of its tenure, and if we, as members of the relevant scientific/psychoanalytic community, are deeply embedded in it as is anyone else, how can we progress to articulate and thereby question the assumptions on which our paradigm is based?

Kuhn notes that almost always those who achieve the fundamental inventions of a new paradigm have either been very young or very new to the field whose paradigms they change. From the vantage point of being neither, I would like to briefly mention some of the recent work that, in my opinion, does articulate and challenge previously unarticulated paradigms that underlie psychoanalytic theory and practice. Among the most important are the work of recent feminist theorists, notably Dorothy Dinnerstein (1976), Nancy Chodorow (1978), and Carol Gilligan (1982).

Dinnerstein is perhaps the most revolutionary of these theorists, as she questions the silent assumptions underlying all developmental theory —such as one-sex child rearing or mother-raised children. She does not question that this is most often the case but does question that this is how it has to be. The paradigm of the family from which all of our developmental theory arises is solidly based on a notion of family in which mothers are almost solely responsible for the care of infants and young children and are the first primary objects to whom these children become attached. Within this paradigm of the family, much of what psychoanalytic theorists have described is remarkably accurate, from the oedipal conflict and its resolution to mother-infant research. However, the theory building derived from these descriptions does not articulate the assumptions that underline the theory. In other words, given these kind of families in this kind of culture, these are the developmental stages we can expect most children to undergo. These unarticulated assumptions color our research as, for example, when, in keeping with our theory that the primary maternal connection is the most important one for an infant or young child, we act in such a way that the mother is the person who is most exclusively devoted to the care of the child, thus insuring "maternal bonding," and then proceed to study the undoubted distress caused when an infant who has been thus parented is suddenly separated from his or her mother. We then use this research to "prove" that young children should be tied even more totally and exclusively to their mothers, thereby producing what may well be a self-fulfilling prophecy.

Feminist theory is only one area in which current paradigms are open to question. It offers to psychoanalysis profound questions regarding our most basic assumptions about nature, norms, and how life is to be lived. It is important also in that it has been so well articulated. Similar questions could be asked, however, about other areas that are central to our theory and practice. We could—and need—to ask to what degree our concepts of mental health and, thus, psychoanalytic goals change with changes in our underlying paradigm. With this, we must question the extent to which we mediate between the political world—the world that deals with the distribution of power and privilege within social systems—and the individual with whom we have negotiated an analytic relationship. Again, it is important to note that I do not speak here of the deliberately manipulative political abuse of psychology or psychiatry. This is to be abhorred, although in some ways these abuses are the easiest to recognize and condemn. I speak, rather, about the well-meaning and well thought out, theoretically based and in no way incorrect way that each of us, via the paradox of being part of the paradigm, perpetuates it by not being able to be outside of it and question it. Thus, in our very attempts to be neutral without being political the goals that we set are usually consonant with the values of a given time and place and consistent with some political or economic need. For example, the value placed on goals of separation and individuation, a *sine qua non* of maturity in Western culture, is not incompatible with the need for a work force that is mobile and is not tied by family attachment or loyalty to place. This same individualism is anathema in certain Eastern cultures where such mobility will be disruptive and destructive to the sociopolitical and economic schema. These values are not explicitly dictated by the powers that be but, rather, emerge in interaction with the larger culture.

Radical psychoanalytic and political groups have criticized psychoanalysis for its value on adjustment, claiming that it enables individuals to accept what they should be working to change. Even, however, substituting, as American psychoanalysis largely has, self-understanding and growth for adjustment may just be putting a new window dressing on the old display, for when we do spell out what constitutes growth and what constitutes fruitful self-awareness, we generally find ourselves back at the traditional and unquestioned model. For example, most models of mental health include some ability to perform productive work. We tend to define as productive that which earns money and to see work as becoming more "productive" as it goes up the hierarchical scale. A bright person holding a factory job at the termination of analysis might be seen as a less successful and less healthy product of analysis than a bright person holding a position as a college professor or attending graduate school. I would venture to say that for most of us, the analysand that we would wish to write up is the one who has made progress or at least not lost ground along the employment or productivity scale to which we, ourselves, subscribe.

Another concept inherent in models of mental health is that of choice. It is a stated and assumed goal of psychoanalysis to help to free the analysand of neurotic binds that make options and choices unavailable to her or him. What often goes unacknowledged in this is that, even without neurotic and character problems, many choices are not available. It should be noted that among our criteria for what constitutes a "good analytic patient" are those that would enable the person, once analyzed, the most freedom of choice—being young, verbal, financially self-sustaining or having the potential to be so, educated, and the like. While the freedom to make choices needs to be an important goal in psychoanalysis, it also becomes important for the analyst to be aware and to help the patient to be aware of where those choices are hampered by outside realities.

The issue of how one deals with relaxation and leisure time is one that we relate to mental health. One of our shared values is the importance of being able to enjoy leisure—time that is not spent in paid labor, time that "belongs" to oneself. A person who cannot do this we label a workaholic, and threaten with the specter of heart disease, ulcers, marital disharmony, and, recently, even cancer. Several assumptions underlie this value: One is a nonscarcity economy. One would be hard-pressed to call a Guatemalan farmer a workaholic, regardless of the long hours put in at subsistence labor. Another is the assumption that gratification does not come from paid labor itself; and in an industrialized world in which work involves increasingly small and repetitive tasks and in which the product of the labor is ever more removed from the tasks that each individual performs, this assumption is warranted, except for a fortunate minority. Therefore, the leisure time that we help our patients to be able to accept and enjoy, whether in the form of hobbies, vacations, or the grown-up toys that have proliferated in the last few years, may be the rewards for the acceptance of performing alienated work. What we may help the well-analyzed person to do is to perform alienated work but not admit it; and thereby we, as well as our patients, can maintain our blindness to some of the realities of the modern workplace.

We need, certainly, to articulate our models for relationships and for the family. Therapeutic or analytic success usually involves as a stated or unstated goal the attainment of a stable, long-term relationship, usually with a heterosexual partner and most usually culminating in marriage (even though we now accept sequential marriages, so long as the sequences are not too frequent and too short-term). Although more than one-third of American children live in single-parent or reconstituted families, we continue to think of intact nuclear families as the norm and any deviation from these as atypical families. Like Postman and Bruner's subjects, we don't notice when this is not the case, not only when it occurs by divorce but, for example, during World War II when a large percentage of the population lived in households where the fathers were absent for months to years. We have not studied the effect of these "broken homes" on delinquency rates, childhood maladjustment, sexual identity, and so on, the way that we have with children of divorce because going off to war fits with our model in a way that divorce does not, so that we do not consider these homes "broken." Similarly, we did not consider the impact of working mothers on children when these mothers were doing war work but stressed the necessity for a full-time mother at home when servicemen were returning from war in need of jobs, many of which had been filled by women.

Carol Stack (1974), in her study of family structure and kinship organization in an urban black ghetto in the United States, describes the kinship-based linking of multiple domestic units, the elastic household boundaries, lifelong bonds to three-generation households, the domestic authority of women, and limitations on the role of the husband or male friend within a woman's kin network that characterizes the population that she studied. Stack sees these as highly adaptive structural features of poor urban black families, a resilient response to the socioeconomic conditions of poverty, unemployment, and access to scarce economic resources. Yet, these same structures often are seen by the mental health establishments as disrupted, chaotic, and generative of psychopathology, in that they deviate from the model of the nuclear family held by the dominant culture.

The analytic model is itself reflective of models in the culture. It has many of the characteristics of relationships between benevolent authorities and subordinates in an essentially patriarchal culture. The authority establishes the rules of the relationship, both practical and relational, among the latter being the clarification of who tells what; whose life becomes known. While there are excellent theoretical and practical reasons for the patient becoming more known than the analyst, it should be noted that this same model characterizes relationships between human beings and the deities that they worship, clergy and their congregations, gurus and their disciples, physicians and their patients, heads of state and their populace, teachers and their students. Every analyst has some horror story about meeting up with a patient when the analyst's child is having a temper tantrum or of being seen somewhat inebriated at a party. These are horror stories because they violate the model and, as such, are seen as disruptive of or anomalous to the process of analysis. Yet, as with scientific anomaly, these moments, when they do become part of the analytic process, can and often do present a novel view of the patient and the process.

In all of the above I have tried to illustrate the thesis that analytic theory and the technique based on it can never be politically neutral, any more than can any other scientific theory, whether in the "hard" or the "soft" sciences; that all of what we look at, whether or not we choose to look at it, and what interpretation we give to what we look at is necessarily based on a complex interactional system of which we, ourselves, are a part. We are, in truth, participant-observers not only in the analytic transaction but also in the world and the specific culture in which that interaction takes place. Our myth of political neutrality assumes that, while we see ourselves as participant-observers in the one (the analytic) transaction and carefully analyze what assumptions, reactions, and interactions of our own we bring into that situation, we somehow manage to perceive ourselves as neutral, as unaffected by the other, as standing outside of the culture and, therefore, as able to enter the analytic transaction "objectively", that is, except for our own personal idiosyncrasies and problems which, hopefully, have been analyzed into awareness.

What are we to do, then? How do we punch our way out of this particular paper bag—the paradox of being part of the paradigm and, therefore, unable to stand outside of it, critique it, and know its impact upon ourselves and our work? Perhaps our very training and perception of ourselves as participant-observers can aid us in this endeavor, if we can extend the meaning of the term to go beyond the analytic interpersonal transaction and understand ourselves to be participant-observers also in our transactions with the world in which we and our patients all live.

Analytic training and supervision have focused on exploring the ways in which the analyst's personal distortions impact on the analysis. Analytic institutes require candidates to undergo their own analyses to this end. Neither the supervision nor training of any major school, however, requires us to as carefully scrutinize the assumptions and distortions in the culture that we share with our patients, our supervisors, and our analysts, so that these continue to influence our theory and our practice without our needing to acknowledge that they do. In this way our professional training becomes rather like an analysis taking place among members of the same family. Assumptions that are shared by all, or at least most members of the family, tend to be seen as givens and are never even articulated. Those members who are dissident often become the "problems." However, in this larger context, we do not have the option of working with a patient or an analyst from another "family." In this sense, we are all members of the same family. It thus becomes imperative for us to relinquish our myth of neutrality and to own, identify, and articulate to the extent that we can, at least for ourselves and sometimes with our patients, what our own and our shared assumptions and values are. We can never be perfectly aware of all of the sociocultural forces acting upon us, any more than we can ever be perfectly aware of all of the countertransferential issues that impact on our work. To be thus would be to give up being a participant, and this would be impossible. But our acknowledgment that they exist, that we are products of a shared history and players in a common drama, although we may have different parts, and seekers whose perceptions are colored by belief and expectation and by the time and place in which we inhabit this planet may help us to name what is rarely named, to question what is rarely questioned, and to emerge not with truth for all time but with a far greater understanding of the lives that we and our patients live in this place and time.

REFERENCES

Bruner, J. S., and Postman, L. 1949. On the perception of inequities: A paradigm. *Journal of Personality,* 18: 206–223.

Chodorow, N. 1978. *The reproduction of mothering.* Berkeley: University of California Press.

Dinnerstein, D. 1976. *The mermaid and the minotaur: Sexual arrangements and human malaise.* New York: Harper & Row.

Gilligan, C. 1982. *In a different voice.* Cambridge: Harvard University Press.

Gould, S. J. 1981. *The mismeasure of man.* New York: W. W. Norton.

Kuhn, T. S. [1962] 1970. *The structure of scientific revolutions.* Chicago: University of Chicago Press.

Levenson, E. A. 1972. *The fallacy of understanding.* New York: Basic Books.

Stack, C. B. 1974. *All our kin.* New York: Harper & Row.

13

THE RECONSTITUTIVE FUNCTION OF PSYCHIC DEATH-STATES

Marjorie L. Carter LaRowe, Ph.D.

He tried disgustedly to keep himself from thinking, his thought moreover was shapeless and without memories and fragmentary as though with each flicker of consciousness he was reborn differently until after all these births once by chance he was reborn as himself.

FERDINANDO CAMON,
The Fifth Estate

This essay explores a specific type of psychotic episode that I have termed *psychic death-states*. Similar states have been described by others, including Bick (1968), Grotstein (1985), and Joseph (1982). The three phases of psychic death-states, their technical management, and the theoretical understanding I have proposed are original and are intended to provide only one means of conceptualizing such states.

Psychic death-states can be defined as periods of unintegration during which the individual perceives himself or herself to be nonhuman or subhuman, for example, a machine, a cancer, or an amoeba. Searles (1960) has suggested that as human beings we have anxiety not merely lest we regress ontogenetically (to an infantile or intrauterine state, for example), but also lest we regress further, phylogenetically as it were, to an animal, vegetable, or even an inorganic state. Psychic death-states do not represent a fragmentation or disintegration of self but instead constitute a separate psychic experience that temporarily replaces the functional self. One patient described her unintegrated experience of being a "vapor" as having "a life and coherence of its own."

From my perspective, such states can be viewed as reenactments of the time(s) in the first months of life when the failure to provide for the newborn was such that its survival was perceived as threatened. I believe that each of us has critical, primitive experiences of sensing we might die, from early on. Gestation and birth are processes made up of biological imperatives; a single developmental failure can result in the demise of the fetus or newborn. I believe we are genetically encoded with this information.

Similarly, postnatal environmental failure can endanger physiological survival. Such failures will occur when there is an overstimulation of need (for nourishment, warmth, touch, and so on) and an inability to self-provide. As Winnicott (1974) has stated, the ego cannot organize against environmental failure in so far as dependence is a living fact. Imagining and hallucination are utilized to overcome the deprivation in fantasy. When these fail, I believe there is a retreat to an (imagined) earlier form of existence when such needs did not occur.

These experiences disrupt the establishment of the core, or unit, self. If the infant is to survive at all, he or she may develop a premature or "precocious self"—to use Boris's (1987) term—as a functional facsimile of the core self that would perish. In a similar manner, Bick (1968) has described the disruption of the primal skin development as leading to a " 'second skin' formation through which dependence on the object is replaced by a pseudoindependence, by the inappropriate use of certain mental functions, or perhaps innate talents for the purpose of creating a substitute for this skin container function" (484). In resorting to the development of a precocious self, the core self demonstrates its inability to survive in the true Darwinian sense—not because it is not fit enough but because it is not fit for the immediate, present environment in which it was born. As Gould (1973) reminds us, "natural selection is a theory of *local* adaption to changing environments" (57).

Later on, when the needs of the unit self are reexperienced and survival is once again at stake, psychic death-states can be viewed as the most primitive representation of the core self. The recurrence of these states may be the result of the effort to secure a different outcome—that is, to give psychic birth to the self. One patient expressed it as follows: "I was born but not brought into being." In analytic work, such states can follow an intense period of inner restructuring that includes an awareness of previously unacknowledged needs and their frustration.

As individuals describe their experience of psychic death-states, three separate phases can be identified: the centered, the transformational, and the emergent. In the centered stage, the individual withdraws from the external world into an objectless feeling state. It is usually reported that a peripheral awareness of the environment continues, but it is irrelevant. For example, the individual may know where he or she is but could, in fact, be anywhere; the physical surrounding does not have a direct bearing on the individual's sense of self. One woman said she could recognize my words when I spoke, but they had no particular meaning and no communication could take place. There is a turning inward of sensory receptors and cross-modal perceptions occur (sounds that are felt in or on the body). I believe this replicates the fluid world of infancy as described by Stern (1985).

Infants do not attend to what domain their experience is occurring in. They take sensations, perceptions, actions, cognition, internal states of motivation and states of consciousness and experience them directly in terms of intensities, shapes, temporal patterns, vitality affect, categorical affects, and hedonic tones. (67)

However, psychic death-states are accompanied by a feeling of panic and terror of unmanageable proportions, which I believe occurs because the direct experiences cannot be organized or patterned. As such, they parallel Bick's (1968) unintegrated state where he describes the infant as in a "frantic search for an object—a light, a voice, a smell, or other sensual object which can hold the attention and thereby be experienced, momentarily at least, as holding the parts of the personality together" (484). But in this phase of the experience there isn't any object.

Ogden (1986) has described a state of "nonexperience" where all experience is emotionally equivalent. It is viewed as a final, superordinate defense against overwhelming and continued stress in infancy where meaning is no longer given to perception. I conjecture that experience cannot be translated into thoughts and meanings when it cannot be arranged or codified in a systematic way. If so, "nonexperience" and similarly described states (Laing 1959, for example) are related to psychic death-states. If not, they represent states (catatonia?) that defy organization and transformation, the means by which one ends the centered phase.

The transformational phase is marked by the effort to establish a primary identification of the self through evidence of bodily sensations or functions. A transforming act (such as self-induced vomiting, bleeding, mutilation) provides this identification. This act serves two central purposes in (1) providing concrete, visceral evidence of the individual being alive and (2) giving somatic form to the psychic event. In addition, it may reactivate the fantasy of relating the functions of one's body to the inner workings of another's (Klein 1952). If so, the transformational act can be considered prototypical of the intra- or extrauterine nurturance experience.

The various transforming acts organize and soothe the individual who now enters the emergent phase. This includes the reexperiencing of the self beyond the functions of the body. There is a sense of reawakening, of recognizing oneself and the immediate situation. The episode is frequently followed by sleep.

Physical death can be fantasized as a psychic rebirth. As discussed, what has not taken place is the unobstructed psychic birth of the infant despite its being physically alive. Instead a psychic death has occurred. Suicide brings with it complete annihilation and the fantasy of a psychic and physical rebirth. Suicide can appear to be a means of mastering the transformational phase—of providing the death that was intended in infancy.

Therapeutic intervention relies on the symbolic alteration of the transforming act into an act of inclusion. It then becomes an experience involving an integrated and integrating other. (Perhaps the lack of integration in the primary caregiver(s) accounts for the most catastrophic of early failures: the need for the infant (patient) to integrate and organize the other.) The inclusionary act commonly involves the giving or taking of a symbolic object related to the transformation. For example, the self-mutilator will give the mutilating instrument to the analyst. The analyst then holds the representation of the transformation (cutting) and the body function (bleeding). There now exists the possibility of the fantasized presence of the analyst at the transformational phase. This process may replace the act itself as the bridge to the emergent phase. It must occur again and again with varying degrees of success before any sign of the unit self can be acknowledged and maintained.

Working against the procreative forces are malignant ones. The act of inclusion can degenerate into an act of collusion of the most perverse and destructive variety. The analyst is then imagined as one who perpetrates and encourages the bodily violence. Optimally, the analyst holds the destructiveness—the body itself—to allow for safe delivery. If the analyst is perceived as joining in the patient's bizarre excitation, the patient is doomed. When viewed as a collaborator, the analyst must use his or her own emergence (integration) to assist the patient in redefining the analyst as a facilitator, not an annihilator. This is always a procedure of painful endurance, one which sometimes never succeeds. Then it appears as if the individual is, for the present, addicted to his or her own psychic death. Joseph (1982) has described similar patients as follows:

> They retreated apparently into themselves and lived out their relationships in this sexualized way, in fantasy, or fantasy expressed in violent body activity. This deeply masochistic state then has a hold on the patient that is much stronger than the pull towards human relationships. (455)

I believe the need to torture the other as a means of exorcising the need to self-torture can be powerfully linked with the need to give life to the self. I do not believe that psychic survival can occur without the direct intervention of another human being. However, one almost thinks at times that the other's survival demands one's own symbolic demise. There is an insidious way in which that which is nurturing becomes unexpectedly lethal. A patient's dream expresses this better:

> I was lying naked on your couch in the office. A large-headed fetus in viscous fluid was crawling up my body. It reached my left breast and bit into it. My breast began to spurt milk copiously, like out of the blow hole of a whale. Then the milk turned to blood.

This woman first associated the dream to a time around age ten when, after masturbating, she tried to cut off her left breast with a razor. In both the conscious and the unconscious states, she has fused life forces (lactation, autoeroticism) with death images (bleeding, self-mutilation). At times this is compounded by an inability to distinguish between the self as subject and the self as object, as well as between the other as subject and object. Such confusions breed multiple transformations from one to the other, often imperceptibly.

This particular woman has had numerous episodes of unintegration. I will present portions from three consecutive sessions during which one such episode occurred. I hope to illustrate how these states can provide a means of reconstruction in the face of threatened dissolution.

In the first of these sessions, the patient said she felt "stuffed" with me "to the point of bursting." This was a marked change from feeling she was being "fed" by my perceived understanding. Now she said we had created a special, secret world where she experienced herself in a way that did not function in reality. This, too, was a distinct shift from previously being able to extend her evolving sense of self beyond the confines of the analytic situation. Now these two world were split. She felt I was obliterating her, that she was unable to communicate clearly

anxiety about the danger of predators and other potential disasters" (315). As such, the death instinct may provide a premature psychic death when internal or external dangers threaten to annihilate. This allows for the possibility of reorganization and reintegration.

In conclusion, I would like to present a patient's poem that gives alternate expression to this process.

I dreamed I was a pair of eyes
Descending into oceans of flora:
Splendid, luminescent,
Down to a darkened landscape of megaliths.
I could not surface.
I was fixed among stone columns
Packed like children's toys in their tomb.
I am the subterranean fetus
Wanting human explusion.

I believe the return to the nonhuman environment carries with it the hope of a secure release into the realm of sustained contact with the self one was taught to fear then bury alive.

REFERENCES

Bick, E. 1968. The experience of the skin in the early object relationships. *International Journal of Psycho-Analysis* 49: 484–86.
Bion, W. R. 1984a. *Attention and interpretation.* London: Maresfield Reprints.
———. 1984b. *Second thoughts.* London: Maresfield Reprints.
Boris, H. 1987. Tolerating nothing. *Contemporary Psychoanalysis* 23: 351–66.
Camon, F. 1987. *The fifth estate.* Marlboro, Vt.: Marlboro Press.
Gould, S. J. 1973. *Ever since Darwin.* New York: W. W. Norton.
Grotstein, J. 1985. A proposed revision for the psychoanalytic concept of the death instinct. In *Yearbook of Psychoanalysis and Psychotherapy,* vol. 1, edited by R. Langs, 299–326. Hillsdale, N.J.: New Concept Press.
Joseph, B. 1982. Addiction to near death. *International Journal of Psycho-Analysis* 62: 449–56.
Khan, M. M. R. 1974. *The privacy of self.* New York: International Universities Press.
Klein, M. 1952. Mutual influences in the development of the ego and the id. In *Envy and gratitude and other works, 1946–1963,* 57–60. New York: Delacorte Press.
Laing, R. D. 1959. *The divided self.* Baltimore: Pelican Press.
Ogden, T. 1986. *The matrix of the mind.* Northvale, N.J.: Jason Aronson.
Searles, H. F. 1960. *The nonhuman environment.* New York: International Universities Press.

Stern, D. N. 1985. *The interpersonal worlds of the infant*. New York: Basic Books.
Winnicott, D. W. 1971. *Therapeutic consultations in child psychiatry*. New York: Basic Books.
———. 1974. The fear of breakdown. *International Review of Psychoanalysis* 1: 103–7.
———. 1975. *Through paediatrics to psychoanalysis*. New York: Basic Books.

INDEX

EDITORS

HOWARD B. SIEGEL is a supervisor at the New York University Post-doctoral Program in Psychoanalysis, and associate professor at Baruch College. He is also supervisor at the Washington Square Institute.

LAURA BARBANEL is the program head at the Graduate Program School of Psychology, Brooklyn College, and is a faculty member and supervisor at the Manhattan Institute for Psychoanalysis.

IRWIN HIRSCH is the director of the Manhattan Institute for Psycho-therapy, and is an associate professor of psychology and a supervisor at the Postdoctoral Program in Psychoanalysis and Psychotherapy at Adelphi University.

JUDITH LASKY is a faculty member and supervisor at both the Institute for Contemporary Psychotherapy and the New Hope Guild Center, Child Therapy Training Program, and is a supervisor at both the City College and Pace University.

HELEN SILVERMAN is a supervisor at Long Island University, works with the Yale University Video Archive for Holocaust Testimonies, and maintains a private practice.

SUSAN WARSHAW is a supervisor at the New York University Post-doctoral Program in Psychoanalysis and Psychotherapy, and is an associate professor at the Ferkauf Graduate School of Psychology. She is also an honorary clinical associate at the Graduate Program in Clinical Psychology, City University.